Robert E. Howard's

ADVENTURES IN AN AGE UNDREAMED OF

System Design
Benn Graybeaton, Nathan Dowdell
& Jay Little

Line Development
Jason Durall & Chris Lites

Writing
Richard August, Jeb Boyt, Jason Durall,
Chris Lites, Kevin Ross, Jesse Scoble,
Devinder Thiara & Anne Toole

Approvals
Patrice Louinet & Jeffrey Shanks

Editing & Proofreading
Jason Durall, Chris Lites, Sally
Christensen & Tim Gray

Cover Artwork
Tom Grindberg

Interior Artwork
Michael Syrigos, Shen Fei, Martin Sobr,
Eli Maffei, André Meister, Johan Fredriksson,
Mateusz Wilma, Jessada Suthi, Aleksi Briclot

Cartography
Tobias Tranell

Art Direction
Mischa Thomas & Richard August

Lead Graphic Design
Michal E. Cross

Layout
Thomas Shook

Additional Graphic Design
Dan Algstrand & Malcolm Wolter

Produced by
Chris Birch

Head of RPG Development
Sam Webb

Publishing Assistant
Virginia Page

Production Manager
Peter Grochulski

Social Media Manager
Salwa Azar

Operations Manager
Rita Birch

Community Support
Lloyd Gyan

With Thanks to
The Robert E. Howard Foundation,
Professor John Kirowan, H.P. Lovecraft,
Fred & Jay at Cabinet Entertainment

Published by
Modiphius Entertainment Ltd.
2nd Floor, 39 Harwood Road,
Fulham, London, SW6 4QP
United Kingdom

Legal

© 2020 Conan Properties International LLC ("CPI"). **Conan**, **Conan The Barbarian**, **Hyboria** and related logos, characters, names, and distinctive likenesses thereof are trademarks or registered trademarks of CPI. All rights reserved. **Robert E. Howard** and related logos, characters, names, and distinctive likenesses thereof are trademarks or registered trademarks of Robert E. Howard Properties Inc. All rights reserved.

The **2d20 system** and Modiphius Logos are copyright Modiphius Entertainment Ltd. 2015–2020. All **2d20 system** text is copyright Modiphius Entertainment Ltd.

Any unauthorised use of copyrighted material is illegal. Any trademarked names are used in a fictional manner; no infringement is intended.

This is a work of fiction. Any similarity with actual people and events, past or present, is purely coincidental and unintentional except for those people and events described in an historical context.

Third printing by Standart Impressa Dariaus ir Girėno g.39. Vilnius 02189, Lithuania.

TABLE OF CONTENTS

Introduction
CONAN THE PIRATE 4

Chapter 1
PIRATE CHARACTERS 6
    Pirate Homelands 6
    Pirate Castes 8
    Pirate Stories 11
    Pirate Archetypes 15
    Pirate Natures 18
    Pirate Educations 20
    Pirate Stories 22
    New Talents 22
    Finishing Touches 23
    Gear & Equipment 26

Chapter 2
GAZETTEER 29
    The Main 29
    The Western Ocean 29
    Zingara 31
    Argos 40
    Southern Shores 46
    Shem 46
    Stygia 48
    Kush 50
    The Black Coast 52
    Northern Wilds 53
    Vanaheim 53
    The Pictish Coast 53
    The Vilayet Sea 55

Chapter 3
EVENTS 56
    Mortal Events 56
    Natural Events 59
    Preternatural Events 60

Chapter 4
MYTH & MAGIC 61
    Sea-Cults 61
    Spells 63
    Ships of the Dead 65
    The Barachan Oracle 67

Chapter 5
ENCOUNTERS 69
    Sea-Dogs and Hardies 69
    Beasts from the Depths of Sea 72
    Monstrous Foes 76
    Famous Pirates and Others 81

Chapter 6
HITHER CAME CONAN... 91

Chapter 7
THE WAY OF THE PIRATE .. 94
    Pirate Organizations 94
    All the Sea's Wealth 97
    A Road of Slaughter 98

Chapter 8
SHIP COMBAT 110
    Borne on the Waves 110
    Ships of the Hyborian Age 120

Chapter 9
A PIRATE OF THE AGE 126
    Zarin the Red 126

Index 129

My good friend, Lord Taverel —

I trust all is well with you, and your estate has been restored to a sense of normalcy. I am still incredulous over the events that transpired when last we met, and the revelations that emerged from that unfortunate incident in Conrad's study between Ketrick and O'Donnel.

As for my own work, I am currently in a state of exhilaration over my recent findings. Proof — in the form of hard archaeological and anthropological evidence — continues to come to light, and I am cultivating sources worldwide to provide me with the scant scraps of evidence pointing at the existence of what von Junzt called the "Hyborian Age".

Yes, it is something of an obsession, but you have never known me to be less than ardent, and meticulous, in my scholarship. From ancient shards of metal, cryptic markings, and engravings in heretofore unidentified ruins, to translations of long-lost texts, I continue to discover conclusive proof of the existence of this heretofore lost epoch of human history. Time and again I find evidences of the Hyborian Age concealed beneath our own history, the forces and cultures that shaped it still evident even now, in the modern world. The evidentiary preponderance ignored by the scholarly and scientific community is staggering, so much so that at times I suspect the presence of some sinister force hellbent upon eradicating the Hyborian Age from the historical record.

But enough. I have spoken at length to you about this, I know, so I will not bore you with my pedantry again. We both know what we know, have seen things far more inexplicable than anything the open-minded souls at the Wanderers Club would countenance, and for men such as we, the jury has returned its verdict on the matter.

The cause of this letter is nonetheless related to this passion of mine, for even on seemingly unrelated matters, the specter of the past looms large. If you recall, several months ago, you set me to investigating the veracity of a journal you came into possession of, a testimony relating to an encounter with your illustrious ancestor, Helen Taverel. I've named the journal for its author, a sailor named Steven Harmer, formerly from a Virginia merchant boat named The Blue Congress. Harmer, as the journal claims, encountered your ancestor Taverel — herself temporarily sailing with The Black Raider — and her crew when he was stranded on a mysterious and unidentified island, one that he luridly dubbed "The Isle of Pirates' Doom". Harmer's journal proved a gripping insight into her experiences as a pirate (for "privateer" is too polite a euphemism for her true role), related by another.

The all-too-recent events regarding that damnable ring caused me to set that research aside for several months, as I must confess that I merely scanned the first few pages and thought it was little other than yet another testimony of a hapless sailor falling unwillingly into the trade of piracy, mostly likely emphasizing his innocence before turning to a life of depravity and murder.

However, when I returned to the journal, I discovered much of interest, and I will confess that the brief work was nonetheless quite the page-turner: perhaps some author like Cooper or Stevenson might craft it into a gripping yarn, suitable for Argossy or even the pulps. Surely it could stand alongside the works of Dumas or Sabatini, perhaps, Stevenson or London at the least.

Harmer's journal, relating to events in the late 17th century, described a landing upon an unnamed (and seemingly still lost) island in the Caribbean Sea. According to Harmer's testimony, Captain Taverel and her crew set ashore and explored. They quickly discovered Harmer, after he found one of their number murdered. Despite these suspicious circumstances, Taverel took him at his word, and he won her confidence by saving her from a would-be assassin among her own crew. Together, Harmer and Taverel explored the island, and there they found the ruins of an ancient and mysterious culture, whose provenance neither could determine. Though they did not find the treasure they sought, and instead barely escaped alive from their rival pirates, the compelling description of the ruin set my imagination afire.

Curious also is the reference to an obscure pirate group of which Taverel is a member: The Red Brotherhood. As you might remember, the group itself is known to me from my own researches into the Hyborian Age, with references to it coming up in the testimony of one of its more illustrious members, a Captain Strom, who was apparently so notorious that he merited inclusion in "The Nemedian Chronicles", which eventually made its way into von Junzt's Unaussprechlichen Kulten.

I've written an article for the Journal about this manuscript and its ties to the Hyborian Age, and have enclosed it for your perusal. My profuse thanks for this inadvertent bounty your request brought me, as it opens yet another door into that bygone era.

So now I return your solicitation with one of my own. I ask that you vouchsafe for me when I ask the fellows of the Wanderers Club for funding to seek out the mysterious "Island of Pirates' Doom" described in the Harmer journal. Those ruins, should they still stand, could be our first chance to walk upon the very ground trod upon by figures such as the pirate captain Strom, and perhaps even by Conan of Cimmeria himself, from his sojourn as a pirate.

I am enclosing a copy of my latest article published within the Journal, an effort at planting the seed of for the expedition I suggest. Your support would be invaluable.

Best regards,

J.K.

July 13, 1936

THE IVORY SKULL: PIRATES AND PIRACY IN THE HYBORIAN AGE

By Prof. John Kirowan (PhD, FRS, FRAI, FRGS)
Guest Lecturer, Department of Anthropology
Miskatonic University
Akham, Massachusetts

The act of waterborne piracy, in its many forms, has been a part of human history since the first primitive boat was placed in the water: the so-called "Sea Peoples" who wrought such devastation upon the Mediterranean were not invaders so much as raiders; the Phoenicians were famed as traders but were not altogether benevolent; Chinese pirates plied Eastern waters and were infamous in their regions; Vikings raided far and wide across England, Europe, the Baltics, their own shores, and far beyond; and more recent history is redolent with accounts of piracy throughout the Age of Sail. Even now, pirates ply their dastardly trade in the remoter corners of the world, from the coasts of Africa to the East, and no waterway can be said to be truly safe from the danger of piracy.

In my ongoing series attempting to illuminate the lost epoch of the "Hyborian Age" I have presented ample evidence that humanity during this period achieved much in the way of cultural development, far before such developments were described in known history, and it is equally true that the people of this age suffered the same depredations, particularly in the form of organized piracy. Echoes of the more famous pirate groups of the Hyborian Age are even found much later in human history, particularly in the form of the Red Brotherhood which plied the seas as recently as the 18th century...

INTRODUCTION
CONAN THE PIRATE

> *The sea and the ways of the sea were never-ending mysteries to Conan, whose homeland was among the high hills of the northern uplands.*
>
> — "Queen of the Black Coast"

Listen to me, dogs, for your life depends on heeding my counsel and obeying my command. While I stand here, I am your king, and you are my subjects. If you feel you have something to say about that, I welcome you to step forward. My steel is ready to answer you.

Nothing? Then let us begin.

I am, if you are new here, your captain. Strom is my name. Some of you know me well, while some of you have recently joined us, borne to this deck by the vessel you see sinking off our starboard bow. Pay no mind to it, though. It represents the past, and I am offering you a new life, as a member of my crew. A life of piracy awaits you, and there is no better place than the *Red Hand* to learn the trade.

With me, you will become a hardened pirate, learn our ways and our secrets, and you will reap the rewards handsomely. With these bold few, we will plunder the fat ships of Argos, Zingara, Shem, and even Stygia, and your name will join mine as we sail beneath our ivory-skulled banner.

It is a bloody and cruel world, to be certain, but here on these blue waves and on this very crimson-stained deck, you will be free in a way you have never known. Free to kill, free to take, to revel and to relish that which you have been denied... free, indeed... to live life to its fullest!

So now, if you have the guts for it, we sail a road of gold upon these wild waters, and we will scribe our names into the pages of history with steel and with blood!

THE PIRATE'S LIFE

If you have any qualms about choosing a life of piracy and slaughter, then turn back away from the sea, for the harsh waters have no patience for the timid and the weak. If you feel you have the mettle within you, then read on.

Chapter 1: Characters

Whether bold, desperate, or simply bloodthirsty, if you find yourself upon the path of the pirate there is no better introduction to the life than within this very chapter. Here are the means to create new pirates and to season even the most experienced of buccaneers, from homelands, castes, stories, new archetypes and talents, education, and natures, to other such elements that make each pirate distinct.

Chapter 2: Gazetteer

Though the Western Ocean is the only place that matters to a pirate, the coasts are nonetheless of some importance, especially the opportunities ports present for larceny and carousing. This chapter describes Zingara, Argos, Shem, Stygia, Kush and the Black Kingdoms, the notorious Baracha Isles, and even touches upon the Pictish coastline and Vanaheim, where piracy is practiced under a different form.

INTRODUCTION

Chapter 3: Events
Though each ship is a fiefdom unto itself, and pirates hold to no kingdom's law, pirates are nonetheless subject to many events that affect those ashore, as well as occurrences peculiar to the life at sea. Here is described the life of a pirate in times of war, strife, and plague.

Chapter 4: Myth & Magic
Pirates are equal measures superstitious and godless, but all respect the other world and the unseen powers that manifest whilst at sea. From ancient curses, dark magic practices of the Picts and those in the Black Kingdoms, to ancient and powerful entities that reside on forgotten islands, these pages describe the myths, superstitions, and folklore common to pirates from north to south.

Chapter 5: Encounters
This chapter chronicles the many colorful and dangerous characters the pirate world is known for. Here are allies — such as the crew of the *Tigress* — rivals, Minions to threaten even the hardiest buccaneers, and monstrous creatures from the very ocean depths.

Chapter 6: Conan the Pirate
Though he was famous for many things, it is his during time as a pirate that Conan of Cimmeria earned the title of "Amra", the Lion. This chronicles the barbarian's hasty introduction into the pirate life and his years of piracy, as welcomed by Bêlit and her vessel, the feared *Tigress*.

Chapter 7: The Way of the Pirate
In these pages are two notorious pirate organizations — the Red Brotherhood and the Zingaran freebooters — and a description of the life of a pirate and crew. Presented are rules for looting and plunder, the pirate code (such as it is), and pirate-themed Carousing tables for the time spent between acts of piracy, both ashore and when in the doldrums. Additional rules cover shipboard combat and the means of surviving the harsh conditions imposed by weather.

Chapter 8: Ship Combat
What would be the life of a pirate without risk? Presented within this chapter are the rules governing ship-to-ship combat, from pursuits to the exchange of missile fire, and the terror of a boarding action. Vessels common to the Western Ocean are described here, as well.

Chapter 9: A Pirate of the Age
Here we describe one particularly notorious pirate who has risen to my attention, though he has yet to join the ranks of the great pirate captains of the age.

> "A carack," answered the seneschal. "It is a carack trimmed and rigged like a craft of the Barachan pirates — look there!"
>
> A chorus of cries below them echoed his ejaculation; the ship had cleared the point and was slanting inward across the bay. And all saw the flag that suddenly broke forth from the masthead — a black flag, with a scarlet skull gleaming in the sun.
>
> — "The Black Stranger"

CHAPTER 1
PIRATE CHARACTERS

"A ship and crew are all I want. As soon as I set foot on the deck, I'll have a ship, and as soon as I can raise the Barachans I'll have a crew. The lads of the Red Brotherhood are eager to ship with me, because I always lead them to rare loot. And as soon as I've set you and the girl ashore on the Zingaran coast, I'll show the dogs some looting! Nay, nay, no thanks! What are a handful of gems to me, when all the loot of the southern seas will be mine for the grasping?"

— Conan, "The Black Stranger"

Many and varied are the souls that set foot on the sea-road, choosing lives of piracy and slaughter, but all are united in that they are pilgrims, caught between the sun and the deep sea. Presented in this chapter is a guide to the creation of pirate player characters, with new background options, as well as new opportunities in the form of talents and even equipment. Cultures central to the pirate lifestyle are found here, along with new names suitable to denizens of those homelands.

Creating pirate characters is exactly as it is in the **Conan** corebook, with the additional step that the gamemaster should determine how the player characters are connected, as described in *Player Pirate Crews* (next page).

PIRATE HOMELANDS

While most folk spend the entirety of their humdrum lives within a dozen miles from the place of their birthplace, dying without seeing anything new, the call to adventure inevitably brings restless rogues to the greatest horizon… the untamed waters of the Western Ocean.

PIRATE HOMELAND, TALENT, AND LANGUAGE			
Roll	Homeland	Talent	Language
1–4	Argos (see page 40)	Sea Raider	Argossean
5–8	The Baracha Isles (page 36)	Sea Raider	Argossean or Zingaran (pick one)
9–11	The Black Coast (see page 52)	Strife	Kushite, Keshan, Punt, or Darfari (pick one)
12–13	Kush (see page 50)	Strife	Kushite
14	Shem (see page 46)	Strife	Shemitish
15	Stygia (see page 48)	Desert-born	Stygian
16	Vanaheim (see page 53)	Winter-born	Nordheimer
17–20	Zingara (see page 31)	Sea Raider	Zingaran

PIRATE CHARACTERS

PLAYER PIRATE CREWS

The biggest question the gamemaster must address before beginning a pirate-based campaign is how the player characters are connected. The character creation guidelines presented herein are suitable for creating pirate characters that can adventure across the world as readily as any others, but a pirate-based campaign assumes that the player characters are a part of a pirate crew, either serving under a captain or with a ship to call their own. Thus, when creating a pirate crew, the gamemaster should determine the nature of the crew and the player characters within it — either by asking the players, deciding for them, or collaboratively.

Different campaign styles are discussed in *Chapter 7: The Way of the Pirate*, and the various relations player characters can have with one another are summarized here.

- **FELLOW CREWMEMBERS:** In a campaign where the player characters are all crew serving under a captain, they may choose from any of the archetypes presented in this sourcebook or other CONAN sourcebooks. If their status seems improbable, such as a Noble Warrior, it is assumed that they have fallen from their prior station prior to or upon embarking on a life of piracy. One or more of the crew may be officers, which should be determined by the players themselves, based on the archetype and skills of the player character. See *Officers*, below. Crewmembers are all expected to have Sailing Expertise and Focus of 1+, or a significant reason they do not.

- **OFFICERS:** The campaign might also be structured so that the player characters fill the roles of the officers of a pirate crew — or the rough equivalent of officers — and jointly serve together under a captain, whether loyally or conspiring against her. In this case, the gamemaster should describe the roles of the officers onboard a pirate vessel (see page 120) and let the players assign the roles to their characters, or create characters with those roles in mind. Generally, Skill Expertise and Focus of 2+ are required for an officer onboard a pirate vessel.

- **CAPTAIN AND CREW:** In this type of structure, one of the player characters serves as the ship's captain and is supported by the other player characters, either as officers or crew. This type of arrangement should be carefully weighed by the gamemaster before being decided, as it places a considerable amount of authority in the hands of one player, which might not be to everyone's tastes. In these cases, the captain should have the following skills with Expertise and Focus of 2+: Command, Melee, and Sailing. It is possible for crew and officers to be more skilled and competent than the captain, but a captain without this basic competency will not survive for very long in the role.

Thus, pirates and sea-reavers alike can hail from coastal lands, as well as the remotest deserts or landlocked kingdoms. The *Pirate Homeland* table provides the most likely choices for pirate player character homelands, and players can pick or roll 1d20 to determine their origin, or select other homelands from the corebook. Homeland talents are all presented in the **Conan** corebook. Many pirate crews are inevitably rogues' galleries assembled without thought to borders or national identities, and the gamemaster is advised to welcome rarities such as Nemedian nobles turned to piracy, Keshan or Darfari corsairs, Khitan freebooters, or even the occasional Cimmerian barbarian turned pirate.

Piracy is present in the Vilayet Sea, as well. The pirate society known as the Red Brotherhood has a presence in the Western Ocean, as well as the Vilayet Sea, hundreds of miles apart. This sourcebook covers pirates and pirate activity in the Western Ocean, while *Conan the Brigand* addresses more fully the Red Brotherhood's presence in the Vilayet Sea.

Vanir practice their own brand of piracy in their northern fjords, sailing dragon-prowed ships up and down their coastline, raiding one another and occasionally striking into Pictland and even further southward. They are described in depth in *Conan the Barbarian*.

PIRATE CASTES

As noted above, you can pick any caste from the **Conan** corebook for your player character's native caste. The new castes below represent those that traditionally produce pirates, and can be chosen or rolled for, as desired by the player. Generally, these should be selected based on the player character's homeland, as many inland nations do not traditionally have these castes.

CASTE DESCRIPTIONS

The following castes are common backgrounds to those that have set to the sea-road.

Corsair

Caste Talents: *Naval Discipline, Reaver*
Skill Gained: Melee

This caste should only apply to player characters from Kush (see page 50) or the Black Coast (see page 52), as it reflects the hereditary corsairs, a time-honored traditional way of life among the people of those kingdoms. Seafaring raiders, corsairs are drafted or chosen for their fierceness and ambition while still young. Corsair expeditions are financed by chiefs or kings, raiding their neighbors and sometimes as far up the coastline as Shem or Argos. Some groups of corsairs go rogue and serve particularly powerful captains, embarking on lives of outright piracy.

CASTE, CASTE TALENTS, SKILL GAINED, SOCIAL STANDING					
Roll	Caste	Caste Talents	Skill	Story	Social Standing
1–4	Corsair	Naval Discipline, Reaver	Melee	Page 11	1
5–8	Fisher	Fisher, Wave-harvester	Craft	Page 12	0
9–12	Marine	Naval Discipline, Salt for Blood	Ranged Weapons	Page 13	1
13–16	Sailor	Call of the Sea, Explorer	Sailing	Page 13	1
17–20	Trader	Sea-trader, Shipbuilder	Society	Page 14	2

PIRATE CHARACTERS

PIRATE ANCIENT BLOODLINES

The *Ancient Bloodline* talent, described on page 17 of the CONAN corebook, describes the effect that these ancient racial traits have on particularly exceptional individuals possessing an attribute of 12+. As described in the rules, these bloodlines manifest when a player character fails any Personality test. The gamemaster gains 1 Doom point, and the player receives an additional d20 for the test (up to the maximum).

Each ancient bloodline is different, and the way these affect their inheritors vary.

- **ARGOS:** Though the root stock is Hyborian, the bloodline of the folk of Argos has blended with an influx from Shem, Zingara, and even Stygia, inheriting ancestral traits from those ancient bloodlines. When this talent becomes active, the Argossean feels a strong sense of competition with others, a desire to get the better of any negotiation, no matter what the cost.

- **THE BLACK COAST AND KUSH:** These ancient bloodlines draw from those great kingdoms south of Stygia, whose ways are so different from the Hyborians. They are a scattered and diverse people, long separated from the rest of the dreaming west by the twin barriers of Stygia and the River Styx. When someone from Kush or the Black Coast exhibits this talent, they are filled with a fierce pride, scoffing at the ways and accomplishments of the upstart Hyborian kingdoms, pale reflections of their own fallen glory.

- **SHEM:** The folk descended from the Sons of Shem suffered much at the hands of their Stygian neighbors, enslaved and brutalized over the course of centuries. When a Personality test is failed, the Shemite with this talent feels a sense of outrage and the desire to dominate, turning the tables on a perceived opponent.

- **STYGIA:** Descended from the Lemurians who fled to the West and supplanted an ancient kingdom, embracing its ways, the Stygian bloodline is an ancient and terrible one, steeped in evil. A Stygian with the *Ancient Bloodline* talent failing a Personality test feels the presence of the Old Serpent and will view any situation they are enmeshed in as an opportunity to do Set's bidding. Though the Stygian is not beholden to commit an evil act, the desire to do so is there and must be suppressed.

- **VANAHEIM:** As described in *Conan the Barbarian*, a Vanir with this talent comes from a lineage that devolved into apedom after the Cataclysm and later returned to the semblance of humanity. A Vanir with this talent failing a Personality test is prone to boastfulness and foolhardy overconfidence.

- **ZINGARA:** Originating in the Valley of Zingg and boasting a bloodline that mixes the Hyborian ancestry with that of the folk of Zingg, this bloodline is expressed in the fashion of extreme boldness, almost rash emotion and feeling. A Zingaran suffering the effects of this talent will take insult over the merest slight, even mistaking honesty for mockery.

As always, the player is free to have the player character act as desired, but the above conditions will color the player characters' perceptions and feelings at the time of the test, as well as those of their allies and foes.

Fisher
Caste Talents: *Fisher, Wave-harvester*
Skill Gained: Craft

Whether using spear, rod, or net, you worked with your family to gather fish for sale and sustenance, for yourselves or others. You may have gathered shellfish in the wet shallows and coastal sands, diving for pearls with knife and bag in hand, or sailed far to sea with great nets or spears to bring back many small fish or one great one. It was hard work, and you learned the trade well, including the skills of woodcarving, knotwork, and the repair of your equipment.

Marine
Caste Talents: *Naval Discipline, Salt for Blood*
Skill Gained: Ranged Weapons

One of your parents — and likely, their parent — served in one of the great navies of the coastal kingdoms, whether Shem, Stygia, Argos, Zingara, or Turan. This parent hunted pirates or acted as a privateer, and battled the navies of neighboring kingdoms in the games of kings. You heard their tales of great sea-battles and bloodletting on the high seas, and knew that one day you would follow them to sea.

Sailor

Caste Talents: *Call of the Sea, Explorer*
Skill Gained: Sailing

Your father was a sailor, whether in a navy or as part of a merchant fleet. He was absent for long stretches of time, sailing up and down the coast of the Western Ocean or the Vilayet Sea. Much of your youth was spent at the docks, waiting to see if he returned, and when he did your ears were filled with tales of piracy and horrors from the deep.

Trader

Caste Talents: *Sea-trader, Shipbuilder*
Skill Gained: Society

Your parents and their parents and those before them made their living from the ocean, whether at a coastal shop, a dockside stand, or through the transport of goods — sometimes illicit items or even slaves — up and down the coast for sale or resale. You've been on many trade voyages, and know your way around the coast.

CASTE TALENTS

The following pirate — and nautical-themed talents are provided for these new castes, and can (at the gamemaster's discretion) be substituted for castes from other coastal homelands.

Call of the Sea

You have always looked to the sea as your destination, your home. You are more comfortable on the deck of a ship than on the streets of towns, and the great and limitless frontier is where you find yourself most at peace. As such, you have an intuitive understanding of the sea and the folk who travel upon it. You can re-roll any failed d20 for Insight or Command tests made against anyone with a naval or ocean-going background (at the gamemaster's discretion).

Explorer

Many ply the waves in search of blood or gold. Some seek adventure upon the waves. You, however, look to the ocean horizon as a place of possibility. You and your family are navigators, and have always sought to explore and chart the seas and expand the knowledge of your immediate coast. Whenever attempting an Observation, Sailing, or Survival test while in unfamiliar waters you can reduce the Difficulty by one step.

Fisher

Some part of your youth was spent on a fishing boat, or diving for fish in the shallow waters near your home. When making Survival or Swim tests in or adjacent to the water, you may add an additional +1d20 to your rolls. Every point of Momentum on the Survival roll provides enough food to feed an additional person for one day.

Naval Discipline

Whether part of a tradition as organized as the naval fleets of Argos, Zingara, Shem, or Stygia, or the corsairs of Kush and the Black Coast, your caste have traditionally served at sea, and view the sea as a battlefield. When at sea, you gain 2 🛡 non-stackable Morale and Cover Soak when fighting alongside at least one other character with this talent that has not suffered any Wounds.

Reaver

Your caste is known for piracy or raiding activities up and down the coast, against your own people, against neighboring countries, or everyone else. Your Reputation is increased by +1 when dealing with anyone with a nautical or pirate background, and you inflict an additional 1 🛡 damage on Threaten attacks against anyone that has heard of you.

Salt for Blood

Your family has had a long tradition of ocean-going and sailing, and you've grown up on the shore, spending as much of your time on or in the water as on land. Swimming tests are reduced by one step of Difficulty.

Sea-trader

Due to your familiarity with the coastal trade routes, you've developed a network of friends and allies in the various port cities, and know your way around such environments. In coastal settlements, you gain the *Tradesman* talent (see page 21 of the **Conan** corebook). When engaging in trade, you gain an additional +1d20 when rolling for Persuade or Discipline tests to get the best deals.

Shipbuilder

The craft of shipbuilding is zealously guarded by the members of your caste, whether they be the hereditary shipwrights of the Vanir; the guilds of Argos, Shem, or Zingara; or the Stygian sect devoted to such labor. You gain the *Sea Raider* talent (see page 15 of the **Conan** corebook) and +1d20 on any Craft test to repair or maintain a watercraft.

Wave-harvester

Your family has always taken its wealth from the sea, whether in the form of fishing or diving for the sea's bounty. When you attempt to dive for pearls, gather a harvest of saleable fish, etc. in familiar waters, you gain the *Hunter* and *Tradesman* talents (see pages 15 and 21 of the **Conan** corebook, respectively).

PIRATE STORIES

As presented on page 22 of the **Conan** corebook, your character's caste influences their background story. Roll or pick a result from these entries. You can choose to answer some of these questions or leave them to be explored later, through play or with answers provided by the gamemaster. The relevant traits all relate to piracy in some fashion, and are used to recover spent Fortune points as described in the corebook.

CORSAIR STORIES

Roll	Event	Trait
1–3	Child of the Chieftain	Humbled Pride
4–6	Famous Ancestor	Shadow of the Past
7–10	From Poisoned Waters	Mysterious Origin
11–14	Left to Vengeance	Calculating
15–17	Steps of the Elder	Suffer No Slight
18–20	Storm-wracked	Catastrophe

Child of the Chieftain

Your mother was chieftain of your village, and you were always expected to take a role amidst her corsairs. You were trained in the fighting arts, and you took your place in the corsair fleet as soon as you were able, rising within its ranks as befits your lineage. But something happened, and now you cannot count on your parent's name. What happened? Why are you not the captain of your own corsair vessel?

Famous Ancestor

Back in your family history was a heroic or particularly fearsome corsair, of whom stories are still told. Perhaps you take after him in some fashion, or perhaps you are nothing like him and have spent your life trying to distinguish yourself from his legendary status. Who was this figure, and what was he known for?

From Poisoned Waters

You were found in a basket, floating down the poisonous Zarkheba River in Kush, which is feared by most. Though this was an ill omen to many, the corsair captain took you aboard and adopted you. You grew up on a corsair galley, and your first steps were upon its decks. The mystery of your birth and abandonment haunt you, though. Have you taken any steps to learn who you are, and where you came from?

Left to Vengeance

Your village was destroyed by corsairs when you were but a child, and your people enslaved to the last man, woman, and child… but for you. When you were an infant your mother hid you beneath the floor-slats of your home as the corsairs struck, and your cries were unheard amidst the screams of the dying. Relatives found you and nurtured you, and when you were old enough to be told, you learned the truth of your birth. What decision did you make?

Steps of the Elder

One of your older siblings — or a particularly beloved aunt or uncle — was a corsair for your chieftain. Her name was spoken of with respect amidst the other corsairs, and many felt that this relative would eventually take control of the corsairs and become the chief. This was not to pass, and one day you awoke to learn she had been slain, her head set upon a spear outside the chieftain's hut. From that day on, your family's name was besmirched, and you found no place in the galleys of your village. What did you do then?

Storm-wracked

The folk of your village still speak of the Great Storm, the one that destroyed your village, shattering huts and walls, waves rushing over the coast and sweeping away hundreds of your kinsfolk and neighbors. That storm left you an orphan. You had little left but the sea, and with the few galleys remaining, you and the survivors set to sea as raiders, preying upon others more fortunate than you. Now you have set aside that life, but for what?

FISHER STORIES

Roll	Event	Trait
1–3	Bitter Rivalry	Betrayed
4–6	Empty Nets	Hard Times
7–10	Lost at Sea	Missing Kin
11–14	Returned to Ruin	Without a Home
15–17	Sailing to the Horizon	Seeker
18–20	Too Big a Fish	Dark Waters

Bitter Rivalry

Your family's fishing business was among the most prosperous in the village, town, or city you dwelled in, each catch yielding more and better than the prior ones. Your family grew wealthy and you grew up thinking that this bounty would continue forever. Then one day, your family's rivals struck, chopping nets and sails and setting fire to your fishing boats. Your family was ruined, and you lost everything. You now fish for the benefit of some other, and you think back of those bygone days of plenitude. What will you do about it, should you learn who was responsible?

Empty Nets

Something happened that caused your source of income to become scarce. It does not matter the reason — whether some strange and terrible tide killed the fish you harvested, or they were fished to extinction — the result is that your once-laden nets drew back empty time and again, and you could no longer ply your trade. Now you have left your home, seeking your fortune on other waters. Was there something unnatural about the scarcity? What was it? More importantly, what will you do now?

Lost at Sea

You grew up fishing alongside your family-members, continuing a generations-long tradition. One day, though, your beloved father's boat did not return. You spent long days waiting at the shore, looking up and down the coastline, and venturing out into the waters yourself in search of him, but found nothing. What happened to him? Did you ever find out? What did you do next?

Returned to Ruin

It was a fishing voyage like any other, miles and miles from the coast because that is where the best catch could be found. Your vessel full of the sea's bounty, you returned homeward. The first sign of trouble was the long trail of smoke wafting from the location of your village, and as you drew near you saw that the beautiful and familiar village of your birth was but fire-blacked ruin. There were far too few bodies, however, and you realized that most had been taken, likely by a slave ship. Who took them? What do you plan to do about it?

Sailing to the Horizon

There was nothing especially tragic about your childhood and youth, and you did not suffer any calamity, no major and dramatic incident that steeled you for the future. And such was the problem. Instead, after too many long hours spent dragging fish from the sea, splicing ropes, repairing nets, and returning home after long hours stinking of fish, you decided you'd had enough. You stole a small boat and set off, as far from home as you could go, and sold it for hard coin. Will you return to the sea, and if so, under what terms?

Too Big a Fish

Though you returned to your village barely alive, washed ashore like a half-drowned rat, no one in your village believed you when you told them what had happened. You and your family were fishing when your net caught something... something big. You pulled at it, and it pulled back. As you sought to cut yourselves free, it rose to the surface, dwarfing your boat with its vast and horrible bulk. You were lucky to be thrown free, the screech of the hull as it bowed and broke filling your ears. What was that terror from the deep? What would you do should you face it again?

PIRATE CHARACTERS

MARINE STORIES

Roll	Event	Trait
1–3	Betrayed by Your Captain	Distrust
4–6	Keelhauled	Suffered an Ordeal
7–10	Mutineer	Outlaw of the Sea
11–14	No Honest Path	Nothing Left to Lose
15–17	The Short Walk or the Pirate Road	Forced into Piracy
18–20	Survivor	Left to Die

Betrayed by Your Captain
You once served your ruler with zeal, joining the ranks of your homeland's navy when you were of age. Your training, though filled with strict discipline and hard drilling, transformed you into a marine — a seaborne fighter, the deck your battlefield. Your captain, however, was not so loyal. She sold you out to enemies of your country, whether another navy, privateers, or pirates! Without the chance to fight, your ship surrendered, and you and your fellow marines were captured. Why did your captain sell you out? How did you escape? What do you plan next?

Keelhauled
Your offense, however severe, did not merit the punishment you received: keelhauling. Your hands were tied to one line, your feet to another, and you were dragged beneath your ship's keel, suffering terribly as barnacles and rough wood scraped at your flesh, your lungs filled with water, and your limbs were wrenched with terrible force. You recovered, however, the fire of hate burning within your breast as your savaged flesh mended. Driven from the navy, now you are free to do as you will. Are you relieved enough to be alive and free, or does the thought of vengeance haunt your every thought?

Mutineer
You entered the navy with the best of intentions, but it became clear as you sailed on that your captain was not worthy of the title. Overly harsh discipline, outbursts of rage, inexplicable orders, brutal punishment, and forced hardship visited upon the entire crew caused morale to plummet. The officers and crew conspired against the captain. Now you find yourself without a ship. Did you support the captain, or stand with the crew? What part did you play? Was the mutiny successful, or was it quashed by the loyalists?

No Honest Path
Your stint in your homeland's navy was spent in loyal service, and you fought valiantly alongside your captain and crew in the defense of your country. But something put an end to that — whether your own actions caused you to lose your rank or you were captured and set free in a foreign land — you are unable to return to the navy. Your training was that of a marine. Life as a merchant guard did not appeal to you, but the life of an outlaw of the sea holds plenty of promise.

The Short Walk or the Pirate Road
Your career as a marine consisted of many years of uneventful sailing and military drilling, practicing armed combat at sea to no avail. Your first encounter with pirates marked the end of your naval service, when your ship was overpowered by a fleet of the blackguards. They captured you and your fellow marines, giving you a choice to join or die. Then they executed your captain and the officers as examples. Some of your companions refused to join the pirate ranks, but you chose wisely. Now there is no turning back.

Survivor
During a great sea-battle, your ship was rammed by another, and its hull was breached. As your vessel took on water, you and your fellow marines were forced into the sea, where you were at the mercy of the enemy. They fired arrows aplenty at you, eventually giving up and leaving you to the sharks while the ships of your own nation retreated, leaving you for dead. You were one of the few who survived, clinging to a section of your vessel's hull. A pirate vessel sighted you, and it was amongst these rogues that you found mercy. Now, at night, memories of that horrific battle play over and again in your memory.

SAILOR STORIES

Roll	Event	Trait
1–3	Crimson Sails	Caught Up into Piracy
4–6	Dishonest Company	Framed
7–10	Dragooned	Unwilling
11–14	Kidnapped!	A Pirate's Life
15–17	Swept Overboard	Marooned
18–20	Turned to Piracy	The Sea Is My Home

Crimson Sails
Your stint as a sailor was relatively uneventful, long days of shipboard life immersed in the day-to-day tasks of keeping a ship functioning. You saw much of the coastline of your own land and others, and you imagined that you'd do this until you were no longer able. Then one day, the crimson sails of a ship of the Red Brotherhood appeared off your vessel's bow, and you fled. The faster ship caught yours, and

your captain and crew surrendered your cargo. The pirates demanded your ship, and you saw that your only chance for survival was to throw in with their lot. Now you serve on the same ship, but under a pirate captain and flag. Will you remain? Do you consider yourself a pirate now, or will you escape when given the chance?

Dishonest Company

Enlisting to serve on a merchant vessel, you quickly grew used to the routine and the occasional danger. You trusted your fellow sailors and you did what you were told. The pay was adequate, and you got to see the world. Unbeknownst to you, though, enough of your fellow crewmembers were unsatisfied with their lot, and on one voyage they chose to seize the ship, killing the captain and claiming the goods onboard as their own. Now crewing a stolen vessel full of trade goods, you went from being an honest sailor to a pirate. Is this the life you want? What will you do?

Dragooned

Frequently, sailors such as yourself put to shore between voyages, residing in cheap dockside taverns and inns, or with kin when you are in a home port. This downtime is generally quite dull, marked by drunkenness and labor, getting the vessel shipshape for the next journey. You either went to sleep in the wrong place, or you were waylaid while walking through town, and the next thing you knew, you were on a pirate ship at sea, dragooned into service. Your new captain told you to serve or to get swimming. You had little doubt that the latter would be difficult with a slit throat.

Kidnapped!

Many children grow up hearing stories of piracy on the Western Ocean, and your childhood was spent listening to such tales, told by relatives who had set to sea. The names of famous pirates and their dastardly acts thrilled you, and though you would likely serve as a common sailor, you craved a life of adventure and even infamy. Then one day, on land, you encountered a landing craft full of these very sorts. They captured you, and eventually made you one of their own.

Swept Overboard

A common sailor, your life was turned upside-down when you were swept overboard during a particularly fierce storm. You do not know if your ship and its crew perished, and you spent long days floating, clinging to a barrel that went overboard with you. Spotting a small, barren island, you made your way there and lasted for a few days, near starvation, before discovering that it was a pirate refuge. Faced with remaining on the island to perish or join the pirates' ranks, you chose the latter, and have not looked back. However, your thoughts often drift back to that time. What was on that island, too small to support life or restock a pirate vessel?

Turned to Piracy

Rare is it that someone sets out to become a pirate, and your case was no exception. Your family were sailors, and your early life was spent sailing and serving on merchant or fishing vessels. Something happened, however, that set you on the path of the reaver, a life of outlawry at sea. Was it misfortune, some unplanned event that forced you to piracy, or did you make a choice that forced your hand?

> *"You know I've commanded bigger ships and more men than you ever did in your life. As for being penniless — what rover isn't, most of the time? I've squandered enough gold in the sea-ports of the world to fill a galleon. You know that, too."*
>
> *"Where are the fine ships and the bold lads you commanded, now?" she sneered.*
>
> *"At the bottom of the sea, mostly," he replied cheerfully. "The Zingarans sank my last ship off the Shemite shore — that's why I joined Zarallo's Free Companions."*
>
> — Conan and Valeria, "Red Nails"

TRADER STORIES

Roll	Event	Trait
1–3	Captured and Set Adrift	Hard Choice
4–6	Crew Became Cargo	Betrayed
7–10	Driven into Destitution	Beggared
11–14	It Walked the Decks	Haunted
15–17	Mutineered!	Past Betrayal
18–20	Restless Natives	Savage Pursuit

Captured and Set Adrift

The greatest threat to trade on the open sea is, of course, piracy, an eventuality that most must contend with. And like all eventualities, it was your turn, as you and your crew faced a black-sailed marauder across the seas. You fled, and it gave chase, pulling upside you and using grapnels to fix you in place. Your captain — if it was not you — did not want to give up the fully laden hold of trade goods, and ordered the crew to fight back. Though the pirates were fewer in

PIRATE CHARACTERS

number, you were no match for their ferocity, and soon they had seized control your ship. Did you fight until you were downed, or surrender early? Did the pirates take your ship and maroon you, or did they leave your ship and merely abscond with the cargo? Were you taken prisoner, ransomed later, or did you join their own ranks and become a pirate?

Crew Became Cargo

Though the slave trade is not the most noble of professions, it is nonetheless tolerated in most kingdoms, and is treated like any other business. Some ships and captains define themselves as slave traders, while yours was one of those who merely transports slave traders and their wares to and fro, without taking on any of the responsibility of capturing slaves, or the soulless task of selling them on the market. A new contract with a slave trader your captain was unfamiliar with took you to a meeting with a much larger slave vessel, and fate turned against you when that ship seized yours, crew and all slaves onboard, to fill their own slave hold. How did you escape? What happened to your own ship?

Driven into Destitution

Life was good as a merchant trader. You and your crew lived comfortably, shares between captain and crew were distributed equitably, and your captain (if it was not you) steered you clear of most pirates and rough weather. It was, sadly, your peers that presented the greatest danger — rival merchant houses allied against yours — who used political leverage to enact usurious taxes, undercutting prices, and even bullying to drive your ship's owner out of business, unable to purchase new trade goods or even offload them at a profit. One day, the tax collectors came to seize your boat. Some of her crew gave up, while others attempted to take it and sail away, presumably to embrace a life of piracy. What did you do?

It Walked the Decks

This trade trip was like any other, transporting a variety of trade goods — copra, mirrors, silks, oil, weapons, slaves, and some other bulk cargo — on a known route along the Western coast to a known harbor, to deal with known merchants and vendors. Something on this voyage, however, was different, with strange and horrific occurrences each night at sea. Sailors went missing, presumably overboard; slaves were murdered bloodily in their chains without witnesses; and the weather and very creatures of sky and sea behaved unnaturally. Then one night, a suspicious captain and crew set a trap for the thing that haunted the ship's deck, and the events after are a bloody, cacophonous nightmare. What was it that caused such horror? What happened next? How did you survive? Did it?

Mutineered!

Trade by sea is generally a lucrative career for all concerned, but on your own vessel, the division of wealth between captain and crew was perhaps not all that it could be. Clandestine meetings in the dead of night and whispers between resentful sailors were all it took to turn a trading ship into a boiling kettle. When it came to the confrontation between the "miserly" captain and crew, which side were you on? Did it come to bloodshed, or more traditionally, with the losing side set adrift in a rowboat? Were you on that boat? What happened to the cargo?

Restless Natives

You were either captain or a crewmember of a trade ship bold enough to sail down past Kush to the less civilized of the Black Kingdoms, or up to the north and trade amongst the Picts. Such daring served you and your company well enough, for a time. Eventually, one of these trade voyages went poorly and your ship was seized, her crew scattered and either killed, captured as slaves, or escaped to make the long and dangerous route home. You were lucky enough to survive, but how did you make it to safety? Are any of your fellow crewmembers alive?

PIRATE ARCHETYPES

Presented here are four new archetypes for characters intent on sailing the high seas. These expand upon those provided in the **Conan** corebook. In addition to equipment, these archetypes include bonds that connect the character to other people or places. You should work with the gamemaster to develop these relationships, either during character generation or during play.

> ## SORCERY AT SEA
>
> Pirates, like most of the folk of the Hyborian Age, have a deep loathing — or outright fear — of sorcery and those who practice it. Like untended fire aboard a ship, the presence of magic is to be avoided at all costs, and rare is the pirate crew that will tolerate any sort of sorcerer in their midst. A sorcery-using character — whether a witch doctor from the Black Kingdoms, a Stygian priestess of Set, or a Zingaran scholar — should expect a great deal of resistance and distrust.
>
> Some powerful pirate captains, however, are rumored to employ magic in support of their actions, such as curses or even weather-magic to foul the sails of their prey and their pursuers. Should the players choose to create a pirate crew and one of the players desires a sorcery-using character, the gamemaster should take special care to create the proper context for such a figure.

GALLEY SLAVE

You were chained to the oar of a slave galley, a punishing life and a certain death. Your skin is burnt dark by the ever-present sun and exposure, and marked with the cruel lines of the lash. However, this experience fills you with a savage determination to survive. Somehow, you won your freedom. Where you go next is up to you. Do you seek vengeance… or will you instead search for glory, loot, and adventure?

CAREER SKILL: +2 Expertise and +2 Focus in the Resistance skill
CAREER TALENT: *Hardy* (see the CONAN corebook, page 78)
MANDATORY SKILLS: +1 Expertise and +1 Focus to Athletics, Discipline, Persuade, and Sailing
ELECTIVE SKILLS: +1 Expertise and +1 Focus to two of the following: Insight, Observation, Stealth
EQUIPMENT:

- A knife or club
- A loincloth, tattered trousers, or similarly worn clothes
- A curious amulet snatched from the neck of one of your brutal slavers

BONDS:

- Loyalty from others enslaved with you
- Enmity from slavers
- Knowledge of the ports and waters of the coast where you were taken

MARINER

You went to sea at a young age, either born on a coast and following a family tradition or through your own volition. Once on the decks, surrounded by a fraternity of sea-goers, you realized you were home, and thus you have stayed. Whether you sailed on fishing boats, merchant vessels, or warships, you know the ropes, and cannot imagine life on land. You thrive under the routine of shipboard duties and chores, and have thrilled when cutlasses came out and the waters ran red beneath the hull of your ship and those it fought.

You know how to sail along the coasts, and you know your way around the docks in the ports that you've visited, far better than you know the streets of the cities beyond. The countryside itself is a strange vista, whereas you find yourself quite at home riding upon the dark waters of the Western Ocean or the Vilayet Sea.

CAREER SKILL: +2 Expertise and +2 Focus in the Sailing skill
CAREER TALENT: *Sailor* (see CONAN corebook, page 81)
MANDATORY SKILLS: +1 Expertise and +1 Focus to Athletics, Craft, Discipline, and Survival
ELECTIVE SKILLS: +1 Expertise and +1 Focus to two of the following: Command, Society, or Stealth
EQUIPMENT:

- A knife
- A few sets of plain traveling clothes
- An appropriate tool kit for your Craft

BONDS:

- Relationships with fellow sea-dogs
- A friend in every port that you've visited with whom you've shared a drink, a throw of the dice, a roll in the hay, a one-sided bargain, or a punch in the face

PIRATE CHARACTERS

MERCHANT CAPTAIN

You've made a living on the sea trading goods along the coast. You may know all the ports along the Western Sea, or you may have merely sailed between Messantia and Asgalun. You're an able seaman, captain, and merchant, ready to either ride out a storm or invest in goods that fetch a fine price in Kordava.

CAREER SKILL: +2 Expertise and +2 Focus in the Society skill

CAREER TALENT: *A Modicum of Comfort* (see the CONAN corebook, page 82)

MANDATORY SKILLS: +1 Expertise and +1 Focus to Command, Insight, Persuade, and Sailing

ELECTIVE SKILLS: +1 Expertise and +1 Focus to two of the following: Craft, Discipline, Observation, or

EQUIPMENT:

- A sword or knife
- Several sets of plain traveling clothes and a suit of decent clothing
- A sea chest
- A share in a small merchant watercraft

BONDS:

- Relationships with investors in your home port
- Relationships with merchants, chandlers, and port officials in any of the ports you frequent

SMUGGLER

You know the secret ways along the coast, the secluded coves, the guards you can readily bribe to look the other way, and how to sneak items into and out of a city. You know how to covertly move goods, whether to avoid the tax collector or some other officious lout. Evading both tax and law, while avoiding the noose, is your reason for being.

CAREER SKILL: +2 Expertise and +2 Focus in the Stealth skill

CAREER TALENT: *Living Shadow* (see the CONAN corebook, page 85)

MANDATORY SKILLS: +1 Expertise and +1 Focus to Discipline, Observation, Persuade, and Thievery

ELECTIVE SKILLS: +1 Expertise and +1 Focus to two of the following: Insight, Sailing, or Society

EQUIPMENT:

- A melee weapon of choice
- Several sets of plain traveling clothes, including at least one set that is dark in color
- One of the following: mule, camel, canoe, or rowboat

BONDS:

- A hiding place — a cave, an abandoned house, or an isolated hut — where you stash your smuggled goods and hide out when you need to lay low
- Relationship with at least one guard or other official who you bribe to look the other way
- Relationships with reliable people willing to work for you at odd hours and under difficult conditions with no questions asked

PIRATE NATURES

The **Conan** corebook presents on page 35–37 a variety of natures suitable for most player characters. However, the life of oceangoing banditry that represents the way of the pirate makes many of these natures less suitable for pirate-oriented games and campaigns. The following natures are presented for use by players and the gamemaster for use with pirate player characters or non-player characters (if desired).

As with other aspects of character creation, roll or pick the nature you'd like your pirate character to have, from the *Nature* table or from the **Conan** corebook. These function in all aspects as the natures in the corebook.

NATURE			
Roll	Nature	Roll	Nature
1–2	Bloodthirsty	11–12	Lustful
3–4	Craven	13–14	Reckless
5–6	Egotistical	15–16	Remorseless
7–8	Greedy	17–18	Ruthless
9–10	Gregarious	19–20	Vain

BLOODTHIRSTY

You crave violence, and feel no hesitation about spilling blood to pursue your goals, whether it is warranted or not. In truth, you need no reason at all to draw steel and sheathe it in flesh.

Attribute Improvement: Add +1 to Brawn
Mandatory Skills: +1 Expertise and +1 Focus to Athletics, Melee, and Parry
Elective Skills: +1 Expertise and +1 Focus to two of the following skills: Animal Handling, Thievery, or Warfare
Talent: One talent associated with any of the above skills

CRAVEN

Violence, danger, risk… these are the sorts of things you try to avoid. While others seek to prove themselves through bold action, you have learned that discretion is the most powerful contributor for your continued survival.

Attribute Improvement: Add +1 to Awareness
Mandatory Skills: +1 Expertise and +1 Focus to Acrobatics, Observation, and Stealth
Elective Skills: +1 Expertise and +1 Focus to two of the following skills: Parry, Persuade, or Thievery
Talent: One talent associated with any of the above skills

EGOTISTICAL

You seek to make a name for yourself, and take offense when others impugn your deeds or character. Though you may not be as famous as you would like to be, you are not willing to let any unkind remark or deed go unanswered.

Attribute Improvement: Add +1 to Personality
Mandatory Skills: +1 Expertise and +1 Focus to Melee, Resistance, and Society
Elective Skills: +1 Expertise and +1 Focus to two of the following skills: Command, Insight, or Persuade
Talent: One talent associated with any of the above skills

GREEDY

Wealth — whether in the form of gold, jewels, property, or other material goods — is all that matters to you. Your every decision is made with an assessment of "What's in this for me?", weighing risk versus reward for maximum profit.

Attribute Improvement: Add +1 to Awareness
Mandatory Skills: +1 Expertise and +1 Focus to Insight, Society, and Thievery
Elective Skills: +1 Expertise and +1 Focus to two of the following skills: Craft, Lore, or Persuade
Talent: One talent associated with any of the above skills

PIRATE CHARACTERS

GREGARIOUS

No matter where someone comes from, there are elements of commonality in everyone, and you take pleasure in reaching out to people in camaraderie, an open palm of friendship. This might be genuine, or your smile might mask the flint in your gaze.

Attribute Improvement: Add +1 to Intelligence
Mandatory Skills: +1 Expertise and +1 Focus to Counsel, Linguistics, and Persuade
Elective Skills: +1 Expertise and +1 Focus to two of the following skills: Animal Handling, Insight, or Society
Talent: One talent associated with any of the above skills

LUSTFUL

Comforts of the flesh are what you crave, whether wantonness or something more specific and perverse. You tend to evaluate others on their potential to satisfy your desires, and have little patience with activities unlikely to result in your pleasure.

Attribute Improvement: Add +1 to Personality
Mandatory Skills: +1 Expertise and +1 Focus to Counsel, Persuade, and Society
Elective Skills: +1 Expertise and +1 Focus to two of the following skills: Athletics, Sorcery, or Thievery
Talent: One talent associated with any of the above skills

RECKLESS

The thrill of adventure drives you, whether the clash of steel between dangerous opponents or the sensation of pitting yourself against the odds. You have always been fortunate, so you are inclined to take ever-greater risks.

Attribute Improvement: Add +1 to Agility
Mandatory Skills: +1 Expertise and +1 Focus to Athletics, Observation, and Survival
Elective Skills: +1 Expertise and +1 Focus to two of the following skills: Melee, Parry, or Thievery
Talent: One talent associated with any of the above skills

REMORSELESS

No matter what the deed, you refuse to feel any guilt over it. If others came to harm through your actions or your inaction, you do not care, nor would you expect others to be concerned about the effects they have over you.

Attribute Improvement: Add +1 to Willpower
Mandatory Skills: +1 Expertise and +1 Focus to Discipline, Melee, and Resistance
Elective Skills: +1 Expertise and +1 Focus to two of the following skills: Observation, Parry, or Survival
Talent: One talent associated with any of the above skills

RUTHLESS

No matter how hard the decision, whatever the cost, you will make it because it is the right thing to do. It does not matter whether your decisions are altruistic or selfish, everything is a calculation, with no emotional weight attached to any aspect of the equation.

Attribute Improvement: Add +1 to Willpower
Mandatory Skills: +1 Expertise and +1 Focus to Command, Discipline, and Insight
Elective Skills: +1 Expertise and +1 Focus to two of the following skills: Lore, Observation, or Survival
Talent: One talent associated with any of the above skills

VAIN

Whether your personal appearance or your reputation — or both — your sense of worth is inextricably tied to the perception of yourself in the mirror or in the eyes of others. Much of your attention is spent grooming, procuring fine garments, or cultivating your growing fame.

Attribute Improvement: Add +1 to Personality
Mandatory Skills: +1 Expertise and +1 Focus to Insight, Persuade, and Society
Elective Skills: +1 Expertise and +1 Focus to two of the following skills: Athletics, Counsel, or Discipline
Talent: One talent associated with any of the above skills

"I think of Life!" he roared. "The dead are dead, and what has passed is done! I have a ship and a fighting crew and a girl with lips like wine, and that's all I ever asked. Lick your wounds, bullies, and break out a cask of ale. You're going to work ship as she never was worked before. Dance and sing while you buckle to it, damn you! To the devil with empty seas! We're bound for waters where the seaports are fat, and the merchant ships are crammed with plunder!"

— Conan, "The Pool of the Black One"

PIRATE EDUCATIONS

The induction into the pirate life is often cruel and marked with hardship, violence, loss, the death of loved ones, and even slavery. While the educations presented on pages 37–40 the **Conan** corebook accommodate a variety of experiences, the entries in the *Education* table are specific to that career path.

EDUCATION			
Roll	Education	Roll	Education
1–2	Adrift	11–12	Mutiny
3–4	Chained to an Oar	13–14	Navigator
5–6	Deserter	15–16	Once a Merchant
7–8	Envoy	17–18	Outlawed on the Shore
9–10	First Mate	19–20	Wounded at Sea

These educations function in all ways as the ones from the **Conan** corebook.

ADRIFT

You were found clinging to a piece of flotsam, no clue to your origin other than your skin color and the language you spoke. How you got there, you do not like to remember. You were taken in by the crew of that vessel — merchant, naval, or pirate — apprenticed in their trades, yet you were always set apart.

Mandatory Skills: +1 Expertise and +1 Focus to Craft, Sailing, and Survival
Elective Skills: +1 Expertise and +1 Focus to two of the following skills: Athletics, Insight, or Observation
Talent: One talent associated with any of the above skills
Equipment: A small keepsake from your past, worn about your neck or concealed somewhere.

CHAINED TO AN OAR

You spent several years chained to an oar on a slave vessel, every day marked with the monotony of punishing labor. Lashed for the slightest lapse, in constant threat of being killed and tossed overboard, a fire grew within you. When you found your chance to escape, you took it.

Mandatory Skills: +1 Expertise and +1 Focus to Athletics, Discipline, and Resistance
Elective Skills: +1 Expertise and +1 Focus to two of the following skills: Craft, Observation, or Sailing
Talent: One talent associated with any of the above skills
Equipment: A manacle around your wrist, to be struck off when your former tormenter is dead.

DESERTER

Life in the navy was one of unwanted discipline and capricious leadership. Your ship met its end in battle against a pirate fleet, and you threw your lot in with the very sea-rogues you hunted. You have not looked back.

Mandatory Skills: +1 Expertise and +1 Focus to Craft, Melee, and Sailing
Elective Skills: +1 Expertise and +1 Focus to two of the following skills: Acrobatics, Athletics, or Observation
Talent: One talent associated with any of the above skills
Equipment: An old lodestone, stolen from the navigator on your former vessel.

ENVOY

Your service at sea was one of diplomacy, attached to a royal ambassador from one of the major seafaring nations. Though you held no title yourself, you accompanied the negotiators and messengers to foreign estates and courts, and learned their ways.

Mandatory Skills: +1 Expertise and +1 Focus to Linguistics, Persuade, and Society
Elective Skills: +1 Expertise and +1 Focus to two of the following skills: Insight, Lore, or Observation
Talent: One talent associated with any of the above skills
Equipment: Papers identifying you as an envoy of a foreign court (choose one).

FIRST MATE

Your service onboard your vessel was exemplary, and you earned your captain's trust. Whether through loyalty, competence, or both, you rose to the position of first mate, serving as your captain's proxy, and at times, the voice of the crew to the captain.

Mandatory Skills: +1 Expertise and +1 Focus to Command, Craft, and Sailing
Elective Skills: +1 Expertise and +1 Focus to two of the following skills: Insight, Persuade, or Survival
Talent: One talent associated with any of the above skills
Equipment: The captain's own gold-hilted cutlass (worth 10 Gold).

PIRATE CHARACTERS

MUTINY

Your apprenticeship was on a merchant vessel or a naval ship under a cruel and unthinking captain, backed by his loyal henchmen. Morale was low, and the crew suffered. You supported your shipmates in a night of bloody mutiny, and with a ship in your possession, the only course left was piracy.

Mandatory Skills: +1 Expertise and +1 Focus to Observation, Persuade, and Sailing
Elective Skills: +1 Expertise and +1 Focus to two of the following skills: Craft, Melee, or Ranged Weapons
Talent: One talent associated with any of the above skills
Equipment: A jeweled earring cut from your captain's ear.

NAVIGATOR

It is rare that a vessel sails the Western Ocean for reasons other than trade, but you were on such a ship. Your captain was tasked with navigating the coastlines and trade routes, mapping currents and winds, as well as seeking any uncharted islands.

Mandatory Skills: +1 Expertise and +1 Focus to Lore, Observation, and Sailing
Elective Skills: +1 Expertise and +1 Focus to two of the following skills: Insight, Linguistics, or Survival
Talent: One talent associated with any of the above skills
Equipment: A set of naval charts, more accurate than any yet made.

ONCE A MERCHANT

You plied the seas on a merchant vessel, sailing the rivers or along the coast, transporting goods to and from various ports. You paid attention to the trade, learning how to read customers, figure risks and expenses, and weigh everything against profit. It ended with pirates. You either joined their ranks or you are your own captain.

Mandatory Skills: +1 Expertise and +1 Focus to Insight, Persuade, and Sailing
Elective Skills: +1 Expertise and +1 Focus to two of the following skills: Craft, Linguistics, or Society
Talent: One talent associated with any of the above skills
Equipment: A leather-bound folio of detailed notes about trade routes.

OUTLAWED ON THE SHORE

Whether a criminal or an exile, you found it expedient to leave your homeland and set to sea, as it limited your enemies' means of striking at you. Originally your sea-passage was to a destination, now it is your home. Several years later, you wonder if it is safe to return to your homeland.

Mandatory Skills: +1 Expertise and +1 Focus to Insight, Observation, and Survival
Elective Skills: +1 Expertise and +1 Focus to two of the following skills: Parry, Sailing, or Thievery
Talent: One talent associated with any of the above skills
Equipment: A signet ring or pendant identifying your lineage.

WOUNDED AT SEA

You served onboard a sea-vessel, whether in the navy, as a trader, or even as a pirate, and you earned your keep in blood. Your first battle nearly cost you your life, and you were wounded so grievously that you were sent ashore to convalesce with a healer. You spent months recovering, but your former crew-mates never returned for you. Now you consider yourself free, to make your own fate.

Mandatory Skills: +1 Expertise and +1 Focus to Craft, Healing, and Sailing
Elective Skills: +1 Expertise and +1 Focus to two of the following skills: Counsel, Melee, or Warfare
Talent: One talent associated with any of the above skills
Equipment: A healer's bag (3 Resources), given you by your former caretakers.

PIRATE STORIES

These tales are either the most notable experience your character has had, or the event that sent them onto the road of the pirate. Pick one or roll for it, and add the relevant improvements. You can choose to elaborate on this before play begins, or afterwards, if it becomes relevant.

NEW TALENTS

The following new talents can be picked by pirate player characters or any who meet the prerequisites.

ACROBATICS TALENTS
Deck Rat

Prerequisite: *Agile*
Maximum Rank: 3
Experience Point Cost: 200

Your training has left you accustomed to maneuvering in the tight and claustrophobic environment below-decks, whether moving quickly to extinguish a fire, defending your ship from attacks, or pursuing victims while you ransack their vessel. As such, you are never inconvenienced by fighting in cramped or close quarters. Each rank in this talent negates one additional step of Difficulty imposed by the environment when attempting to act in such conditions. This talent applies to any such conditions (darkness, lack of room, etc.), as well as to any physical or perception-based skills attempted.

Swashbuckler

Prerequisite: *Deck Rat, Nimble as a Cat*
Maximum Ranks: 3
Experience Point Cost: 400

You know your way around the rigging of any sea vessel and can perform astonishing feats of agility and movement by swinging or rapidly climbing from rope-to-rope, using the rigging as if it were solid ground. You gain +1d20 for any Acrobatics or Athletics test while climbing the rigging of a ship, and whenever you are on a vessel with adequate mast and rigging, you may use a Move Action to swing to any zone on that vessel or an adjacent zone, such as a dock or the deck of another ship.

MELEE TALENT
Fighting Dirty

Prerequisite: *No Mercy*
Maximum Ranks: 3
Experience Point Cost: 200

Pirates rarely fight with any honor, and you've learned a gruesome array of brutal and dirty tricks to employ against your opponents. Once per turn after you make a successful melee attack, you quickly follow through with an immediate second attack, an instinctive dirty trick. This costs 1 Momentum and is assumed to be part of the initial attack, though damage is calculated separately. This trick (eye gouge, groin kick, elbow, spit in the eye, etc.) causes X ♦ damage with the Stun Quality, where X is the number of Ranks in this talent. *Fighting Dirty* cannot cause a Wound.

	PIRATE STORY	
Roll	Select War Story	Skill Improvements
1–2	Survived a famous sea battle (winning side)	+1 Expertise and Focus to Command and Warfare
3–4	Survived an outbreak	+1 Expertise and Focus to Healing and Resistance
5–6	Lost (and found) at sea	+1 Expertise and Focus to Observation and Survival
7–8	Marooned	+1 Expertise and Focus to Resistance and Survival
9–10	Survived a pirate raid	+1 Expertise and Focus to Stealth and Thievery
11–12	Shipwrecked	+1 Expertise and Focus to Athletics and Sailing
13–14	Saw a mysterious sea creature	+1 Expertise and Focus to Lore and Observation
15–16	Ship seized by pirates	+1 Expertise and Focus to Parry and Sailing
17–18	Survived a famous sea battle (losing side)	+1 Expertise and Focus to Ranged Weapons and Parry
19–20	Mistaken for a famous pirate	+1 Expertise and Focus to Persuade and Society

PARRY TALENT
Boarding Action

Prerequisite: *Deflection*
Maximum Ranks: 3
Experience Point Cost: 200

Pirates are experts at boarding unfriendly craft and know all the best places to seek cover. When boarding a hostile vessel, you count as having Reach 4 and Cover Soak 1 per rank of the talent for the round you board the vessel. You must be aware of the presence of opponents onboard, and be able to move freely to take cover, for this talent to work.

RESISTANCE TALENT
Strength from the Sea

Prerequisite: *Hardy*
Experience Point Cost: 200

You're used to being on a ship in the roughest of weather. You never get seasick and you can ignore any additional levels of Difficulty from stormy weather or rough seas, save for the roughest of hurricanes or maelstroms.

SURVIVAL TALENT
Lodestone

Prerequisite: None
Experience Point Cost: 200

You have a knack for navigation, and know the skies well enough to navigate day or night without difficulty. If the constellations are visible to you, you gain one free use of the Obtain Information Momentum spend when using the Survival skill to attempt to chart a course or to find your bearings. The information from the Momentum spend must relate to your current location and a potential path from there to another destination.

> *He swept the ships in the harbor with an appreciative glance, then lifted his head and stared beyond the bay, far into the blue haze of the distance where sea met sky. And his memory sped beyond that horizon, to the golden seas of the south, under flaming suns, where laws were not and life ran hotly. Some vagrant scent of spice or palm woke clear-etched images of strange coasts where mangroves grew and drums thundered, of ships locked in battle and decks running blood, of smoke and flame and the crying of slaughter…*
>
> — The Hour of the Dragon

NEW LANGUAGE: PIRATE CODE

Pirates throughout the Main — whether Argosseans in the Red Brotherhood, Zingaran buccaneers, or even the Black Corsairs — frequently have need to signal one another from ship-to-ship, ship-to-shore, or shore-to-ship. There is a variety of these methods, ranging from smoke signals, drum codes, pidgin dialects they can speak amongst outsiders without fear of being understood, or even colored rockets containing explosive powder (see page 164 of the CONAN corebook).

A pirate character may choose "Pirate Code" as their additional language in *Step Nine: Finishing Touches* of character creation ("Languages", page 44 of the CONAN corebook), or as a new language whenever one is learned.

Though the specifics of these codes are often unique to each pirate group, they are similar enough that a character knowing one form of pirate code is assumed to be able to understand and communicate in any other pirate code with a successful Simple (D0) Linguistics roll.

FINISHING TOUCHES

All other aspects of character generation from the **Conan** corebook are unchanged and should be consulted when completing your character. The following sections cover aspects specific to the content in this book, including additional names for the countries covered, pirate titles, and appearances of the folk described herein.

PIRATE NAMES

The following names are provided for player or gamemaster use, expanding those found on page 48 of the **Conan** corebook.

Zingarans with noble names (or those with pretenses to nobility) use surnames, usually the name of their family, their house, or even their home town (often one and the same) with a "de" linking them. For example, a Zingaran grandee might announce herself as Aurelia de Palma.

PIRATE NICKNAMES

Many pirates have titles appended to their names, based on some personal quirk, affectation, or deed they have committed. When creating a pirate character, you may choose or roll on the following chart for one of these nicknames or titles. First, roll 1🎲. If the result is 1–2, add a prefix to

PIRATE SAMPLE CHARACTER NAMES

Homeland	Male	Female
Argos	Abas, Anaxos, Bracus, Davos, Kallias, Leontis, Lysandros, Maro, Oresus, Stolos, Theoros, Tychaeus	Anysia, Charis, Cilissa, Demetria, Helice, Ianessa, Melita, Nyssa, Roxanne, Sophia, Thetis, Zita
The Black Coast	Adebayo, Adedji, Adeoye, Amaku, Bengu, Bunda, Enanga, Kamara, K'Gari, Makara, N'Komo, Okunnu	Ayana, Behare, Erza, Hamere, Katura, Maiba, Massasi, Nehanda, Ntara, Ntuli, Saba, Zenzele
Kush	Adagala, Karanja, Kashta, Kassaye, Khama, Matano, Mayanja, Morake, Mshila, Mwangi, Okondo, Zenyami	Ghida, Ghnima, Hasna, Hassiba, Karimala, Najet, Nezha, Tafat, Tanest, Tiziri, Wrina, Zergha
Shem	Abibaal, Agga, Ahaz, Ibni-Addu, Megalaros, Naram-Sin, Ninus, Obares, Shopak, Turbaza, Ur-Nammu, Zabdas	Aishah, Aya, Elisheba, Izevel, Mariamne, Maesa, Ninki, Nisaba, Semiramis, Siduri, Silili, Tanit
Stygia	Amenakht, Anen, Apophis, Harnakhte, Hemaka, Inarus, Kenamun, Menmet-Ra, Panas, Penamun, Rahotep	Ahwere, Asenath, Henut, Hesepti, Inuhue, Maharet, Senebtisi, Senet, Sitre, Taheret, Timat, Weret
Zingara (personal names)	Allande, Amadeo, Arano, Belasco, Elazar, Flavio, Gergori, Luciano, Marcelo, Nunio, Rogellio, Valerio	Alegria, Anabela, Aurelia, Belicia, Eliana, Esmerelda, Ligia, Lucia, Nidia, Sabina, Valentina, Zabaleta
Zingara (surnames)	Acosta, Aguerre, Alvarez, Castanos, Delezon, Ferrara, Galvez, Karavacca, Kervera, Montilla, Moreno, Palma, Peralta, Sandoval, Solera, Truxillo, Valadez, Valencia, Zarate, Zelaya	

your name. If there is no result (a roll of 3–4), add a suffix. If an effect is rolled, roll or pick two prefixes and combine them to form a nickname, such as "Bloody Bracus, the Bold".

PIRATE NICKNAMES

Roll	Prefix	Suffix
1–2	Big	...the Bold
3–4	Black	...the Bloody
5–6	Bloody	...the Lucky
7–8	Dead	...the Brave
9–10	Grim	...the Foolish
11–12	Little	...the Blessed
13–14	Lucky	...the Cursed
15–16	Old	...the Fortunate
17–18	Red	...the Dire
19–20	Scurvy	...the Hunted

APPEARANCE

Many and varied are the crews of pirate vessels, though the root stock of the seafaring nations is somewhat easy to distinguish. If you are creating a character from one of the coastal nations, these guidelines may help you describe your character:

- **Argos:** Argosseans are generally olive-skinned and average of build. Their hair ranges from light brown to glossy black, and eye color is usually brown, grey, or green. Their noses are straight and often have a slight nasal bump, and their eyelashes are frequently so dark they seem as if they are wearing kohl.

- **The Black Coast:** Denizens of the Black Coast are tall and ebon-skinned, black — or brown-eyed, and they style their hair in a variety of fashions based on their immediate tribe and rank within their village. Some wear body paint or indulge in scarification, while others pierce their earlobes, noses, and even lips with rings and sharpened pieces of horn, bone, or precious metal. In build, they tend to be slender and long-limbed, with some exceptions.

- **Kush:** Kushites are divided into two primary social castes, the Gallah and the Chaga. The Gallah are the minority, and are ebon-skinned giants, with black eyes, hair, and features common throughout the Black Kingdoms. The Chaga are descended from Stygian ancestors, and are lighter-skinned than the Gallah and bear strong resemblance to their Stygian forebears.

- **Shem:** Shemites range in coloration greatly, from light brown complexions to pale white. Dark hair and eyes are common, though some of the pale-skinned

PIRATE CHARACTERS

Shemites have blue eyes. They are slighter than the Hyborian races, and are strong-featured, often with curly hair and beards.

- **Stygia:** Descended from the Lemurians of old, the people of Stygia are dusky-skinned, with hawklike features, tall and broad builds, dark hair, and glittering black eyes. Some of their older bloodlines bear the admixture of Acheron, and are pale-skinned. Shaved heads are common among men and women, with hair replaced by elaborate enameled wigs and head-pieces.

- **Zingara:** Zingarans are generally swarthy-skinned compared to most Hyborians due to the Pictish influx in their ancestry, and have eyes that are brown, green, or dark gray. They are average in build, tending towards being compact, and are hot-headed and passionate as a rule. Their hair is usually dark, though blonde hair is not rare.

> *They were characteristic Argossean sailors, short and stockily built. Conan towered above them, and no two of them could match his strength. They were hardy and robust, but his was the endurance and vitality of a wolf, his thews steeled and his nerves whetted by the hardness of his life in the world's wastelands.*
>
> — "Queen of the Black Coast"

These features are readily visible to casual onlookers, but can be concealed or disguised. None have any in-game effects: they are merely cosmetic. If they would normally seem to cause some disability, your character has long since managed to compensate for it.

Clothing

Pirates tend to wear a ragged motley of whatever they have, either from their former lives, garments of common sailors, or augmented with bits of finery snatched from those they have stolen from. Head-scarves are common, as are loose shirts, billowing leggings, and sandals. Sleeveless vests are often worn in warmer climes, and baldrics or sashes help support the weight of weapons.

Pirates often have tattoos, scarification, and their teeth may be replaced with gold ones, symbols of rough times and testament to the poor medical treatment afforded by their lifestyle. That said, they tend to flaunt their wealth whenever possible, so earrings, necklaces, rings, and other signs of plunder are worn, removed only to pay debts or when captured. Some pirates with experience in traditional navies often wear elements of their former uniforms, decorated in barbaric and uncouth fashion.

Distinguishing Feature

At your discretion, your character may have a distinguishing feature, some unique element of appearance that marks them and makes them especially memorable. You can roll or pick from this table if desired.

Roll	DISTINGUISHING FEATURE
	Feature
1	Long scar (or series of scars) on face.
2	Visible burn marks, including loss of hair.
3	Unnatural hair coloration.
4	Bald with a tattooed scalp.
5	Ritual scarring on cheeks and forehead.
6	Vivid stripes of white in hair and/or facial hair.
7	Long scar leading from corner of mouth.
8	Deep scarring on cheeks from some disease.
9	Several gold or silver teeth.
10	Reddish-purple stain visible on face.
11	Forked beard (if male). Roll again if female.
12	Eyes unnaturally light.
13	Missing a lot of teeth.
14	One eye milky white, looks blind but is otherwise functional.
15	Missing 1🔥+1 fingers.
16	Hideous scar across throat.
17	Deep notch cut out of one ear.
18	Nose broken several times.
19	Missing an ear.
20	Missing one eye.

GEAR & EQUIPMENT

Bandits of the waves, pirates have access to a wide variety of gear, armor, and weaponry, stolen from others or picked up in one of the many port markets they frequent. Sea-vessels provide a regular base of operations for their crew, and as such the average pirate may have more personal possessions than many other types of player characters.

If pirates dwell on the ship they crew, they may (player choice) have a small footlocker, satchel bag, cask, nook, or, in the case of the captain or first mate, a cabin within which to store their personal effects. Additionally, most sea-vessels are equipped with adequate tools and other sundries to function, giving a pirate player character group a potentially wider range of readily available equipment.

PIRATE EQUIPMENT

Most of the items in the **Conan** corebook are available to pirate player characters. A few items are unique to the pirate lifestyle, and are described below.

Pirate Weapons

For the most part, pirates tend to fight with one-handed weapons, allowing a free hand for holding onto ropes or for finding purchase when decks lurch. Particularly valuable are those items that have a dual purpose for work as well as fighting; thus, most pirate weapons are tools first and foremost.

Weapons in the **Conan** corebook that pirates favor are one-handed swords and knives, hatchets, and spears (though used in melee, rarely thrown). Another weapon is the two-handed scimitar, a greater version of the normal scimitar, favored by strong pirates and used more on the shore than in shipboard combat.

Several new weapons are presented here for pirate player characters, generally fishing and boat-handling tools put to use as improvised weapons.

- The **boarding axe**, a one-handed long-handled axe with either a spike or hammer on the reverse, used to cut ropes or hack through doors, put to brutal use as a weapon.
- The **belaying pin** is a foot-long wooden truncheon used to secure ropes, serving as an improvised club or potential parrying weapon.
- The **gaff** is a wickedly curved hook mounted on a handle or a pole, used to hook fish or ropes, and is often used as an improvised weapon.
- The **boarding pike** is one of the few two-handed melee weapons favored by pirates, a long spear with a head backed with a rear-facing hook, used to pull ships together, manipulate ropes, and to present a wall of sharp steel to repel boarders.
- The **marlin spike** is a thick, tapered metal bar up to a foot long, used in rigging to secure lines or even to help untie tight knots, useful as an improvised dagger or light club.

Ranged weapons favored by pirates include slings, crossbows, and bows. Sling stones, especially, are easy to replace, and some ships may have barrels of rocks suitable for throwing, kept at the ready. Bows are used less frequently in poor weather, as wet bow-strings are less effective and occasionally dangerous. Whenever a pirate vessel seizes another, any weapons are confiscated and stored for later use. For naval vessels, it is another story: they often use arrow-fire more regularly, counting on dockside quartermasters to replenish their supplies.

Weapons like throwing axes, throwing knives, and javelins are less popular, as missing with one of these can mean striking an ally or losing it overboard.

PIRATE WEAPONS							
Weapon	Reach	Damage	Size	Qualities	Availability	Cost	Encumbrance
Axe, Boarding	2	3⚔	1H	Intense, Piercing 1	1	3	1
Belaying Pin	1	2⚔	1H	Improvised, Non-lethal	1	1	1
Gaff	1	3⚔	2H	Improvised, Vicious 1	1	3	2
Pike, Boarding	3	4⚔	2H	Piercing 1, Vicious 1	1	4	2
Scimitar, Two-handed	3	4⚔	2H	Intense, Vicious 1	1	6	2
Spike, Marlin	1	3⚔	1H	Improvised, Stun	1	1	1

Pirate Armor

Due to the dangers of drowning, few pirates wear anything other than the lightest of armors, preferring to sacrifice protection for mobility, whether climbing yardarms, leaping from one ship-deck to another, or rapidly scrambling through below-decks in pursuit of loot or hidden foes. Shields are used infrequently, favored in the initial exchange of missile fire and set aside when boarding actions begin. In shipboard combat, it is often difficult to use anything larger than a buckler or medium shield.

The sole type of armor worn more frequently at sea than on land is the **buff coat**, a frequently sleeveless, knee-length coat of thin, tough cow — or elk-hide, boiled and stiffened, flaring below the breast and providing a light and sturdy alternative to metal armor. These are left their "buff" tan color or are stained and decorated, sometimes paired with cloth sleeves. The one advantage the buff coat has over other types of light armor is that it is possible to layer a breastplate and sleeves above or below it, adding that armor's value to the torso hit location.

Pirate Gear

Pirates use the same sort of gear common to fishermen, sailors, and others who ply the oceans for trade or war, though they are traditionally poorly equipped and accustomed to dealing with substandard equipment, making do or jury-rigging when they do not possess the right item. Nonetheless, several items of gear may be of use to pirate and oceangoing characters, and are described here.

Most are self-explanatory, and yield +1d20 when used for the appropriate skill.

- A **grappling hook** can be used for Climbing or Sailing, bringing one ship closer to another.

- A great **spyglass** removes up to three levels of Difficulty for Observation tests due to range, and a small spyglass removes one level.

- An **astrolabe** is useful for finding one's location and plotting a course across the ocean.

		PIRATE ARMOR					
Armor Type	Item	Hit Locations Covered	Armor Soak	Qualities	Availability	Cost	Encumbrance
Heavy Clothing	Buff Coat	Torso, Arms	1	—	1	3	2

KITS AND MISCELLANEOUS GEAR

Skill or Activity	Item	Type	Availability	Cost	Encumbrance
Athletics	Grappling Hook	Tools	2	1	1
Observation	Spyglass, Great	Tools	2	5	1
Observation	Spyglass, Small	Tools	2	3	—
Sailing	Signal Rocket	Tool	2	1	1
Survival	Astrolabe	Tools	2	5	—
Survival	Fishing Gear	Tools	1	1	—
Survival	Lodestone	Tools	1	2	—
Survival	Nautical Charts	Library	2	5	2
Command	Finery, Captain's	Tools	1	5	1

- **Fishing gear** can be used to add +1d20 to Survival attempts when fishing.

- A **lodestone** is also useful for determining which direction true north is at, and thus navigating based on that knowledge.

- **Nautical charts** describe the oceanic currents and weather patterns, and chart the location of islands, coasts, and ports.

- A **signal rocket** is created using the Alchemy skill, and incorporates explosive powder to propel the rocket into the air a great distance before it explodes in a brilliant display of sparks, flame, and smoke. These come in a variety of colors and sizes, and are used by pirate vessels to communicate with one another easily at nightfall or when a simple signal is desired. It adds to the Sailing skill only when communicating with other vessels.

- **Captain's finery** is a rough term describing a style common to Zingara and, to a lesser extent, Argos. It encompasses a flamboyant mix of crass and opulent garments designed to impress lackeys and sailors, as well as striking a suitable impression with those encountered during acts of piracy. Zingaran captain's finery is especially gaudy, with wide-brimmed hats, slashed and puffed sleeves, high boots, and open-fronted silk shirts.

Siege Weapons

Weapons used against ships are ultimately grand-scale versions of hand-to-hand weapons, using the same principles. They range from the ballista — an immense arbalest with internal winch — to the catapult and trebuchet, essentially large-scale slings. These are described more fully in *Conan the Mercenary*, though they are summarized in the ship-to-ship combat system described in *Chapter 8: Ship Combat*.

CHAPTER 2
GAZETTEER

> *Here there was no loot — no towns to sack nor ships to burn. The men murmured, though they did not let their murmurings reach the ears of their implacable master, who tramped the poop day and night in gloomy majesty, or pored over ancient charts and time-yellowed maps, reading in tomes that were crumbling masses of worm-eaten parchment. At times he talked to Sancha, wildly it seemed to her, of lost continents, and fabulous isles dreaming unguessed amidst the blue foam of nameless gulfs, where horned dragons guarded treasures gathered by pre-human kings, long, long ago.*
>
> — "The Pool of the Black One"

The world of the pirate is one of the open sea and the coast, and rarely any deeper inland than that which can be reached within a quick walk from the waterfront. This chapter provides an overview of the coastal cities and kingdoms along the Western Sea, from the Baracha Isles and the Pictish Coast in the north to the Black Kingdoms in the south. These countries and regions are discussed briefly in the **Conan** corebook, and their coastal regions are expanded upon here.

Though most of these kingdoms and regions are a part of the coast of the Western Ocean, they are arranged into **The Main**; consisting of the Western Ocean, Zingara, and Argos; **The Southern Shores**; which include Shem, Stygia, Kush, and **The Black Coast**; and **The Northern Wilds**, a stretch that covers Vanaheim and the Pictish Coast. The Vilayet Sea is also mentioned in brief.

THE MAIN

THE WESTERN OCEAN

The Western Sea itself is the greatest body of water in the world, defining the coastline from north to south, and it once covered the world entirely at the time of the Cataclysm, sparing only a few small island chains and regions from its embrace. It is vast, and though its dimensions and character from the snowy wastelands north of Vanaheim down to the uttermost jungles south of the Black Coast are known, few have ventured to chart what lies to its uttermost west.

Explorers and particularly daring traders have sailed forth west from the coast of the Thurian continent, and though some have encountered mysterious lost islands forgotten by humankind and lived to speak of what they found, none have ever returned from voyages further west.

Countless are the islands found in the Western Ocean, and the adventure generator in the *Conan Gamemaster's Toolkit* and the ruins generator in *Ancient Ruins & Cursed Cities* allow the gamemaster to create them easily. Following are two examples of islands, each lost in legend and suitable for explorers who stray far from the continent and into unknown waters.

THE ISLE OF THE BLACK ONES

Many weeks of sail west from the Baracha Isles is a small tropical island, identified only in ancient maps and hinted at in the mysterious *Books of Skelos*, pleasant in semblance and horrifying in its true nature. The jungle itself is redolent of spices and bountiful with many fruits, including a golden variety that is particularly tasty, and possesses a narcotic effect not unlike that of the gas of the black lotus, which brings on sleep (**Conan** corebook, page 166).

> *He desired to learn if this island were indeed that mentioned in the mysterious Book of Skelos, whereon, nameless sages aver, strange monsters guard crypts filled with hieroglyph-carven gold. Nor, for murky reasons of his own, did he wish to share his knowledge, if it were true, with any one, much less his own crew.*
>
> — "The Pool of the Black One"

This island, surrounded with white sand, grassy slopes, and verdant jungle, hides the ruins of an ancient culture of a mysterious race known only as the Black Ones, ebon-skinned giants of inhuman appearance and diabolical practices. The jungle hides their home city, a veritable metropolis of greenish stone towers and bizarrely configured circular walls, all of it overgrown with grass and vines. The Black Ones' strange and inscrutable worship concerns a black stone-ringed pool filled with greenish water in the center of a courtyard surrounded with semi-translucent green stone. The Black Ones place their victims into the pool, which inflicts a terrible transformation upon the victim into a tiny figurine, not much bigger than a man's hand. The walls surrounding the pool of the Black One are filled with hundreds of such figurines, the sad and terrible fate of the many who have found the island and met their ends there.

The Black Ones are described on page 77.

THE ISLE OF PIRATES' DOOM

This innocuous isle lies scores of miles from the Pictish coastline. Remnants of huts and prior habitations on the beach indicate that the island has been dwelt upon before, though there is no sign of any natives in these rude huts, their whereabouts or fate a mystery. The sole remaining inhabitants are insects, birds, and venomous serpents. One of the island's secrets is a majestic waterfall, behind which is a concealed cavern, large enough to hide a small force within. The eastern side of the island is dominated by swamps almost too dense and miserable to allow passage.

Deep within these swamps, however, is an ancient temple, ruined even before the Cataclysm, yet made so stoutly that it will likely endure deluges to come. The few scraps of rumors about this mysterious island are that the temple hides a bounty of precious stones, but their exact nature — whether gems or merely sacred rocks — is unknown.

Inside the temple is a great altar that no doubt had been stained crimson time and time again with ritual knives plunging into innocent flesh, and suspended above it on a thin column is balanced a huge block of a disquieting nature, fashioned of yellowish stone shot through with veins of red. Close examination of the altar and a successful Daunting (D3) Observation test will reveal that the lid is cunningly hinged to slide away from the altar, revealing a gleaming red stone inside its hollow. Legends say that it is priceless beyond compare, while a cunning pirate may do well to remember that such easy rewards often belie fiendish traps. Setting off the trap is immediately fatal to anyone failing a Daunting (D3) Acrobatics test, so great is the weight and size of the block.

THE ISLE OF BAL-SAGOTH

Situated at least two weeks away from the shores of even Pictland, its exact location unknown, this island, lost to time, is inhabited by a people descended directly from those of long-vanished, pre-Cataclysmic Atlantis, untouched by the calamity that drowned that kingdom for millennia. The island is rich and lush, a tropical paradise, with ample food to be picked as desired. A species of huge, flightless birds menaces the coast, though the breed is nearly extinct. Huge apes graze amidst the jungle foliage, but are essentially harmless unless attacked.

The island's primary inhabitants, though, are a race of brown-skinned folk, powerful in magic, and they know this island as "Bal-Sagoth". They are tall and slim, and wear barbaric finery including brightly-colored feathers, bejeweled gold and silver armlets and leglets. Though they wear no armor, their small shields are chased with silver and their spears, hatchets, and daggers are of the finest steel. Their king wears a golden chain upon which depends a curious jade carving. The city is wealthy beyond compare, furnished in fine wood, marble, gold, silk, and other such fine substances, never having known the depredations of invasions or catastrophe.

The people of Bal-Sagoth worship many gods: the greatest of all is Gol-goroth, "the god of darkness who sits forever in the Temple of Shadows". And thus, though they have a king, the truest power in Bal-Sagoth's society is that of a hereditary priesthood. These strange and terrible men and women know secrets of dark sorcery, controlling demons and other entities from the Outermost Dark, inherited from their ancestors and bound to their wills. The labyrinths below the fair city boast unspeakable horrors and nameless monstrosities, all controlled by the priests, and they have mastered the arts of creating life and altering its very nature, spawning unholy hybrids of human and beast.

> *So they progressed through the forest, now losing sight of the distant city as treetops obstructed the view, now seeing it again. And at last they came out on the low shelving banks of a broad blue lagoon and the full beauty of the landscape burst upon their eyes. From the opposite shores the country sloped upward in long gentle undulations which broke like great slow waves at the foot of a range of blue hills a few miles away. These wide swells were covered with deep grass and many groves of trees, while miles away on either hand there was seen curving away into the distance the strip of thick forest which Brunhild said belted the whole island. And among those blue dreaming hills brooded the age-old city of Bal-Sagoth, its white walls and sapphire towers clean-cut against the morning sky. The suggestion of great distance had been an illusion.*
>
> — "The Gods of Bal-Sagoth"

From time to time, the folk of Bal-Sagoth must contend with raids from the Vanir, whether sailing there by intent or happening across the isle by accident, but they are always victorious and manage to drive the red-bearded reavers away

ZINGARA

Zingara is home to many proud, noble families that possess most of the country's wealth, linked through a complex network of alliances, marriages, and rivalries. The land is a prosperous one, wealthy in mineral resources, boasting a robust agricultural economy, and possessing a lengthy coastline allowing her navies and fishing fleets to dominate the sea-front, making them a naval power second only to Argos. But her passionate, fiery people are her greatest wealth, and in Zingara flourishes an elaborate code of chivalry as well as a complex social order that manages to keep rival houses balanced against one another while a relatively powerless king nonetheless rules over all.

The prevailing winds along the Zingaran coast are to the southeast, aiding ships sailing toward Argos and other southerly destinations. Bounded to the north with the Black River and Pictland, bisected by the Thunder and Shirki Rivers, and bounded to the south by the Khorotas River across which is Argos, Zingara is surrounded by water. Even its northeast border is formed by the Alimane River, which separates it from Poitain, a province nominally held by Aquilonia but more Zingaran in temperament than the folk of Poitain would like to admit.

This relative security is both a blessing and a bane, as it means that Zingara's borders are relatively secure from invaders, but it is also difficult for the country to expand, and her proud and ambitious noble houses turn against one another with the lack of breathing room. Aquilonia has pushed aggressively into the Bossonian Marches and beyond to satisfy the greed and ambition of her nobility. Zingara, on the other hand, has nowhere to go but into Pict-held land to their immediate north, lest they wish to dispute borders with Aquilonia or Argos (more than is already the case). Her southern plantations are the heart of her agricultural wealth, and to endanger them would be the death-knell of the country, so the king of Zingara must play noble houses against one another to keep them in check.

Each of these noble houses is led by a "prince", a title denoting noble blood but not directly descended from the king. Valerio, the current king, is supported by a web of alliances among these princes. He has little authority of his own and instead must call upon the princes for military aid and other support. King Valerio is accountable to a council of nobles, made up of representatives from the oldest and most prominent of noble houses. If Valerio fails to abide by the council's guidance, the nobles can call for a vote of confidence in the king. Calling for such a vote often ushers in a period of anarchy as the princes contend among themselves for the throne, both politically and militarily. These periods of uncertainty and unrest can last a few weeks or go on for several years. Each king is also required to marry a priestess chosen from among a line of sacred soothsayers (see page 34), regardless of whether he is already married, in which case he takes the priestess as a second wife. King Valerio has such an arrangement in place, though he shows little of these two wives much attention.

Zingarans traditionally have black hair, brown eyes, and dark complexions, though the Hyborian influence means that dark blondes with dark eyes are not uncommon. Men and women are distinguished from one another by their exotic habits, particularly their brightly colored clothing. They favor broad, colorful sashes or scarves and gold jewelry, particularly hooped earrings. The fashions in the capital city of Kordava change almost as quickly as does its politics.

THE LAND OF ZINGARA

The fertile Zingg Valley, along the lower Black River, was first settled by a farming people more than a thousand years ago. Their simple villages were conquered by a tribe of Picts that remained and settled in the valley. Their villages were in turn invaded by a tribe of Hyborians on their migration west. From the mixture of these three peoples, Zingara was formed. Now, the valley is home to numerous farms, vineyards, and noble estates. It is the heart of the country, where most of its population and its farmlands and vineyards can be found. Many of these farms are immense plantations, hereditarily owned by the noble houses, a primary source of their great wealth. These plantations depend heavily upon slave labor, and the Zingaran slave trade exists primarily to feed this great need, funneling slaves into the countryside from markets in Hyperborea, Koth, Zingara, Argos, Shem, Stygia, and the Black Coast.

North of the Black River, the farmland soon gives way to forested mountains marked by fortified towers. The logging camps and mines in these hills are frequently raided by Picts who come down from the north in search of metals and other valuable goods. Between the Black and Thunder Rivers lie grasslands spotted with fortified ranches and great herds of cattle and horses. On the Thunder River, just upstream from where it joins the Shirki River as it flows down from Aquilonia, lies the city of Astura. It is a city known both as a military garrison and as an important stop for traders traveling between Zingara and Aquilonia, as well as points further east. The Thunder, Shirki, and Alimane Rivers in this area are renowned for the bandits that line their banks and the pirates that ply their waters. The borderlands between Zingara, Aquilonia, and Argos offer great opportunities to brigands and smugglers, and there is usually an ample supply of unemployed soldiers and mercenaries willing to earn some coin through raiding, smuggling, or other jobs where few questions are asked.

East of the Thunder River are the marches where Zingara fights back and forth with Argos for control of the lands. The fortified towns and keeps in this border region often change hands. A traveler is more likely to find a ruined or abandoned homestead than an occupied one. This area is crossed by a caravan road that runs south from Poitain to Messantia in Argos. The road passes through a wood that lies between the coast and the hills that mark the border with Argos. Beneath the black boughs of that forest, ghouls roam at night, and it is said that deep in that wood there are the ruins of an ancient, accursed city through which the ghouls flit like shadows.

The political alliances in this area are even more fluid. As Zingara and Argos shift between war and peace, the noble families may war against Argos one year and then ally with them the next for aid in raids against their rivals. Mercenary companies can often find work here, as some noble is almost always looking to take advantage of a rival's weakness or shore up his own defenses. The lower Thunder River is frequently plagued by attacks from Argos and from pirates.

POLITICS IN ZINGARA

To an outsider, the political state of Zingara at any given time is at best opaque and more often completely inscrutable. Zingara is less a kingdom than a series of ever-shifting alliances and vendettas. While a nominal ruler ofttimes sits upon a throne, true power lies in the great noble houses whose lineage is a mix of blood ties and long-held grudges. The houses support the ruler or do not, as is their choice and whim. It is due to this tempestuous relationship that Zingara does not regularly muster a mighty navy like Argos, but instead a flotilla of aligned house fleets, bound temporarily to a single purpose. That said, all Zingarans tend to view an attack on one as an attack on all, and there is no better way to get them all to cooperate — at least for a time — than to threaten Zingara with foreign invasion.

Naturally, however, these scheming houses are not above plotting with outside powers if they see it to their advantage. There are, it is said, more layers to Zingaran politics than steps down to the abyss of Hell. An outlander has little chance of picking up the nuances of feuds and alliances without considerable experience. A few mercenary companies from outside Zingara have some success in using this complex political structure for constant employment, hired when these rivalries come to bloodshed.

The Great Houses

The noble families of Zingara are all, theoretically, related in some complex way. By tradition, however, each house holds its own customs, seal, troops, and navy. They nominally answer when the king or queen calls, but only when it is advantageous to them. Feuds between certain houses have lasted for decades and even centuries, though marriage bonds are sometimes used to foster better will. But the Zingaran heart is a raging sun of passion. As surely as they love deeply, they hate deeply, as well. They forget neither friend nor betrayer, and any perceived slight can cause calamity between the aristocratic bloodlines that comprise the real power of Zingara.

> *Galbro nodded. He was well aware of the enmity which existed between the pirates and the Zingaran buccaneers. The pirates were mainly Argossean sailors, turned outlaw; to the ancient feud between Argos and Zingara was added, in the case of the freebooters, the rivalry of opposing interests. Both breeds preyed on the shipping and the coastal towns; and they preyed on one another with equal rapacity.*
>
> — "The Black Stranger"

ZINGARAN STYLE

Immodest, outlandish, and often considered an arrogant people, Zingarans would likely claim all such traits with pride. While such claims may be arguable, it is well known to all that Zingaran culture and technology are among the most advanced of the age. They produced a unique dueling style all their own and do build and captain impressive fleets of ships. Ironically, it is that indomitable will alone preventing Zingara from being the preeminent empire upon the Western Sea. Zingarans are not easily cowed nor easily led, a strength and weakness at once.

Zingaran Art

The finest painters in the world hail from Zingara. Their style has revolutionized the art of the current period, or so any Zingaran painter would have you believe. Murals depicting great victories at sea, legendary vendettas, and lost loves sit aside portraits of near lifelike realism.

Poetry, too, is a thing as valued as gold to some Zingarans, for it reflects the passion of the heart. A poem can last a thousand years whereas gold will fade, find other hands, and be forgotten as being owned by the dead. But a poem takes on immortality and any suitor, of either gender, must try to put their passion into words. While the male is most commonly the pursuer of the female in other nations, this is not so in Zingara. Women often write the finest poetry. Perhaps not uncoincidentally, they also make fierce warriors.

Like the people themselves, Zingaran art is flashy if not opulent. They are fond of gilding items, displays of wealth, and pantaloons which bloom like sails in a good wind. Jewelry is common to men and women alike, from the head to toe. When not worn loose and cascading in curls, hair is held in place by fine oils and perfumes from as far away as Vendhya and Khitai. More than one rough-and-ready Hyborian has made the mistake of thinking a Zingaran a dandy and, in the duel which follows, finding the Zingaran poniard pierces the heart as readily as their odes to love.

Zingaran Culture

As their politics is complex, Zingaran culture is equally multifarious. There is no caste system, but a series of cues, mostly in the form of accent and apparel, that allow any Zingaran to readily ascertain the stature of a given fellow citizen. Even the poorest families, though, have great pride and storied histories, and nobles respect this. To dismiss one's bloodline, however seemingly humble, is taboo in Zingara.

Moreover, through great acts and deeds, as well as clever business sense — legal or otherwise — any woman or man can rise to a name of rank. Perhaps, they can even marry into one of the noble houses who have title but now lack in concomitant wealth.

As previously noted by travelers, scholars, and the less-than-humble Zingaran people, the flame in one's heart is all-defining. Life is short, and those who burn brightest make the most of their time on Earth, while those whose candle is dim cast small, mouse-like shadows on history. For many Zingaran nobles, skill in poetry and music is as important as skill with the sword.

The Zingaran heart pushes them to epic feats of greatness and equally memorable debacles. Both results are regarded with pride in posterity. This is not something one often finds in other lands. For, in Zingara, the intent is the thing. The result, while important, is less so than the fire under which a task was taken. There are as many tales of blazing love as there are unrequited love, and mournful poems of the spurned are classics, as well.

Practically, this means Zingarans are passionate in all their relations. They are strong and willful, like a gale summoned up before an unwary outsider. They hug and clasp arms with strangers. They display passion for mates publicly and with abandon. They forgive no slight and forget no debt. The Zingaran culture is built on a system of honor which puzzles most other races.

Two kinds of blood bonds mark Zingaran culture — the blood oath and the blood debt. The blood oath is taken between lovers who become betrothed, those kept apart by rivalry, and great friends. A noble house is essentially a series of blood oaths stretching back in time to one's ancestors. Zingarans do not make such oaths easily, and breaking them can make a given citizen, possibly an entire family, a pariah for all time. Practical marriages between houses rarely take blood oaths but instead consider these marriages transactional. However, if two lovers marry and weld two houses together in such passion, anyone that breaks that bond becomes hated by all. Philandering is a serious mistake in Zingara — if you have declared your love by such an oath. If not, one takes and leaves as many lovers as one likes.

The other side of this coin is the blood debt. A blood debt is a vendetta. It might exist between two individuals, two families, or entire houses. Such blood debts stretch back decades and even centuries. Great houses feud and rarely do they reconcile. It is only in the greater service of Zingara that they temporarily set aside a blood debt to combat a common threat.

Once blood debt is sworn, the two parties can never be friends, never family, never anything more than enemies. One of the great Zingaran tragedies, written by Count Trystero some three hundred years ago, tells the tale of two young lovers whose families had a blood debt against one another. Their loved burned very brightly but all too brief and, in the end, carnage was left behind them. Most see such an end as tragic, but a Zingaran sees it as the embodiment of all their blood's fire. Still a blood debt is a blood debt, and the enemy remains the enemy in the end. At least, most of the time.

There are stories of houses whose feuds were overcome by love, but all these are tales far distant from now and mostly ascribed as poetic legend.

MITRA WORSHIP IN ZINGARA

Though Zingarans are not Hyborian in descent, they are nonetheless almost entirely worshippers of Mitra, the eminent god associated with the Hyborian people. However, the Zingaran people are not overly devout — their invocation of Mitra's name is more custom than act of fealty — and the church of Mitra serves more as a political entity than a godly one.

The church's prime responsibility, in practice, is keeping records of house marriages, births, deaths, and grievances. When two houses argue and the king will not intercede, the matter is settled by arbiters from the church of Mitra. While this is recognized as a religious judgement, all know it is, in fact, one handed down by priests who are more barrister than cleric. Despite this, they are rarely corrupt.

Temples exist, but serve practical, political, and community purpose more than faith. Offerings to Mitra are an acknowledgement of an agreed-upon system which keeps

Zingara free from constant internecine warfare — which would surely destroy it. The average Zingaran's faith is in the system itself and the incorruptible, neutral nature of their clergy, not in the god himself, who is regarded as distant and unknowable.

Zingaran priestesses of Mitra enjoy a special distinction as soothsayers and oracles, and many priests of Mitra chafe at the respect given to these women by the noble families.

KORDAVA

Kordava, the capital city of Zingara, lies near where the Black River flows into the Western Sea. The palace in Kordava, from which King Valerio holds court, is known for its crystal floor and for its opulent gardens lined with arched passages. Poets have called it "the pearl upon the shore" for the way its white walls shine above the bay. The fountains and fragrant blooms of the palace gardens have been praised effusively in song and script, and have played host to innumerable trysts, duels, and intrigues. One of the most noted sites in the gardens is the Fount of the Four Lions of Zingara. The lion statues also function as a water clock, with the water pouring from their mouths shifting each hour from one lion to another.

Many Hyborian languages are spoken aloud in the streets of Kordava, as merchants and travelers are drawn there by the city's wealth and vibrant life. The taverns of the city are filled with song and performances by the city's famous dancers late into the night. Brawls between groups of nobles present more of a danger than do thieves. The city guard answers to the royal court, but tread carefully when dealing with the bravos from the prominent noble houses.

Most buildings in the city are made from stone quarried locally or imported from other areas of Zingara. The harbor of Kordava is protected by a stout, stone breakwater that is often used as a site for hanging Barachan pirates as an example to others.

The merchants of Kordava deal in goods from all along the coast of the Western Sea, from Vanaheim to the Black Kingdoms. Inland trade routes connect Kordava to Aquilonia and countries further east. The city has four major markets. The Royal Market and Fish Market are near the docks. The Royal Market specializes in imported goods, and the Fish Market features seafood and other consumables. The North Market is just inside the Zingg Gate on the north side of the city, and it features a wide variety of goods and foods brought in both by local farmers and craftsmen and by traders arriving from the east along the road from Astura and Aquilonia. The Horse Market is near the East Gate. There, one may find Zingara's famous horses and all manner of other livestock. Additional smaller and more informal markets are set up from time to time outside the city's gates by those who want to avoid the fees charged for bringing goods into the city. The artisans of Kordava are noted for their fine leatherwork. Leather goods and the famed Zingaran wines are Kordava's main exports.

> ### THE PRISON OF VALETTA
>
> Valetta Island, located several miles off the Zingaran coast and just west of Kordava, is a small and stark island, an oblong barely a mile across and half a mile at its widest point. There is only one small beach, and the rest of the coastline is sheer cliffsides and rocky inclines too steep for any but goats or the greatest climbers. In profile, Valetta Island itself almost seems as it were broken off, and the upper expanse consists of slopes and small pools, perhaps fed by rainwater. Standing high and proud at the peak of the highest point on the island is an ancient redoubt, made in some forgotten epoch of human history, perhaps even before the Cataclysm.
>
> Many have held this fort and used it for various purposes, but for the past few centuries it has been used as a prison, housing enemies of the Zingaran noble houses, its king, or the church of Mitra — whether captives of war, traitors, criminals, or sometimes even unwelcome bastard sons of the king. The catacombs beneath the Valetta's prison feature many small cells, and it is said that those in the most remote of these are housed those who will never see the light of day again, their names forever stricken from memory.
>
> Escape from Valetta is said to be impossible, though many have tried. It is manned by a relatively small garrison, who put prisoners to work in the tiny fields and gardens that support the island's populace, with a single ship allowed to come ashore to deliver new prisoners and supplies that cannot be produced on the island.
>
> Should the gamemaster wish to send the player characters to an inescapable prison, whether sentenced there or with the goal of freeing one of its prisoners, Valetta is just the place for such an endeavor.

TORAGIS

This city's great wealth has faded, but almost a hundred years ago it was considered the wealthiest of Zingaran cities, the center of its great merchant guilds and warehouses, Zingara's major port closest to Messantia in Argos, and usually the first stop for north-going trade vessels. The city's supremacy in the Zingaran economy made it many enemies in the rival great cities, and the small number of noble houses that controlled the port were envied openly, despised privately. The king himself was subject to the whims of the masters of Toragis, and chafed at having mere merchant-princes dictate policy to him. The warehouses charged usurious fees to their rivals, and in time the whole city grew complacent in its wealth. They built magnificent buildings, decorated the wide boulevards with statues, and created a cosmopolitan marvel to those with wealth, though the stark divide between those controlling the money and those working for it was severe.

Unfortunately, the port's prime position and display of ostentatious wealth made it a primary target for piracy, and it earned no goodwill from the king when it was raided repeatedly by pirates from the Barachas, a concentrated effort that seemed almost as if guided by outside forces. Barachan pirate fleets struck time and again, harrying the shipping lanes in and out from Toragis until none but the most desperate would venture there, and over the course of a handful of years the city became destitute, the great houses divesting and moving to less auspicious holdings in Kordava and Valadelad. The conspiracy that brought down Toragis is an open secret amidst the noble houses, abetted as it was by King Taurino, great-grandfather of Valerio. Speaking publicly about this crime is considered treasonous, however, and will be met by torture and execution.

VALADELAD

The formal capital in days gone by, Valadelad is now a smaller port town and home to House Calari, of whom former kings and queens claim their descent. An ancient palace, once that of the king of a unified Zingara (barely imaginable now), is buried somewhere beneath the modern streets and parapets overlooking the sea. The legendary wealth of that vanished king brings many treasure hunters.

> *To the south, only the Alimane separated the plains of Poitain from the plains of Zingara, and not once but a thousand times had that river run red.*
>
> — The Hour of the Dragon

As a port town, Valadelad is under constant threat from the likes of the Red Brotherhood and burned by them more than once in the last century. The Zingaran royal navy keeps ships and sailors in the port. However, the Brotherhood has a clever pirate among them who intends to draw the ships away from Valadelad by staging a false attack on Kordava. If successful, the town would have only a small contingent to defend itself. News of this plot could bring many rewards if House Calari knew about it.

THE BARACHA ISLES

The Baracha Isles lie southwest of the coast of Zingara. The scattered, volcanic islands are home to hardy fisher folk, hermits, and the Red Brotherhood of the Barachan pirates. The islands are covered in jungle thick with wild pigs, cattle, and other beasts. The waters in the area can be treacherous for those unfamiliar with the islands, their swift, treacherous currents and the many partially-submerged rocks and reefs that can open a hole in any boat. The prevailing winds are from the southwest.

The pirate haven of Tortage is described in the **Conan** corebook on page 227 and on page 39 of this chapter. Legendarily, it is a city where practically anything can be bought and sold, often multiple times in a single day. The Red Brotherhood comes here to sell goods that they've seized from ships, villages, and towns all along the Western Sea. Traders come to Tortage both to buy plunder from the Red Brotherhood and to sell in return ship's supplies, weapons, and copious amounts of ale and wine. Some traders also offer information on ships and towns that may be raided in exchange for protection from the Red Brotherhood. Most of the traders come to Tortage from Argos, but a few Zingaran traders will brave the voyage to what can be hostile waters. Traders from ports as distant as Stygia and even the occasional Vanir will make their way to Tortage, seeking opportunity.

Several fishing villages are scattered through the isles. The fisher folk of the Barachas are a mixed lot, their heritages drawn from Zingara, Argos, Picts, and even older races. The fishing families are hardy and self-reliant, though they are usually eager to trade with any passing ship. But, guests can easily overstay their welcome. The villagers follow a variety of old faiths, generally gods obscure or forbidden in other civilized lands. Each year at midsummer, they have a great roving festival where they spend a week or more sailing from village to village in brightly decorated boats. Each village in turn hosts feasts, games, and dancing. Recently, missionaries of Mitra have traveled through the isles seeking converts, tolerated out of superstition or for their value as sources of amusement. Mitra's missionaries have had scarce better luck with the fishing folk than they have had with the pirates.

Pirate camps can be found throughout the isles. Most of these ruins are transitory camps with tents and other simple shelters. A few, though, are more permanent with a wooden stockade, a blockhouse, or a stone tower. Many ruins are hidden in the jungles that cover the isles. Most ruins are the remains of pirate encampments. There are tales aplenty of far older structures half-buried in the jungle, far older than even humankind.

1. Ruins
2. Degenerates
3. Sunken Ship
4. Volcano
5. Native, Tobosans
6. Ruins, Inhabited
7. Natives, Serpent-Men
8. Ancient Ruins
9. Ruins
10. Pyramid
11. The Great Sargasso
12. Isle of Lost Ships
13. Docks/Seatown
14. Tortage, The Real City
15. Ruins, Fort
16. Ruins

THE JAGGED, BROKEN ISLES

The Cataclysm rent the world in pieces, and no more so is this evident than in the Barachan Isles where the remains of an entire island empire lie broken — a cenotaph of the Thurian Age. Among the rough islands, many of which have yet to be charted, are the vestiges of that vanished civilization as well as what rose in their place — mostly degenerate throwbacks, cast out of civilization and back into barbarism. As they are explored, it is becoming evident that the islands serve not only as redoubts for pirates, but as vaults for things long forgotten, ages long past, and creatures older than the idea of man.

A breakdown of specific locations in the Baracha Isles follows below. Each location is keyed to the map.

A FRACTURED ARCHIPELAGO

One should not make the mistake of thinking of the Baracha Isles as any locale unified in government, ethnicity, language, or anything else. No government nor ruler holds sway, and the "native" populations are not at all the same in physical characteristics, culture, or race. The inhabitants of these isles seem as if they were tossed together in a random amalgam when the Great Cataclysm upended the world. Today, each isle is like unto a world and each indigenous inhabitant a specimen of a rare, perhaps lost race. The rest of the scant populace are those fleeing from other cultures, other worlds, and former lives.

1. Ruins

Standing stones, thirty feet tall and calculated to the confluence of stars above… as they were 100,000 years ago.

2. Degenerates

Tall, lanky, rope-muscled people with tawny hair on head and body. They fell from a much higher state, and date to the early pre-Cataclysmic period. These degenerate men live in the time-eroded ruins of their former civilization. They are cannibals and worship a god of the Outer Dark whose crude visage is carved from native rock in effigy.

3. Sunken Ship

A carrack, by the looks of it. It lies in pristine, clear water. She might have sunk yesterday, only she sank while Atlantis was still above the sea. Her markings are clear, her spar unbroken. No fish nor any other sea-life disturb this large vessel. Her cargo is intact, and a great wealth it would be, yet no one has dived upon the ship and lived. It is said that the sea itself seems to age men to dust in a matter of seconds in the water around this accursed wreck.

4. Volcano

Tobosa, as the natives call it, means "land-breaker" in the native tongue. The natives here, a short, pale-skinned group with dark hair, believe Tobosa was the cause and heart of the Cataclysm. They worship the god they say lives inside. Tobosa is an active volcano.

5. Natives, Tobosans

Supposed descendants of a Valusian colony that barely survived the Cataclysm, the Tobosan culture and mythos is obsessed with that central event. They are an apocalyptic, cult-like tribe, sacrificing members to the volcano at precise dates which no longer coincide with the stars as they now appear. They occasionally substitute others as sacrifices, rather than their own people.

6. Ruins, Inhabited

Like others in the Barachas, this island is dotted with ruins of an ancient — though known — provenance. This was once a slave trading post for the Zingarans, a neutral port and open market where any ships could land and peruse slaves brought from a dozen different countries, with every color of skin and language. The market was destroyed by a slave uprising, and the slavers murdered to a man, all ships in the port captured, their owners executed on the slave market grounds. Now it is a small fishing village made up entirely of the descendants of slaves, a free-town where all are equal. Though the Barachan pirates are not especially liked there, they are allowed to land periodically and recruit to swell their numbers.

7. Native, Serpent-Men

In the secret corners of the world lie civilizations, or their survivors, from ages long past. Among these are the ancient serpent-men, once foe to the mighty King Kull of Valusia. This island, whose true name is unpronounceable to a human tongue, is one of the few refuges of these sons of Set. Perhaps they conduct their business much as they did millennia ago — no human has returned to speak of their ways.

8. Ancient Ruins

This ziggurat-like structure is comprised entirely of a blue, translucent stone. To all appearances, it could be glass, so perfect is its polish and sheen. Anyone approaching the structure sees visions of a black, inky horror being forced into the center of the ziggurat. The creatures forcing it inside are not human, but serpent-men. The mental anguish of such a vision requires a Dire (D4) Resolve test to resist. Failure inflicts 6 🕈 mental damage.

9. Ruins

Rounded by time, these ruins are all but unidentifiable. The jungle has swallowed them to the point where much of this complex now appears as natural hills. However, there is a plain metal disc in the center of the site. It is made of an unknown type of metal, but cracked from the Cataclysm. Foolish or brave explorers could lift it with a lever or pulley system. Below, some one hundred feet down, lies a large metal casket. The casket is locked from the outside and bound in chains as thick as a man's arm.

10. Pyramid

This pyramid looks nothing like those found in Stygia. Instead, it is a stepped structure with strange symbols mounting the walls. The steps appear carved from obsidian. Despite its apparent age, the pyramid has no overgrowth. Indeed, the area immediately surrounding the structure is devoid of plant and animal life.

11. The Great Sargasso

Sailors who work the seas long enough hear tales of a vast sargasso which captures ships like a spider in its web. The holds of these ships, the legends say, hold riches from across eons. In most cases, this is a tale dismissed of a drunken evening in the swaying hold of a ship.

In this case, however, it is true. The Great Sargasso has ensnared ships from the dawn of time. Each is like an insect suspended in amber, for it is as if no time passes here. The ships themselves are connected via a series of walkways, evidence that someone still uses them. Each ship is pristine save for parts visibly removed on purpose. Who knows what sort of village might be built from these varied parts upon yonder shore. And if the ships do not age, what of the men who sailed them? Could they be alive as well?

12. Isle of Lost Ships

This is the isle where the crews of the Sargasso ships went to settle. They indeed have not aged, nor can they reproduce. Instead, they are a kind of menagerie collected by an insane god, trapped on this island and in time. Valusians and Commorians, Acheronians and Argosseans live in uneasy, strange alliances trying to get off the island. Yet, no matter what ship they build, it always brings them back here. Many are convinced they have found hell. Should any player characters be unfortunate enough to suffer a similar fate, the humans on the island speak of other sentient beings, also trapped, who come from ages far older than that of man or any of his ancestors.

GAZETTEER

13. Docks/Seatown

This large town has no name. Much of it is slung out over the open ocean on a stone bridge which, by all rights, should not support the weight. Stilt homes made of local wood also surround the stone in relatively shallow water. The natives wear bronze armor and have high technology but speak an unknown language. They permit no one to enter the interior of the island.

14. Tortage, The Real City

See *Tortage*, see below.

15. Ruins, Fort

Hundreds of years ago, King Osoro of Zingara sought to establish peace in the troubled region in and around the Baracha Isles, and his forces constructed a fortress and port on this island. Osoro's intent was to provide a safe harbor for Zingara's warships and naval vessels, from which they could eradicate piracy in the Barachas once and forever. The fortress stood for several months, until it was wiped out utterly by a massing of pirate vessels the Western Sea had never seen, every man and woman on the island put to death, their heads arrayed upon the broken walls. Chagrined and (more importantly) driven to near bankruptcy by the endeavor, the king ordered the fortress abandoned. It has remained empty ever since, save for the occasional pirate gang using it as a hideout.

16. Deserted Village

This was once a small fishing village named Abdera, originally founded by a small colony of Argosseans. Rarely more than a few hundred people, the island nonetheless prospered on the fishing trade and on pearl diving, and was mostly self-sufficient. Several decades ago, a ship of no known kingdom landed offshore, and sent a longship ashore, the crew meeting with the villagers. Within days, all in the village had contracted a disease unknown to any within the area, and in weeks, the village was a place of death. The black ship that brought plague to Abdera is still moored offshore, derelict, and the pirates of the Barachas give the island a wide berth.

TORTAGE

What only pirates know — for those who learned of it, and are not pirates, were killed — is that the Tortage on the southern end of the isle of the same name is but a decoy, the semi-public face of the infamous pirate haven. The actual city is far larger, secreted within a bay on the northern end of the island where the winds blow harshest and the waves break ships piloted by anyone who is not a master sailor.

This "true Tortage" rests on the foundations of an older, nameless, pre-Cataclysmic city. Part of present-day Tortage reaches out to sea on the cyclopean rocks which once served as that city's foundation. The people and culture of that civilization are long forgotten, and their monuments are but an armature around which present Tortage has grown. The city itself is like coral slowly wreathing a sunken vessel, accumulating in layers and tiers, a haphazard structure of shanties built atop each other in a sweaty, tropic riot of humanity. From her docks, one espies the lights of the city like a horde of will-o-the-wisps beckoning in the jungle night.

Here, in the real Tortage, there is nothing which cannot be sold. A hundred fences work the town, and everyone is but a temporary citizen. Even those that live here permanently never feel settled, for such if the life of a freebooter and scoundrel.

Inns, bars, and brothels predominate as businesses, and many of the staples of normal civilized towns are not found here. All weapons sold are stolen, never forged. There are no artists here, but there are fortunes in pillaged art. Everything is for sale, but it is all, as the locals say with a wry smile, "imported".

Indeed, even Zamora the Accursed has claim to more legitimacy that Tortage. Here, there are no municipal services. Waste is thrown over the sides of stilt houses into a deep, fetid ravine which is, not coincidentally, a place where unfortunate bodies are dumped. There is no law in Tortage but that of one's sword arm and guile.

Likewise, no one person rules the city. There is no council to which one appeals, no authority to which one complains. You set foot in the city at your own risk, trusting only your reputation to afford any protection. As such a situation suggests, the less skilled are eaten alive by the thieves, killers, and other desperate residents of Tortage. Parents on the coasts of Argos and Shem warn their children to behave lest they send them to Tortage. Even hardy naval officers, experienced in bloody warfare, feel lumps form in their throat when mentioning the city by name. If there is a central font for all the evil and rapaciousness inherent in man, it is Tortage itself.

A hundred languages find the ear along any street or canal in the city. Men and women whose origins range from far off the steaming forests of Khitai to the frozen wastes of Hyperborea are all found here. It is a mélange of cast-offs, the leavings of a blacksmith whose mistakes are melted down into rude iron. Places are known by ideograms on shingles rather than the written word, so multifarious is the shifting population. The place is an interzone between the world on the Thurian continent and the wild, riotous freedom of a life lived on the razor's edge of death.

Disease is not uncommon given the lack of any proper sanitation, but regulars seem possessed of some inurement to the malodorous humors which stalk the night. After a few weeks, a newcomer may even get used to the smell of decay as effluvia is ever present in the nostrils.

The secret harbor hides Tortage from any not in the know, for the currents speed a boat past the town and the jungle hides it from view. From sea, the bay disappears, as if an illusion. All the untrained eye can see is a wall of weathered cliff and green foliage.

The other town, the decoy, is also hidden, but has been burned once before. There is only one crime in Tortage: revealing its location. There is only one punishment, death by drowning in the human-waste-choked ravine. That is a spectacle many tenants of this foul place attend. There is no sympathy here, no mercy, and no price too cheap to sully one's remnant dignity, sense of self, or honor.

That is exactly the way the denizens prefer it.

THE TRALLIBES

Located at the northernmost coast of Zingara, the Trallibes are a group of islands beset with rough waters and unusually strong winds. Left alone by the Zingaran people, they are still inhabited by Picts of the Kraken sea-tribe, who ply the waters between the islands in dugout canoes. Though these Picts sometimes war with those of other islands and villages, they are united in their hatred of the Zingarans, and attack — however ineffectually — any ships passing too close to their waters.

Zingaran sailors and pirates of the Barachas alike tell wild stories about strange and terrible rituals they have seen the Picts taking part on, wildly debauched ceremonies in which strange fires shine from the coasts of these islands and cephalopods surge out of the waters and onto land to take part, but none dare to go close enough to confirm the truth of these tales.

ARGOS

The rich country of Argos lies on the western coast, a powerful ocean nation whose economic might is derived from its bustling ports. Its main rival is the country of Zingara, to the northwest across the Khorotas River and beyond a low mountain range. Directly to the north sits Aquilonia. Argos has stood at times in Aquilonia's shadow as full vassal or nominal ally depending on how strongly Aquilonia can enforce its imperial desires. To the northeast is the nation of Ophir, while directly east of Argos lie Koth and Shem.

The wealth of Argos flows from the monopoly of oceanic trade along the western coast. There are rumors that daring merchants have established routes as far as Vendhya and even Khitai, but no verified proof of such an endeavor. Their powerful navy enforces their rights and keeps piracy in

check. Argossean vessels, from small fishing ships to grand trading galleys, sail secure in the knowledge pirates would seek softer targets rather than risk the wrath of the royal navy.

The ports of Argos are open to all ships during times of peace. All are welcome to trade there and to make use of available services, provided the harbor master's dues are paid. The fees are kicked up to the royal coffers, and in turn are used to keep the royal navy afloat.

While much of the trade is above board and conducted per strict regulations, a persistent search can always find merchant houses who are more interested in profit than following the rules. These shady merchants tend to avoid asking where goods came from, provided of course there is no proof that they originated from Argossean vessels.

THE HISTORY OF ARGOS

Argos claims to be descended from the blood of ancient Acheron and the Bori, like most of the northern nations. They, however, took to the waters early and in time mixed with the blood of the island empires of the Thurian Age. As they settled along the coast of the Western Sea, their bloodline spread to the lands to the south along their trading networks. In time, small city-states emerged, each with pride in their history and culture. However, they did not have the same level of infighting as in Zingara. It is said by some that "in Argos, trade supersedes even war". These city-states agreed for mutual benefit to establish a capital in Messantia, and built a national navy to protect her.

The coasts of Argos boast of many other rich port cities grown prosperous from the bounty of the sea and protection of the navy, such as Corypho, Leprium, and Dhilos. In addition to these magnificent city-states, many small fishing villages dot the coastline and continue to produce competent sailors to eventually find service in the merchant or royal fleets.

THE KING OF ARGOS

Atreus, king of Argos, sits upon the throne in Messantia, ruling from the largest, and possibly wealthiest, trading city in the Hyborian Age. All the port cities pay into a naval fund that is governed by the king, who also claims the title "Commander of the Navy". It is King Atreus' duty to safeguard the trading routes, stamp out piracy, and protect Argos from attacks from the sea. The noble houses of Argos only have merchant fleets and wage political intrigue through economic means. Atreus, however, does not command trading fleets and thus is maintained this unique balance of power between the king and the merchant dynasties.

When dealing with foreign powers, Argos wields trade as a powerful weapon to dissuade or persuade their neighbors. Land invasions by the Picts are not a concern as Argos is buffered by Aquilonia and Zingara to the north, and Ophir's border with Argos is relatively small and easily defended. Koth and Shem are blocked by mountain ranges, and Zingara's own government and navy are plagued by infighting too strongly to be much of a menace at sea.

Argos also encompasses a rich hinterland that provides fertile land for farming, and great forests that provide lumber for shipbuilding. Their marriage to the sea, however, dominates all politics, and such assets are considered secondary.

ARGOSSEAN CURRENTS

As the premier power in this section of the Western Sea, Argossean influence spreads far. Its textiles, pottery, oils, and more find port in a hundred cities, villages, and small towns across the continent. Where their economic strength finds purchase, their cultural ways likewise influence those around them. The Khorotas and Tybor Rivers are great arteries for bringing goods inland to its ports, and the carrying trade goods to the sea.

Argossean Art

As a seaborne power, it is little surprise that Argossean art centers around the ocean which provides it with food, transportation… life. All creatures of the Western Sea, from fish and crabs, to sharks and monsters of legend are reflected in their art. Even a simple plate, hardened in a Messantian kiln, is like to have a repeating motif of waves or fish. Waves, also, are a recurring pattern found on Argossean art, buildings, and armor and shields. Stylized as a simplified, recurring curve, the wavy double lines of Argos immediately mark their vessels, their works, and their military. This style is sometimes forged, so prized is the pottery of the kingdom.

Argossean Culture

Again, the tides of the ocean and moon pull and tug at all aspects of Argossean life and culture. Fishing is not only a means for life but a sacred rite. Holidays tend around seasonal highs of fish, tidal patterns, and the like. Argosseans themselves often attribute themselves with a sea-like nature — fluid and shifting to the needs of the wind and the world. Where calamity, social upheaval, and the like have great effect on their neighbors, there is a fatalistic nature to the Argossean character which makes them readily adaptable.

One does not live generations along the coasts without weathering the vagaries of mother nature. This malleability extends to almost all aspects of Argossean culture, as well. Permanence is not generally in their nature. The Messantian king takes a wife as a contracted arrangement, but the commoners take mates. Complicated webs of relations and family, impossible to track by the standards of most nations, are common in Argos. A man or woman may have

> ### THAALA — ELEMENTAL FORCE OF THE SEA
>
> Before Anu and Mitra, before the host of gods whose names have risen and faded over this age, Argosseans speak of Thaala, less god than force. Thaala is the sea, quite literally, from its white breakers to its blackest depths. She predates Argos, and her holy ones are more animists than priests. Shrines to Thaala decorate the mantles of many houses, and both private and semi-public ceremonies honor her.
>
> There is, of course, more to Thaala than that. The lay members rarely know this, and even priests may be in the dark, but Thaala is only a mask for Mother Hydra, the Great Old One who rules the sea with her consort, Dagon. It is this godlike being of the Outer Dark they worship, and his taint hangs about Messantia like the stench of a rotting fish.
>
> In sea caves at the edges of the cliffs east of the city, dwellers of the deep couple with humans in profane rites which produce hybrid offspring. Along the low docks, in neighborhoods where strangers are unwelcome, some folk take on a certain look, aspects of fish with thick lips, slit eyes, and even scale-like skin. This is all, of course, rumor, for who would have made it far into these ranks and lived to tell an outsider?

several of what most nations term "spouses", though they may freely break with them at any time.

For this reason, few individuals possess property save at the aristocratic level. A man or woman's belongings are cataloged and recorded by scribes. It is said that the need to retain such vast amounts of information led to the birth of writing in Argos, which Argosseans claim was the first writing of this Age.

Same-sex relationships are common in Argos, and many Argosseans have partners of both genders. Like the sea, Argosseans are a tempestuous lot, and their poetry is full of love odes, their vendettas often over spurned lovers and rival courtships.

THE MITRAN FAITH

The official religion of Argos is worship of Mitra. The Mitran priests wield considerable power in society and serve as a secondary political structure to bind the merchant city-states of Argos into a cohesive nation. They do not have any fighting orders or military power, and rely on the king to defend the faithful. Another of the king's titles is "Defender of the Faith".

Mitra's priests also serve as teachers, judges, lawyers, and many other civil functions in Argossean society. Many second and further-down-the-line noble sons have found purpose in the Mitran Orders and been of great service to Argos. The **Conan** sourcebook *Nameless Cults* has additional information on Mitra and his worship.

Most of the major ports of Argos are cosmopolitan, and, as such, small followings of other gods are common and tolerated. Temples raised and dedicated to other gods must pay a religious tax to the king and acquire a license to operate. Some taverns frequented by foreigners might house a small altar to ancient or strange gods of the sea, invoked for whatever protection sailors might procure for their next voyage. Likewise, the many small fishing villages might also pay homage to local deities or old customs, praying for calm waters, good winds, and abundance of fish.

Anu was once a predominant deity in Argos, as can be seen on old frescoes in long tumbled palaces of former rulers. Bull jumping, a rare form of sport, is still practiced today. Anu's influence is present but remains small in Mitra's light.

There are places, however, where even the light of Mitra does not reach. There are, as ever, dark corners of the Earth in Argos and even in the sea she claims as her own. In that vast, roiling darkness, the Outer Dark itself reflects in both reality and metaphor. If one peers closely into the ocean, the void peers back. The god Dagon thus has adherents in Argos. They worship in secret, some cultists even offering themselves up to breeding with the hideous dwellers of the deep (see page 336 of the **Conan** corebook). They are not above kidnapping, either, though rarely does the cult take natives of Argos. They have an infrequent, but reliable, trade in slaves with pirates of the Baracha Isles. It is even said those islands house a colony of dweller hybrids and cultists who aim to raise Dagon from the sea and take all of Argos in his name. Only fools believe such rumors, but the wise heed them.

THE ARGOSSEAN NAVY

The royal navy is the pride of Argos. No other sea power that can contest it. Zingara has many ships and a large merchant fleet, but its core is politically fragmented and on the high seas it cannot match Argos militarily or economically. That said, both sides support privateers and freebooters used against each other, and their spies seek news of each other's trade routes and naval actions. Argos often gets the better end of this, and has collected many Zingaran ransoms as proof.

King Atreus is not just Commander of the Navy in name — in practice, all heirs to the throne receive extensive schooling in naval tactics, and serve in command positions in the royal navy before ascension to the throne. This is a longstanding tradition of the country, and if an heir proves to be a weak sailing man, it is thought he will make a weak king. Thus, the heir-apparent is often in command aboard the capital ship of the royal navy, and this is true now, with Atreus' son Orestes.

In times of war, the king might step back on board the capital ship, especially if the heir is very young, inexperienced, or incompetent. The general division in wartime has the king deciding strategy from the capital while tactical execution is left to the heir and his captains.

The royal navy is funded by a system of taxes collected from all ports and trade that happens in Argos. The merchant houses are responsible for collection and bookkeeping with oversight by the royal accountants. Cheating the taxes is considered a treasonous act, as it directly undermines the security of the nation. In practice, cheating is rare, as punishment is harsh and most Argosseans understand that a strong navy is key to their wealth. The tax business has, however, led to a secondary business of litigation to determine what exactly is owed to the crown.

The merchant fleet is much larger in total than the royal navy, but owned by a dozen dynastic noble houses. The houses have absolute command over their merchant fleets and sail the seas as they please, provided of course they do not engage in overt piracy. In wartime, the king can press the houses to convert the various carracks, galleys, and galleons into temporary fighting ships to bolster the royal navy. For the duration of the war, the houses are expected to provide the ships, crew, and care, but these are commanded by the authority of the king. In this manner Argos can float a massive fleet very quickly and is why it remains the master of the Western Sea.

One final arena in which the royal navy has considerable sway involves the rewarding of shipwright contracts. Various houses can find themselves dropped from service or gifted with the royal naval contracts in the political games between the king and the merchant houses.

THE ARGOSSEAN ARMY

Argos has only a minor standing army, essentially an extension of King Atreus' own forces based in Messantia. Most larger cities have a city guard, primarily loyal to the merchant princes that rule each city, while remote areas might have a local magistrate to enforce the king's laws. As a sea power, and an even greater economic power, Argos has little need of a standing militia, and so it employs mercenary armies primarily when needing to marshal larger forces.

THE FREEBOOTERS

The term "freebooter" does not distinguish a single organization so much as it describes a way of life. Even in malleable Argos, codes and laws hold the civilized world together. Freebooters reject these codes, ignore these laws, and take to the sea, from which they take what they want. Still, it would be a mistake to think they have no code; only, it is of their own making and often shifts with the winds of fortune.

A man or woman who has sailed with a group of freebooters may well consider them friends. Hospitality and safe passage is expected among all this subculture's adherents. However, when it comes to booty, even these loose codes go the way of bodies to the sea. Gold, reflected in the eye of avarice, sparkles especially bright to the freebooter. One may call another friend and still stab them in the back for the right treasure.

Argos has a curious relationship with freebooters. While they disrupt trade, kill, and steal, most Argosseans have some affinity with them. Their way of life is, perhaps, the extreme extension of the Argossean nature of free seas, full sails, and a life blown by the winds of fate.

> *He entered the city unquestioned, merging himself with the throngs that poured continually in and out of this great commercial center. No walls surrounded Messantia. The sea and the ships of the sea guarded the great southern trading city.*
>
> *It was evening when Conan rode leisurely through the streets that marched down to the waterfront. At the ends of these streets he saw the wharves and the masts and sails of ships. He smelled salt water for the first time in years, heard the thrum of cordage and the creak of spars in the breeze that was kicking up whitecaps out beyond the headlands. Again the urge of far wandering tugged at his heart.*
>
> — The Hour of the Dragon

MESSANTIA, CAPITAL OF ARGOS

The capital of Argos is also the wealthiest port in the western world. Her spires tower at the edge of a cliff face overlooking the great ocean whose fury and foam break against the rock wall of the sea kingdom. Mighty gates, guarded by a chain said to have been forged by Anu himself, hold back the great waves against the lower docks.

Messantia is a feat of engineering unique in the world. The likes of such a fastness upon the sea has not been seen since the days of Acheron. Sheathed in white marble, the walls and tallest buildings of the city shine in the sun and sparkle under a full moon. "There is a wonder which catches in one's throat", said the famed Nemedian historian Astreas upon his approach to the city from the sea.

Beyond the gates, there are marvels just as great, but they abut slums and rookeries which are ever the darker hallmark of civilized men. Just as other great cities, within its walls are contained the whole of human experience — from gluttonous pleasure to abject misery — conferred upon its residents based on their wealth or lack thereof.

A Gull's View of Messantia

Whirling above the docks and towers, are the ever-present gulls, white against the blue sky. Sailors refer to them as "flying rats", though there is no bounty on their heads like those of the four-legged vermin. But what a gull sees are streets laid out in precise order, ranging like the spokes of half a wagon wheel, extending from a central hub upon which the city revolves, the flat of this semi-circle its harbor-front and docks.

The great Square of Anu is flanked by olive trees, dominated by a large fountain and open space — a fact that causes developers no end of ire, for the property is worth a king's ransom. But no king or queen of Argos would ever befoul the square with trade or buildings.

Yet, given the nature of the cliff's topography, Messantia cannot easily expand, and so the city is densely packed, as the eye of the gull can see plainly. Heading north, one finds the bulk of the slums crash against the lowest edge of the city like the tide breaks upon the rocks, though as the gull flies above, it circles over the docksides where some slums fester, built on unstable and sometimes swampy land.

The gull then flies over the brightly tented markets to alight at the highest point in the city, the great palace which sits atop the apex of the cliff. From there, the salt air fills its lungs and it, too, feels mastery over the vast sea it surveys. Of course, both king and gull know the sea is commanded by no creature of the Earth, however so either might pretend.

No walls guard this city: only the cliffs and the sea and the mighty Argossean navy keep it safe.

Merchants of the Sea

One must always remember that the true princes of the sea are those who possess its wealth. While a king or queen of Argos rules in name, and sometimes by dictum, they do not do so without the permission of the merchants. Argos is not wealthy without their trade, and it is not powerful without its wealth.

Pages in silken livery come to greet travelers who would have the ear of a merchant of note. Rituals are understood between trading men, of which the rude adventurer is like to be ignorant. The class of merchant, in Argos, is one of near nobility. It is better, they say, to insult a savage outlander in a tavern than to misbehave before a great trading lord.

The Messantian Docks

The grand docks of Messantia range along the entirety of its seaward edge. As Astreas once put it, "The whole city life tumbles before me as the ship slides from the rough-hewn poverty of the tenements, past working-class houses with flat roofs and shingled sides, up to the merchant docks, where white stone meets sea and one can smell the salt in the air as surely as the commerce."

While Astreas takes too much pleasure in his observations, they are correct. The docks range from the sordid end to the rich, and all manner of ships find port here. Pirates, however, are unwelcome. Any known vessel which robs the seas upon which Argos relies is like to find its end here. Privateers, however, are another matter. Argos employs a great many such scum against their chief foe, Zingara.

Whilst the well-bred man or woman may easily find the allure of the clean, white marble docks welcoming, those of a piratical bent find much of their business plays out in the shanty town overlooking the low harbor on the western end of the city. Here, one can unload stolen goods — with care — or find a new ship upon which to crew, leaving their true past and name behind them.

Upon any of the docks one tastes the salt in the air, hears the creaking spars and whistling winches pulling up sail, all as the men and women of the sea size up the ocean-worthiness of the new visitors.

> *It was a logical destination; all the sea-ports of Argos were cosmopolitan, in strong contrast with the inland provinces, and Messantia was the most polyglot of all. Craft of all the maritime nations rode in its harbor, and refugees and fugitives from many lands gathered there. Laws were lax; for Messantia thrived on the trade of the sea, and her citizens found it profitable to be somewhat blind in their dealings with seamen.*
>
> *It was not only legitimate trade that flowed into Messantia; smugglers and buccaneers played their part. All this Conan knew well, for had he not, in the days of old when he was a Barachan pirate, sailed by night into the harbor of Messantia to discharge strange cargoes? Most of the pirates of the Barachan Isles — small islands off the southwestern coast of Zingara — were Argossean sailors, and as long as they confined their attentions to the shipping of other nations, the authorities of Argos were not too strict in their interpretation of sea-laws.*
>
> — The Hour of the Dragon

SOUTHERN SHORES

SHEM

The plains of Shem stretch inland from the Western Sea, eventually giving way to desert in the east. Shem is largely temperate year-round. Snowfall is rare; drought, more common. These lowlands provide ample fields for grazing, and the frequent floods from small rivers along the coast leave fertile soil for crops when the waters recede. The farmlands along the shore separate the few ports and harbors as thoroughly as any border.

Coastal Shem is more a military and economic alliance than a sovereign nation. In contrast to the nomads roaming the eastern desert, this collection of city-states is bound by a common culture and history. Even so, their differences have more than once brought them to the brink of war. Only the ever-present threat of Stygia to the south keeps this tender alliance in check.

In ancient times, these city-states grew out of a need to store food in times of plenty, to offset bad harvests. Priest-kings prayed to their patron deities for rain, while building and maintaining extensive irrigation networks. Ziggurat temples sprung up, giving priests a stairway to heaven, as well as offering safety during the floods. Wealth accumulated atop these ziggurats, with fine statues and silver and golden jewelry imported from distant lands. Their system of writing upon clay tablets developed to keep track of these offerings to the deity and ensure everyone contributed to the constant wars between the states.

> *They sighted the coast of Shem — long rolling meadowlands with the white crowns of the towers of cities in the distance, and horsemen with blue-black beards and hooked noses, who sat their steeds along the shore and eyed the galley with suspicion. She did not put in; there was scant profit in trade with the sons of Shem.*
>
> — "Queen of the Black Coast"

One such war left their guard down against outside threats. Stygia seized the opportunity and swept through Shem, sacking the cities as they went. This nascent empire extended all the way to Acheron. The Stygians proved a harsh master to the Shemites. They stripped away the treasures held within the ziggurats, burned the temples that gave audience to the gods, and carried the wealth back to Stygia. Priests and nobles of royal families were made into slaves, and all were subjugated under the Stygian yoke. Impoverished Shemite peasants labored to feed the Stygian empire. Any personal wealth they might have had was stolen by greedy, cruel nobles. To this day, Shemites value treasure so highly because they equate it with freedom.

Eventually, Acheron fell, bringing with it hordes of barbarians that ultimately destroyed the Stygian empire. The city-states of Shem regained their sovereignty, and something else. Centuries of suffering under a common enemy turned former foes into allies. The warring period of Shem had come to an end.

Today's military depends largely on its archers and its specialized warriors called *asshuri*, mercenaries loyal to their home city-state, but also available to those who will pay for their services. With Shem's vast expanses of flat land, few armies can sneak up on a Shemite stronghold, making ranged attacks critical. Shemite archers skilled in their regional variant of the longbow can decimate an army still a mile away. Most of Shem's cities likewise have an array of ranged weapons armed and ready on their walls.

Each city in Shem boasts its own patron deity, laws, and cultural norms, though the differences are often lost on outsiders. Native Shemites share the same ivory skin and thick, black hair, and all value treasure for its ability to grant freedom, often mistaken for greed by foreigners. Shemite society consists of three classes of people: property owners (which include nobles and priests), freed men, and slaves. Sacred rituals held atop the local ziggurat keep this society in order.

COASTAL SHEM

Shem boasts many settlements within striking distance of the Western Sea. The ports serve the great trading kingdom, carrying goods not only from Shem, but the far East.

Asgalun

Asgalun is one of the pre-eminent city-states, with the largest harbor along the coast. Its inland ziggurat stands at the center of a vast fields and grazing meadows. Here, the goddess Ishtar reigns supreme, granting her faithful fertile lands and wombs. Her cult is celebrated by a high priestess, who performs the sacred dance of seduction to lure her godly bridegroom. Their symbolic coupling yields the harvest.

The city, however, has long been ruled by princes. A recent coup overthrew a long-standing dynasty; its members were either sold into slavery or escaped to exile. Since then, Ishtar has been kind, and an era of prosperity has brought gold and gems to port, along with slaves as far south as Keshan.

Devotees who wish Ishtar to grant them special favor commission statues of themselves to stand in her chapel and worship her in their absence. The statues, standing with eyes wide, hands clasped, give passersby an uncanny feeling of being watched. Craftsman of these statues learn their trade through a secret guild in Asgalun. Rarely do these statues leave the city.

Men and women may both own property, leading to even greater demand for land and the trappings of wealth. Unfortunately, men and women may both incur debt, and more than a few slaves working the fields or offering fruit in the market stalls were once proud citizens of Asgalun.

Akkad

Akkad sits not far from the sea, along an inlet. The inhabitants keep to themselves, as they have a secret they guard jealously. Their goddess in the flesh, Ashtoreth, lives atop the ziggurat on the rise overlooking the city. Rumors of the goddess have reached cities throughout Shem, but few believe it. But the faithful who make the difficult journey to Akkad swear that they have caught a glimpse of her Holiness, high up in her chapel.

The prince rules the city, but relies heavily on the advice of the goddess. Like all citizens, he consults with her like an oracle. They have their questions and concerns written upon a clay tablet. They send this up to the chapel via a tray, along with a small offering of food, drink, or treasure. The tablet returns with the verdict of the goddess inscribed upon it, interpreted by the priest who receives it. Many decisions of state have been made at the base of the ziggurat.

The tray, operated by rope and pulley, is the only avenue for communicating with the goddess. After the first two levels of the temple, no stairs continue further up to the chapel. She subsists solely on the offerings of the faithful. Once a year, the people celebrate the Festival of the Goddess, with feasting and music, sending up offerings to the goddess until she is sated. The festival culminates in a ritual wedding. Stairs are built to the top tier of the ziggurat, and the high priest, ritually cleansed and prepared, ascends the stairs as the goddess's bridegroom. If their wedding night is a success, the next morning he returns with a child, and the city is blessed for the coming year.

The people's dedication to the goddess and the relative protection of the alcove and inlet has left the town relatively untouched by outside influence. The inlet is difficult to navigate, and the few overland routes connect Akkad to city-states far more prestigious than her. Akkad's irrigation system ensures the people grow enough to eat. The waters have carved out a stone quarry, where harvesters climb down to pick out exposed precious stones. Besides the goddess, these stones are the only source of fame for Akkad.

> *No longer they sailed past steep cliffs with blue hills marching behind them. Now the shore was the edge of broad meadowlands which barely rose above the water's edge and swept away and away into the hazy distance. Here were few harbors and fewer ports, but the green plain was dotted with the cities of the Shemites; green sea, lapping the rim of the green plains, and the zikkurats of the cities gleaming whitely in the sun, some small in the distance.*
>
> *Through the grazing-lands moved the herds of cattle, and squat, broad riders with cylindrical helmets and curled blue-black beards, with bows in their hands. This was the shore of the lands of Shem, where there was no law save as each city-state could enforce its own. Far to the eastward, Conan knew, the meadowlands gave way to desert, where there were no cities and the nomadic tribes roamed unhindered.*
>
> — **The Hour of the Dragon**

STYGIA

The Stygian coast lies between Shem and Kush. The largest coastal city, Khemi, makes for an imposing gateway to a desert kingdom filled with horrors and dark magic, utterly dependent on the life-giving Styx River that flows through its heart. Sailors recognize Stygian waters by the black marble castles looming on the shore, the black war galleys at port, and the pleasure galleys that ply the waters outside her ports — scantily-clad prostitutes onboard beckoning the witless to forbidden delights within or back upon the Stygian shore (and there, likely the fates of enslavement or death).

The priests of Set perpetuate the myth that they have kept a fist on the reins of Stygia for 10,000 years. Instead, the balance of power between the coastal and inland dwellers along the Styx has shifted in a struggle for control for millennia. Currently, the power rests with Thoth-Amon in the inland capital of Luxur. The sorcerer is leader of the sorcerous cabal known as the Black Ring, his power feared throughout the land, second only to King Ctesphon. But Thoth-Amon has many enemies, and his influence does not protect him against conspiracy...

Stygia's capital city, Luxur, is described along with the inland stretches of Stygia, in *Conan the Adventurer*.

> *Strangers were not welcome in the cities of Stygia; tolerated only when they came as ambassadors or licensed traders. But even then the latter were not allowed ashore after dark. And now there were no Hyborian ships in the harbor at all.*
>
> — The Hour of the Dragon

COASTAL STYGIA

Much of Stygia is arid desert, though the land flanking the Styx River is lush and fertile, populated much more densely than its inland reaches. The coastline is dotted with smallish fishing villages, small ports, and other habitations, as well as abandoned ruins stretching back to ages before even Acheron. Her ports are open capriciously to outside traders, sometimes closed abruptly for unexplained reasons, any foreigners in the towns given only moments to vacate or be faced with ruinous fines or imprisonment and confiscation of goods.

Only two major cities distinguish the Stygian coast, each located at its uttermost north at the mouth of the Styx River, and at its southernmost reach in the soft border the kingdom shares with Kush. Between these two great cosmopolitan centers, Stygian war galleys relentlessly patrol the coast, striking fiercely at any potential pirate vessels they encounter, though they are stretched too thin to catch any but the most reckless of buccaneers. These serpent-prowed ships, serving King Ctesphon, are of the Stygian navy but are eager to strike at foreign merchant vessels, making them little better than privateers. For all this, however, the trade with Stygia is among the most lucrative up and down the coast, and thus many traders and merchant captains — as well as smugglers — brave the dangers inherent when dealing with Stygia, or even passing by the hostile shores en route north or south.

Not far from the coast of Stygia, near Khemi, is an island fortress, built centuries ago as a redoubt for Stygian kings and queens, its exact location kept a state secret. The last Stygian king to hold court there was Tothmekri. While the royal court was away in Khemi, the island was raided by the Zingaran pirate Tranicos, who escaped to the north with an unimaginable treasure. Despite being pursued, Tranicos escaped and the humiliation of this loss haunted Tothmekri to the end of his days. Shortly after Tothmekri's death, the island was abandoned, and now lies in disrepair. However, its secrets are said to be warded by demon sorcery, as well as attended by serpents beyond counting. To sail within miles of the island is to court death, and all Stygian war galleys watch the island for trespassers.

Karnath

Karnath in the south is one of the oldest human habitations in the known world. It is said by some Stygians that the first men lived here, and they were not Stygians but pale men like those that inhabit the north. Such is heresy in all but Karnath, where, in addition to Set, a strange green idol is worshipped. It sits in a temple whose façade shows bas-reliefs of a great lake from which frog-like creatures emerge into the world of humankind. Following the whole of the temple's perimeter, a mighty city is depicted, one apparently hundreds of feet high and wide enough to allow multiple chariots to pass. None of this, save the curious statue that some call "Bokrug", remains.

Priests of the statue claim visions of the past, when a great lake sat here and the sea was some distance away. There, they say, the first men came and cast down the alien, gelatinous denizens of a city unnamed. Upon the ruins of that city was the great city depicted on the temple built, though it vanished millennia and millennia before the Cataclysm. Why the priests of Set allow the worship of this false idol is unknown. Mysterious also is the reason why the long-abandoned mines in the area show no signs of ever having yielded minerals. The sea alone is bounty for Karnath.

As a port, it is remarkable only for its oddly foreign architecture. Bits of it look like nothing of Stygian design or, indeed, of any known culture. The people are dusky-skinned Stygians, but some small proportion of them have curious blue eyes. The port thrives, as does rumor along the docks: tales of strange green lights seen under the sea, and a green mist into which fated ships disappear, not far off the coast of Karnath.

South of Karnath is Zabhela, in Kush, described on page 50.

Khemi

Black-walled Khemi is the greatest of Stygian cities and its most important and cosmopolitan, though by no stretch is it welcome to outsiders. Geographically, the city and its port are set between two man-made prongs of land, product of an immense undertaking. These flank the harbor to either side and are adorned with looming black castles and a defensive wall. The city itself is not much different, with oppressive architecture looming above narrow streets, barely wide enough to allow the passage of the bronze chariots or palanquins favored by Stygian nobles and priests. The arid heat causes most inhabitants to sleep in open gardens and abodes atop the city's flat-roofed buildings, in whatever luxury they might afford.

The strength of Stygia's trade is not with foreign vessels that might reach it through this port, but instead the network of ports and trade towns eastward, along the Styx River, doing business in Shemite ports as well as Stygian. Thus the port of Khemi is small and empty for a city of its size and prominence. More fishermen use the port than traders, and rarely are foreigners present, other than slaves from Shem or the Black Kingdoms.

After dark the shops and stalls close, leaving the gloomy, black-walled streets abandoned to shadows and worse. The horrific stories carried by coastal traders — describing giant serpents slithering through the darkened streets of Khemi at night, released from the temples of Set, and taking whatever human prey they desire — are enough to keep even a hardy sailor from venturing too far into the city proper. Thus, few visitors care overmuch about anything past the docks, much less after dark; and the city itself, like much of Stygia, is a mystery to outsiders.

These stories are true: the great pythons are equivalent to the giant constrictors described on page 329 of the ***Conan*** corebook. These creatures are said to be sacred and are untouchable, and those they consume are considered sacrifices to Set, and thus inviolate, with death to any who bring harm to a holy serpent.

> *So at last they passed the mouth of a broad river that mingled its flow with the ocean, and saw the great black walls and towers of Khemi rise against the southern horizon.*
>
> *The river was the Styx, the real border of Stygia. Khemi was Stygia's greatest port, and at that time her most important city. The king dwelt at more ancient Luxur, but in Khemi reigned the priestcraft; though men said the center of their dark religion lay far inland, in a mysterious, deserted city near the bank of the Styx. This river, springing from some nameless source far in the unknown lands south of Stygia, ran northward for a thousand miles before it turned and flowed westward for some hundreds of miles, to empty at last into the ocean.*
>
> — The Hour of the Dragon

The Great Pyramid of Set

The Great Pyramid of Set lies a short distance outside Khemi in the desert. Its black marble walls make it hard to differentiate from the darkness that surrounds it at night. Only priests of Set may enter, or the victims they take with them. Inside this pyramid lies an endless maze of horrors of which few know the true extent.

The entrance poses a challenge to any who would enter. Two sphinx statues, lions with the faces of women, flank the doorway to its interior. A priest stands ready, lit by only one light, to prevent any unwelcome visitors. He offers one of any number of hand signals. Each must be returned with a corresponding hand signal, or else guards will be summoned in great number.

Within the pyramid, the narrow corridor of marble slopes down gently, lit by cressets, baskets of burning oil. The corridor continues to a fork. Priests of Set know to turn right and continue down to find the vast Chamber of the Dead. Among a forest of columns rest the sarcophagi holding millennia-old remains of the priests of Set. Hundreds of faces carved on wood and stone stare out at the altar, awaiting the day that they will rise again in service to Set.

Around this central hall, a second floor overlooks the altar, offering lower priests a vantage point to watch the rituals that take place. Other entrances to the central room branch off from the ground and the second floor. The Chamber of the Dead stands at the center of a labyrinth of dark corridors that stretch off in every direction.

The fork near the entrance also leads off to the left. This main corridor continues, with doors leading off in one direction or another. The further down it goes, the more archways lead off into darkness, often filled with serpents of Set, waiting for a sacrifice. Sections of this maze lie behind secret doors, activated by a word of magic or knowledge of its mechanism.

Deep within this area lies the lair of Princess Akivasha. Before Set ruled Stygia and the Kushites moved north, she ruled. She seduced an ancient and forgotten god, and in return gained everlasting life as a vampire. She must return to her sarcophagus by day and feeds on sacrifices at night. Akivasha rules the pyramid underworld, but she is not alone. Jackals are said to guard the dead. The children of Set lurk in the dark hallways, as well as other creatures so dark they have disappeared from memory.

Akivasha herself appears in the pages of *Conan the Adventurer*.

KUSH

Kush stands in the shadows of Stygia. A land filled with riches in copper, golden ornaments, pearls and ivory, Kush is a fabled destination for both trader and pirate. History speaks of a time when Stygia conquered Kush, and its ruling class of Chagas are their descendants. The relationship between the two countries proves to be much more complex.

KUSHITE HISTORY

In prehistoric times, Kushites lived inland along the river, surviving on subsistence farming and the fruit of the river. They buried their dead under pyramid-shaped thatch roofs, though these tombs are lost to time. A long period of drought and lower-than-average yield pushed the Kushites up the coast. They settled along the lands just south of Stygia. The elites of Kush intermixed with the natives, who were known for their ivory skin and lust for villainy. These natives have fallen into legend, and few remember a time before the Stygians chose Set as their god and master.

The Kushites that remained behind in Kush developed their own culture. They took to pearling along the coast and hunting elephants inland for ivory. They traded for dried meats and wood that did not grow easily on the savannah. It would be the discovery and mining of copper that would bring back their cousins in the north.

The Stygians, now followers of Set, had long forgotten their connection to Kush. They came not with open arms to greet their neighbors, but bearing arms to crush them. The peaceful Kushites, though plenty in number, proved to have too few warriors to fend off the bronze spears and magic of the priests of Set. For centuries, the Stygians ruled over Kush, turning the lands into a brutal kingdom where the Stygian rulers forced Kushites into practical slavery. Stygian practices were adopted after a fashion, and burials outside the city consisted of pyramids slightly taller than a man.

GAZETTEER

Centuries of laboring in copper mines, however, had taught the Kushites not only how to work, but how to forge copper into bronze weapons. A coup in far-away Stygia weakened the empire as it began to demand more from its southern colonies. The Stygian rulers in Kush, now called Chagas, grated under the rule of a distant land most had never seen, while the original Kushites, the Gallahs, yearned for freedom. The two groups united against the true Stygians.

Stygia tried to reconquer Kush, but was repelled each time. The Gallahs that built pyramids now built high walls that no chariot could conquer. Kush's army of spearmen proved to be formidable against the Stygian chariot. Furthermore, constant political intrigue in Stygia made it difficult to summon the will to lead another campaign against Kush. In the end, the ruling Chagas negotiated a peace for a price that only the Gallahs would pay — in enslaved bodies that would man the oars of Stygian galleys, and in blood for the altars of Set.

KUSH TODAY

Kush has grown into a kingdom of peace and plenitude, which only the Chagas enjoy. Its capital, Shumballa, lies along a river in the center of the Savannah. El Shebbeh, the walled city center, protects the Chagas from the rabble, allowing them to luxuriate on silken couches surrounded by tapestries and the finest goods from across the known world. Outside this walled enclosure lies Punt, whose thatched hovels more closely resemble prehistoric huts than the homes of the Chaga elites.

Chagas still worship Set, and offer sacrifice to the Great Pyramid in the north. A few of the nobles have even mastered in secret the demon-god's sorcery. In contrast, the Gallah worship Jullah in his aspect as a god of the moon. They worship him through simple offerings of bronze and fruits of the harvest. Jullah boasts no high priests, as the Chagas massacred, then outlawed, them millennia ago. Instead, people often consult witch-finders, shaman-like people who wield both the power of Set and Jullah, for guidance and counsel. This aspect of Jullah differs from that worshipped elsewhere, and his other role as a lord of beasts is known, but emphasized less.

Bronze spear-heads have slowly been replaced with those of iron, used to enforce the will of the Chagas more than protect the Kushites from outside invaders. Chaga horsemen can ride in the thousands to suppress any unrest. Even so, the king of Kush has proved weak and Gallah that question their subservient state have met in secret to conspire against him. At the same time, a noble named Tuthmes has planted a Nemedian woman, a slave and a spy, within the court of the king. He intends to use her to control the king and take his place.

The real power behind the throne, however, is the king's sister Tananda, who likewise has plans of her own, involving intrigue with the priests of Set in Stygia. Tananda, El Shebbeh, Punt, and the rest of Kush are described more fully in *Conan the Adventurer*.

THE KUSHITE COAST

The coast of Kush seems to lie far from the court of intrigue in the interior. Small fishing and pearling villages dot the coastline. The cavalry and spearmen of the city hold little sway here. Even so, pirate raids occur only sporadically, because Stygian galleys often patrol the waters, an outcome of the tributary treaty between Kush and Stygia.

A secret lies on the coast, hidden to all but those who know the seas. Hieron, a once-great Kushite capital, has sunk into the waters at the edge of the coast. The statue of an ancient Stygian ruler in the shallows marks what remains of a palace entrance. While much of the city has sunk underwater, pockets of air may still exist in ancient halls, as well as in the sealed tombs of the Kushite pyramid graves.

Rumors among the fishing villages speak of treasure still lying within, awaiting anyone brave enough to enter. They also speak of Set-related horrors that survive in the city's underwater grave. Rumors hint that the serpent children of Set are amphibious and dwell underwater, feasting upon sailors that come too close to the shore.

Lately, some bold groups of pirates have also taken up residence in parts of the ruins, and feed any trespassers to these children of Set. They search the ruins for treasure, so they know where to lay traps for any who might trespass into their territory.

THE PORT OF ZABHELA

On the Kushite coast, Zabhela is a small city of questionable affiliation. It is a free port, with all the guarantee of secrecy and danger that entails. Her docks are home to rats that locals claim are vampiric, and her shanty-like waterfront abodes smell of sex, sweat, and the lotus blossoms of the East. The air is always warm and damp, clinging like a leech. Those unused to life in the south are like to fare poorly in Zabhela.

It also serves as the country's main port for trade, and it is here in the town market that enterprising traders from the north haggle with merchants and vendors to offload their wares, and exchange them for precious goods like peacock feathers, ivory, rare woods, diamonds, and slaves.

While the city nominally gives fealty to the Kushite rulers, it has just as much stake in scurvy dogs like Zarallo's band, the Red Brotherhood, numerous slavers, and Stygian spies. If one has the right connections, however, it is possible to lay low and evade the navies of Zingara, Stygia, and Argos… at least until a fellow throat-slitter finds out how much the bounty on one's head is.

DAVU — THE CITY OF FOREVER

Davu the Dreamer, Pillar of the World, King of Kings, the Golden Promise. There are many names for the ruler of the forgotten city that lies deep in the jungles of the Black Kingdoms. It is so remote that it has not had contact with the outside world for thousands of years. The city is populated by ape-men who are the only subjects of Davu, equivalent to the degenerates (page 315, CONAN corebook).

Eons ago, these people ruled the world, mastering all manner of science and magic. Immortality was in their grasp. They reached further and further into the cosmic mysteries, their greed and curiosity insatiable. From the yonder they contacted ancient powers beyond sanity.

The Cataclysm was the only way to save the world from complete destruction. A small group in one city led by their ruler was all that remained of the once-great civilization. In time, all evidence of their existence was buried. The king outlawed study of all knowledge, keeping the knowledge of immortality for himself. As the centuries rolled by, the people devolved to a former state of savagery, eventually degenerating into the ape-men that wander the lost city. The ape-men continue to worship the alabaster figure of the sleeping king on his marble throne, unable to even dream of the greatness they once had.

The City of Forever runs automated by a science long forgotten, able to provide food, water and protection for its denizens. Davu dreams on still, someday to waken and become the Golden Promise which will usher humanity to a new enlightened state.

Small towns and villages dot this landscape, whose inhabitants survive mostly by hunting, fishing, and simple farming. Most of the region has only advanced technologically as far as bronze-smithing. Therefore, iron tools and weapons are highly desired by the coastal trading villages. The area has constant tribal warfare. Blood feuds go back generations.

The many peoples that make up the Black Coast have varied customs and gods. Some continue to worship the old ones, some revere their ancestors, and a village or two has even been known to have been converted to see the light of Mitra (trade from Argos no doubt playing some part in the conversion). Only a few tribes practice cannibalism, and those are mostly confined to the interior of the Black Kingdoms, but the whole region is often labeled by the West as such. Animism also plays a large part in the spiritualism of the tribes.

Despite the lack of civilization in the conventional sense as defined by the Hyborians, or perhaps because of it, this region has produced numerous warriors and pirates of note, and *Chapter Five: Encounters* describes figures from this area. Ships from Zingara, Argos, Shem, and even Stygia regularly come on recruiting missions to the Black Coast. They find many willing natives looking to escape the villages and earn a share of booty. Some tribesmen have continued further up the coast and taken on mercenary roles in the armies of Kush, Stygia, and even those further west.

The uttermost south of the Black Coast is said to be a place of fire, with intense and bright light gleaming so fiercely that no ship may pass through. Others claim that it is but a trick of the sun, and that the coast rounds to the east, and passage may be had to eventually emerge on the other side of the continent, particularly the shores of far-off Khitai and another ocean, across which are even stranger and more remote lands.

THE BLACK COAST

The Black Coast is a loosely defined area south of Stygia. Its immediate neighbors to the north are Kush, Darfar, and Keshan. Towards the northeast are Punt and Zembabwei. Some would include the Kingdoms of Kush and Zembabwei in the sweeping generalization of the Black Coast, but each is a clearly defined kingdom. The majority of the Black Coast consists of small principalities, towns, and villages that the West refers to as the Black Kingdoms. The major, known cities are the coastal principalities Kulalo, Abobi, and Yanyoga.

Little else is known of this area and even more is lost to antiquity. Heavy jungle dominates the central geography of the region, and, as one approaches the coast, the terrain becomes marshy swampland and flooded plains.

THE SOUTHERN ISLES

Southwest off the coast of Abombi lie the Southern Isles — a chain of about a dozen major islands and hundreds of smaller ones. The tribes that inhabit these isles take to the waters more readily than their coastal cousins, though mostly on skiffs and small fishing boats. They lack the technology and culture for true sailing vessels. The Isles were the favorite recruiting grounds for Bêlit (**Conan** corebook, page 354) and the crew of the *Tigress* (see pages 88–90), who came from the Suba tribe.

POLITICS ON THE BLACK COAST

As there are hundreds of tribes and language groups, there is no centralized political structure along the Black Coast.

Constant territorial warfare and lack of technology generally prevent empire-building. Alliances are temporary and maintained by marriage, trade, coercion, and persuasion. At most, a leader might rise to have influence over a region of a few towns for a short time and call themselves king or queen. The jungles and marshes have nothing to offer other empires, and thus they keep their distance rather than waste resources in attempting conquest. At most, a few villages might have established long-term seasonal arrangements for trade with Argos and such.

The major tribes of the coast are the Suba, Kacha, Hakrao, Wanje, and Sweta.

TRADE ON THE BLACK COAST

Trade is the main source of wealth for the Black Coast. Argos is the dominant trading partner, bringing in finished goods such as cheap jewelry, silks, sugar, iron tools, and arms. In return, ivory, copra, copper ore, pearls, slaves, and exotic animals find their way to markets in Messantia and Kordava, borne there by all-too-eager merchants from Argos or Zingara.

THE ZARKHEBA RIVER

The Zarkheba River lies just south of Kush and would be a major transit from the Black Coast to the interior if not for its dangerous reputation. The waters of the river are rumored to be poisonous and home to giant man-eating serpents that can snatch a man right off the deck of a ship. Nothing can be seen in the black murky depths, and no animals come to drink at its banks. The river is avoided by all, except the most foolhardy or brave.

Down the river, just out of sight of the coast, stands an altar in the ruins of a long-forgotten city. The jungle has encroached heavily on the city ruins and only the altar dedicated to the old ones defies being overgrown. Many have sought its treasure, and none have lived to claim it. Should any dare to venture up the Zarkheba to this site, they will likely be harried by great serpents along the way (**Conan** corebook, page 330), and most likely giant hyenas (page 79 of this sourcebook), and the degenerate winged ones (**Conan** corebook, page 344).

NORTHERN WILDS

VANAHEIM

Far to the north lie the fjords and shores of ice-bound Vanaheim. This land's fierce barbaric inhabitants prey upon one another primarily in their dragon-prowed ships, but at times they venture further south and strike trade with the Picts for whale's teeth, hides, tusks, and amber, or more likely they venture even further south to Zingara and Argos. There, these northerners trade for things they cannot manufacture in their harsh and desolate homeland, like cloth, gold, and iron, and are happy to sell their captured neighbors, the Æsir, into slavery in the south. Their visits, however, are so rare that for the most part they are unknown amidst the folk of the dreaming west, who think the north is naught but unassailable ice. It is from the coast that most Vanir leave their homeland, for the passage through Pictland and Cimmeria is likely a death-sentence.

Vanaheim is discussed in greater detail in the **Conan** corebook on pages 209–210, and in the pages of *Conan the Barbarian*.

THE PICTISH COAST

The wild Pictish coastline has few settlements. The storm-lashed stretch of land is marked by rocky headlands and dense, jungle-like forest, with occasional pockets of sandy beach. The prevailing winds come out of the southwest. However, during the winter and spring, great storms can come tearing down from the north.

The Pict tribes along the coast are as likely to kill you as to trade with you. But, there are great natural riches of furs, timber, minerals, and more to be found there. And, the isolation along the coast can also be valuable. Pirate crews often set up brief camps along the beaches of the Pictish coast while they careen and repair their ships, and venture inland for water and food or even to trade with the Picts. From time to time, hermits who have wandered into the wild seeking isolation for religious, political, or sorcerous purposes will inhabit a cave or hovel along the Pictish coast. Vanir raiders occasionally venture south to trade or pillage here, though they frequently end up skirmishing with the savage Picts for one reason or another.

The Pict tribes that live along or near the coast include the Cormorant, Osprey, Seal, Shark, and Toucan, though there are likely others, as the boundaries between the tribes shift frequently. Tribal lands are usually marked with blazes on trees, skulls, feathers, claws, or other symbols of a tribe. Those that wander inland may also encounter clearings with simple stone altars stained black with the blood of creatures sacrificed to the ancient animal god, Jhebbal Sag. Some of the tribes even go to sea in canoes to fish, hunt whales, and raid nearby villages, taking slaves and plunder as they have for thousands of years, before the emergence of modern piracy.

One of the few attempts at settlement along the coast is Count Valenso's stockade at Korvela Bay (following).

KORVELA BAY

A natural bay flanked by two pincers of land, Korvela has a primitive beauty to offer. The price for such a view is living along the Pictish coast, as unwelcome and isolated a place as any in on the continent. It is for this reason that Count Valenso, a Zingaran outcast, ventured here. He made a wooden fort, rebuilding his beloved home of Korzetta Castle in rough wood pillaged from the wreck of his ship, and established his household anew.

Nearly two hundred men-at-arms, crafters, servants, and retainers accompanied Valenso to this place, and their vessel wrecked upon their arrival. Now they have made a home here, a fortress surrounded with a wall to keep the wilderness out. Valenso and his household are the only population known to dwell in Korvela Bay, save for the Picts who lurk outside and threaten them from time to time. Valenso broods, and none of those who came with him knows the terrible secret that drove him so far from civilization, a curse that he fears may find him again… in the form of the Black Stranger.

The wooden palisades are strong, the archers behind them sure and their aim true, but it may only be a matter of time before the savagery of the Picts, or the dark curse that hangs about the bay, turns this small bastion of civilization into crimson-stained ashes, eventually to mingle with the finely grained sand of the beach below.

Valenso is described on page 85 and the Black Stranger, his supernatural nemesis, is on page 78.

> *"Ships from Zingara occasionally come and trade weapons and ornaments and wine to the coastal tribes for skins and copper ore and gold dust. Sometimes they trade ostrich plumes they got from the Stygians, who in turn got them from the black tribes of Kush, which lies south of Stygia. The Pictish shamans place great store by them. But there's much risk in such trade. The Picts are too likely to try to seize the ship. And the coast is dangerous to ships. I've sailed along it when I was with the pirates of the Barachan Isles, which lie southwest of Zingara."*
>
> — Conan, "Beyond the Black River"

THE TREASURE CAVE OF TRANICOS

Located several miles from Korvela Bay is a curiosity in the howling Pictish wilderness: a rocky hill with a strong and obvious ridge, from which a series of hand-holds are carven into the rocky cliff-face above. At the top of this rude ladder is a cavern, set with wooden beams for support, and at the very end of that tunnel is a stout, iron-bound wooden door.

Beyond that door is a chamber filled with iron-bound wooden chests filled with antiquated garments and oddments, and at one end is an arched door leading into an apparent dining hall, incredibly furnished with a long ebony table, lit by a dully glowing jewel set upon an ivory pedestal in its center. A strange and sluggish blue mist plays about the room, despite the lack of an air current. About the table sit twelve men, all clad in pirate regalia from a century ago, and strewn before them on the table lies a fortune in brilliant jewels. Surrounding these captains of old are more chests, holding impossible amounts of wealth in the form of gold, jewels, objects of art, and other priceless items.

The occupants of the dining room are none other than Bloody Tranicos, a Zingaran pirate of old, who stole from King Tothmekri of Stygia a fortune and fled with it to a land where none would ever find him… Pictland. Picts of all tribes avoid this place entirely, for it figures prominently into an old story they tell of a wizard of their people who cursed a group of interlopers, and left them to suffer eternally, trapped in a chamber warded by a smoke devil.

The exact location of this treasure trove is lost to most, though there are rumors of a map at loose in the world, divided into three pieces so that none might know the entirety of the means of finding Tranicos' last redoubt.

> *She felt that it was not by chance that this sail was beating up this lonely coast. There was no harbor town to the north, though one sailed to the ultimate shores of ice; and the nearest port to the south was a thousand miles away. What brought this stranger to lonely Korvela Bay?*
>
> — "The Black Stranger"

THE LONG BLACK COAST OF DEATH

Not to be confused with the Black Coast — which forms the eastern border of Kush and the Black Kingdoms — this is a fog-shrouded stretch of beach in Pictland, feared and avoided by the Picts themselves, inhabited seemingly by naught but abnormally huge black-shelled spider crabs. Visitors to this stretch of land may find the crabs eerily organized, almost as if they are watching, and even more bold explorers will discover the unthinkable — set high into the cliffsides above the coast is a complex and bafflingly alien city of black stone, apparently fashioned by the crabs themselves and revealing a frighteningly sophisticated level of culture and science.

THE VILAYET SEA

Described as little more than "a Hyrkanian lake", the Vilayet Sea is primarily held by purple-sailed Turanian fleets, dominating all trade therein. Its eastern shores are primarily steppes, uninhabited for great stretches, inhabited as they are by a species of lean-bodied, cannibalistic gray apes. The many islands of the Vilayet are known for the greenish-black stone, iron-hard, which is found only there, and many strange ruins made of the material lure the unwary or unwise. The reedy southern reaches of the Vilayet are filled with marshes though to be haunted with primordial monsters almost forgotten in human memory — giant serpents and worse.

Despite this, the Vilayet's southern waters are haven to a branch of the Red Brotherhood, allied only in name to the group that sails upon the Western Sea. To the north, the only resistance to Turan's fleets are the occasional small band of Hyrkanian buccaneers, as rough a gang as any of their brethren on the Western Sea. Other pirates and pirate fraternities also ply the Vilayet, but ultimately their existence is of little relevance to those who sail the Western Sea. Pirates sometimes travel between the two great bodies of water, to flee enemies or to try their fortune upon unfamiliar waves, but there is no commerce between pirates in either place, and no direct waterway connects the seas. The Vilayet Sea, its coastline, and the surrounding countries are addressed thoroughly in *Conan the Wanderer*, which covers Hyrkania and Turan.

CHAPTER 3
EVENTS

> *The life was uncertain, dream-like, with sharp contrasts of battle, pillage, murder, and flight. Zaporavo's red visions made it even more uncertain than that of the average freebooter. No one knew what he planned next. Now they had left all charted coasts behind and were plunging further and further into that unknown billowy waste ordinarily shunned by seafarers, and into which, since the beginnings of Time, ships had ventured, only to vanish from the sight of man for ever. All known lands lay behind them, and day upon day the blue surging immensity lay empty to their sight.*
>
> — "The Pool of the Black One"

The high seas are the lifeline of commerce, the speediest means by which to transport goods and connect countries and cities via ports. But the sea is a tempestuous mistress, offering bounty and calm waters one day, and maelstroms the next. So, too, the human vagaries of this world apply equally to land and sea. Just as humankind can barely master wild nature on land, it has less power over the ocean, and time and tide make fools of those who claim to control the seas.

The Trade, as piracy is known amidst those who practice it, is an ancient tradition, predating even the Cataclysm. Pirates from the islands of Lemuria, a realm of the Thurian Age, preyed upon the vessels of the mainland, and even the ancient Valusian king Kull had been a pirate at one stint of his illustrious career. Despite the flood washing away all trace of that ancient world but for some remnant bloodlines and the unkillable Picts, the tradition of piracy rose again, a natural outgrowth of humankind's base nature, and the world was once again plagued by the practice.

This chapter addresses the many events that affect the world of the pirate, the sailor, and any that ply the seas for trade, travel, or adventure.

MORTAL EVENTS

No matter how far one might roam throughout the world, there is never a foe both so common and deadly as other humans. Monsters and maelstroms crush ships like dry winter wood and send sailors to their doom without pity or discretion, but mankind is the rare creation that takes pleasure in killing, and discriminates against itself. The following events are those inflicted by humankind upon itself, one country to another, or a group against its rivals, or even its own members.

WAR AT SEA!

For any nation set upon the coasts of the Western Ocean, the travel routes are vital to trade and prosperity, the source of income and much-needed goods beyond local ability to produce. It is little surprise, then, that these sea-lanes are frequently coveted by each country's neighbors. Every trade lane possessed fills the coffers of the king. When Zingara establishes a swift lane to Stygia, Argos likely loses coin.

EVENTS

However, not every shipping lane is worth a war for: if it were, naval warfare would be incessant, and no goods would ever see landfall. This is not the case. Yet the navies of Argos, Zingara, Shem, and Stygia are ever ready to disrupt trade in times of war, and sink all enemy vessels if their masters so say. At such times, sailors and mercenaries are paid well, or even captured and pressed into service by needful captains. A hapless individual could easily pass out in a Messantian tavern only to wake aboard an Argossean galley, forced to row a carrack's mighty oars. Though there are laws against forcing a free person into slavery, there is little recourse once chains are locked about wrists and ankles and a ship leaves a port.

Of primary concern are the nations of Argos and Zingara, for each are aggressive, scheming naval powers. Argos has the advantage of stability and more ships, but Zingara, when threatened, unites quickly against a common foe on the ocean. Their navy is unreliable in times of peace, but devastating when focused on returning a slight or avenging an injury. Zingarans wonder, wistfully, at the scope of an endeavor that would marshal such a grand armada, and sharpen their swords in hopes that such a day will come.

Men and women of adventure may become embroiled in such wars in many ways. A few examples follow below.

Pressed into Service

As noted above, not all members of a given navy are willing. In times of war, kings and queens press and conscript many into service. Often, these are citizens who are duty-bound to serve, but not every captain is so careful finding replacement crew, and authorities often look the other way when hard coin finds its way into their eager palms.

Player characters might easily find themselves caught between two undesirable options. Perhaps their larcenous ways have earned them a hanging, yet their jailer or judge offers service in the navy as alternative. Or, as mentioned, Argossean and Zingaran kidnappers make good money abducting strangers to sell to needy captains. One need not be a slave to find oneself forced to row great oars, or trim the bright sails of a foreign nation.

Privateers

War is neither a pleasant nor honest business. Piracy is ill-tolerated by most nations — unless said pirates work for them. Privateers are common in times of war. They are given legal, though sometimes dubious, authority to attack and steal from enemy vessels. These ships prey upon any vessels who sail under the wrong flag, and inflict losses in both goods, ships, and manpower upon a nation's enemy.

Privateers are mercenaries of the seas, though have little of the honor or bond their land-bound counterparts evidence. For, at the end of the day, most privateers were pirates first and care not for the concerns of a kingdom, but only for the loot they might obtain. It is always a precarious relationship, and even naval officers commissioned as privateers may turn upon their ruler when pickings are slim.

A Spy's Life for Me

Spies are vital in any war, and no less so in naval engagements. The side that knows where the enemy lurks has the advantage. While both Zingara and Argos station fleets near their major ports, there are hundreds of other targets to defend. Each nation must spread their ships judiciously, and each assumes that they cannot defend their entire coastline. Further, a well-executed ploy can draw forces away from one of the larger ports to join a perceived battle.

In all these cases, spies do the work of collecting information and transferring it to those who would make good use of it. Wandering sorts, such as many player characters, fit in easily in the harbors, in the waterfront dives, and on the motley crews of merchant ships. They may easily trade information gathered in such locales for coin or other rewards when in a port whose king has need of such knowledge, and many are the spymasters or naval captains willing to hire player characters to go where they cannot.

Merchants of the more unscrupulous bent will often ply pirates and oceangoing rogues with coin and promise of more for information about what cargoes are shipping to and from their ports, what their rivals are expecting to receive, or what they are shipping out. In rare cases, too, the royal court will become involved in such skullduggery, using pirates clandestinely as instruments of brute force, causing ruin to disfavored merchants or rival noble houses.

Truer still is that pirates themselves seek to know information about the movement of the navies and rival ships, and will pay even more generous coin to those who can provide such intelligence. Player characters associated with a particular pirate vessel might find a rival captain willing to give handsomely for information about the player characters' captain, especially when it comes to the whereabouts of hidden caches of loot and supplies.

AGAINST THE PIRATES

While the rulers of the great ocean-faring kingdoms of the world would never deign to call actions against pirates a "war", they nevertheless often conduct war upon such sea dogs in all but name. No king can long resist the haranguing crowds wanting food and silk and wine. When pirates prey too heavily upon the powers of the Western Ocean, those powers strike back with the quickness and deadliness of a Stygian cobra.

When piracy bites too heavily into the coffers of a kingdom, the king is obliged to respond. Further, this is one case where rival naval powers might collude to stop a common foe. For pirates, a group that welcomes wanderers

and sell-swords like the player characters, such times are more dangerous than normal… and their normal level of "dangerous" is very high indeed.

Being hunted by Argossean and Zingaran ships is nothing to take lightly. If those two navies war against the Red Brotherhood, the Barachans, or anyone else, the pirates are almost always on the defensive. A pirate relies on surprise and overwhelming might against a single vessel. They are not in the business of stand-up fights against trained naval warriors and well-armed ships.

Of course, there are brilliant and mad examples of pirates who take the challenge as a dare and chance for glory rather than good reason to hide and let the storms blow over.

PIRATES UNITE!

Sea dogs are, by nature, a treacherous lot. One rarely trusts the next person, to say nothing of an unfamiliar pirate vessel. However, there exist codes on the sea even for such scum as this and, on occasion, the basest of men may rally under a common flag… at least in theory.

In the dives and houses of ill-fame in Tortage are myriad stories of "pirate armies" that once defeated Argos, or Stygia, or even lost Acheron. Pirates and sailors alike are known for tall tales and yarns both long and implausible. But what if such a story inspired a singular pirate to unite disparate cutthroats for more gold and glory? In an event such as this, a charismatic leader emerges from the seas to not only wreak havoc in their name, but to rally others to their bloody pillaging. At first, such a group begins as a thorn in the side of a great kingdom, but, over time, it could grow into an army of its own.

To date, these tales remain legends, and the nature of the pirate is one antithetical to long cooperation. Yet a character of steely glare and iron will could forge such dogs into a genuine force to be reckoned with. Perhaps the player characters themselves have such a freebooter amidst their ranks?

STYGIA RISES ON THE SEA

Stygia is an undisputed power along its coast and, further south, along the famed Black Coast. Any pirate operating in these waters knows well the capabilities of the Stygian navy. Yet Stygia does not oft venture beyond its waters, preferring instead to scheme against powers inland. That, however, is merely recent custom, for the libraries of Khemi and Luxor tell of times when Stygia dominated the Western Ocean while Argos and Zingara were still in the throes of barbarism. Old Stygia sat in the shadow of Acheron, and that, perhaps, kept it in check. But Acheron is long dead and, while Stygia has not the same power it once held, it grows in strength every day — grows and molts like the serpents who slither through the Khemi night.

EVENTS

One day, Stygia may strike from the sea. There is much gold in the shipping lanes of Argos and Zingara that, if taken by Stygia, could fuel a northern expansion and the long-sought crusade against the followers of Bori and now Mitra.

Such an expansion would lead to open war. Argos and Zingara might ally with each other or with Stygia against the other. Shem, meanwhile, waits such a conflict out and avoids direct conflict with their neighbor across the Styx, which would be ruinous. Shipping then becomes precarious; goods rise in price and so pirates covet them more. The black market, run by the dog-brothers of the ocean, becomes the supplemental source for basic goods. Opportunities for pirates and privateers suddenly abound. An entire campaign might revolve around Stygia's attempted domination of the Western Ocean, involving war, piracy, lost treasures, and secrets even Set himself looks upon only in the dark.

NATURAL EVENTS

History reminds us always of the power of nature. The Great Cataclysm forever altered the world and led to the age in which humankind now finds itself. On land, the dangers are many but, overall, known. Not so on the sea. Its nigh-fathomless depths hold the entire history of the world, and creatures long past their age still lurk there. Not a single sailor worth their salt lacks a tale of a great sea monster or white squall. Buy them a jack of wine and let them tell it. Even the most seemingly impossible may turn out to be true.

TYPHOON SEASON

People of the coasts and the sea alike are familiar with the stormy season that visits in summer months. It is a dangerous time for anyone near the water, and even more hazardous for those who sail her. Ships are wrecked, fortunes are lost, and small villages are wiped clean from the map.

Yet trade persists, even in dire circumstances. Pay increases, slightly, for those that crew ships during typhoon season, and pirates become rarer. That is the trade-off nature offers. While weather can sink a vessel, or simply scare the crew near to death, it can also blow ships far off course. There are many legends of sailors whose ships were cast about by angry winds, only to wind up in places so strange no one would believe them.

THE WIDENING GYRE

Tales of whirlpools, abyssal gyres, and the like populate the lore of sailors. Some of these are verifiable phenomena, but others speak of wells in the ocean so deep that those

---

LIFE'S CONSTANT WOES
Strife

Civil unrest can be as dangerous as war and even more unpredictable. Zingara is famous for the fractious nature of its princes, but no country is immune to strife. Even the famous autocrats of Stygia must deal with slave revolts and power struggles, but their solutions simply lean toward poison and sorcery over brawling in the streets. Civil unrest can come about due to political turmoil, famine, disease, or natural disaster. Zingara is known for the ongoing political disputes and duels between its would-be rulers. Argos sees conflicts between its wealthy merchants, privileged nobles, and laborers. Strife can also create waves of refugees that spill over into adjacent lands, creating yet another destabilizing effect. The city-states of Shem, meanwhile, are at a near-constant state of rivalry, set aside only when threatened from without.

Strife can create opportunities for adventure as one faction seeks to gain advantage over another or when a losing side seeks to escape the retribution from the victors. Smugglers thrive on strife that creates demands for weapons, food, and other goods. Such strife makes transporting information, refugees, diplomats, and spies even more profitable. Strife creates uncertainty and unrest that can destroy a merchant's fortune or create opportunities to gain fabulous wealth.

Plague

Most cities of the day have poor sanitation, crowded conditions, and limited medical care that make them ripe for outbreaks of disease. Ships may avoid a city where there is an outbreak of plague, and ships coming from the city may be turned away by other ports. Yet, ships are also great incubators of disease that can spread quickly through the people on board. A ship filled with the sick may not be able to find a port, or a trader might encounter a ship drifting listlessly after its crew was overcome by disease.

In the cities, the sick may be quarantined or exiled, either driven out or shipped to some isolated island or mountain valley. Fear of the plague may spark riots that result in fire or other wanton destruction intended to purge sickness, or just the sick themselves, from a city.

Plague can also create a demand for medicines, and even in these harsh times there are missionaries of Mitra and other religious orders dedicated to caring for the sick. A physician or a missionary may seek a ship to take them to a city where there is an outbreak of plague or to go in search of needed medicine. Ship captains are not known for their altruism, so, for the sick, hefty bags of local coin are the difference between life and death.

pulled into them wind up on the other side of the world… or another world altogether. Such ideas may seem mad to landlubbers, but the seasoned sailor knows there are stranger things in the depths of the sea than can be found anywhere but the Outer Dark.

FROM OUT OF THE ICY PAST

Sea monsters are an essential part of any tall tale. There isn't a sailor around that hasn't heard one and few who would not claim to have seen such a beast with their own eyes. While there is little doubt that malicious entities from vast gulfs of space sleep beneath the bottle-green waves of the Western Ocean, most so-called sea serpents are holdovers from eras even earlier than the Thurian Age.

Some few scholars have tried to catalogue such beasts but, like the mythical creatures on land, the accounts are conflicting and often rather impossible to believe. Still, the dusty tomes of Numalia's library, Tarantia's archives, and other lyceums and scriptoriums readily offer up drawings and eyewitness accounts of such creatures.

In the vast, inky black of the ocean are creatures older than humanity, older than those sentient beings which presaged humanity, perhaps as old as some of the beings of the Outer Dark that came to this planet long before the memory of any creature now living. Such species are monsters in all but name, and few sailors would care to define a difference between an ancient sea beast and a demon summoned from hell… the results are so often the same, after all.

PRETERNATURAL EVENTS

The unknown is what man fears most and, of those things unknown, the most frightening is that which is inherently unknowable. A sea creature might be explained, a war may be unexpected, but one can wrap one's mind about it. Not so with the unnatural, not so with things which fall to Earth from the dark voids above. These are things which cannot be known and, for those who try, madness often prevails.

THE GREAT SARGASSO

Ships have become stuck in sargassos since man clawed his way back to civilization after the Cataclysm. They are dangerous and often trap a ship so thoroughly that the crew aboard can starve. Yet out there is a Great Sargasso, by this some wild-eyed sailors swear. They refuse to return to the ocean, instead drowning in wine and reluctantly telling their tale for more of the same. Such sad men and women are best ignored by those of keener minds… and yet there is something to their stories that hooks the mind like fish, that catches at the wonder of the unknown and drags a person headlong into the depths of the sea in search of answers.

There are a hundred variations of the legend of the Great Sargasso, but they all have common features. It is to these points, like iceberg tips above the cold water, which adventurers cling to. They speak of a vast Sargasso as old as time. In its web are caught up all manner of ships — many of them not of this age or perhaps even of this world. Sailors aver that Atlantean vessels sit enmeshed next to Valusian galleons. Some describe ships of such alien geometries that they could scarcely be recognized. Each of these vessels is preserved, untouched by time. Their decks are quiet, their treasure holds full. One merely must find the Great Sargasso to loot such a trove, though this is no small thing.

Some of these tales go further. Some say that the crews of these ships, too, have not died, but instead persisted through the eons. They live together, in some city made of parts of their former vessels, which lies like a spider at the heart of the Sargasso. There, if you believe the besotted tale-teller, they worship a god like no other and have access to times and events that have yet to happen. So say the stories.

THE GREAT OLD ONE WAKES

Of all the nameless terrors of the world, none are as feared or unknowable as the Great Old Ones. They are beyond our space and time, beyond our ken, and beyond any petty notions of human power. At least one, it is said, sleeps in the depths of the ocean, though none can say where. Perhaps he is alone. Perhaps others wait below. Perhaps there exist cities built with cyclopean blocks and alien geometry which exist yet above the waves. Perhaps we are best off not knowing.

If one of these entities, these gods, awoke, it would disrupt the entire world. For what could stand against these creatures? Men know not if their gods exist; Crom and Mitra might alike be tales told to explain the rules of a world man does not yet understand. But the Great Old Ones? They have left strange ruins across this world, birthed cults older than the language of any kingdom, and driven men mad from the first time they dragged themselves out of abject barbarism. The Old Ones are quite real, and they neither answer prayers nor bestow favor upon their worshippers. Their wants are not inherently understandable by sane minds, and those minds loosed from sanity can no longer explain their motives in any human tongue.

If but one of these ancient edifices or necropoli rises from out of the ocean, all the kingdoms of the world united together would be unable to stand against it.

CHAPTER 4
MYTH & MAGIC

> "This was the temple of the old ones," she said. "Look — you can see the channels for the blood along the sides of the altar, and the rains of ten thousand years have not washed the dark stains from them. The walls have all fallen away, but this stone block defies time and the elements."
>
> — Bêlit, "Queen of the Black Coast"

From the dawn of time, the sea has represented many things to humankind. Some hypothesize that its murky depths are the source of all life, and many cultures believe in sending their dead into the sea, returning them to that primeval birthplace. Myths and legends abound about the sea, and its vastness and unknowable depths contain mysteries beyond human reckoning.

As such, there are few in the Hyborian Age more superstitious than sailors or pirates. Those who brave the seas do so knowing that, as they step from the solidity of earth and stone to the unstable wooden decks of triremes and biremes, they also step into myth, into the raw stuff of history and legend. For that is what waits on the high seas. Beyond the dangers of storms, the querulousness of waves and elements, the wretched conditions of life aboard ship, beyond all that there is the danger of those things which land dwellers have forgotten. Civilizations swallowed by the ocean — perhaps commanded by envious gods — whose wealth and genius can still be found by those brave enough to search or unlucky enough to cast a net into the wrong current.

The sea is vast and dangerous and unknowable. There is much beyond the comforting boundaries formed by steep cliffs and beaches, better left to the cold embrace of the deep. When mariners finally return to land, their minds are filled with the strange things they have heard and seen, and the loosening effects of ale and rum can coax tales from unwilling lips.

This chapter describes some of the mysterious elements of magic, worship, and other enchantment relating to the Western Sea, the lands along its coast, those who sail upon its surface, and some other entities who move beneath its waters.

SEA-CULTS

Many are the secret societies and cults operating in the lands adjacent to the Western Sea, or upon its waters. Described here are two cults of sorcerous practitioners, and their secrets.

SOOTHSAYERS OF ZINGG

An ancient cult persists in Zingara, consisting of an unbroken line of soothsayers that predates the arrival of the Bori. All these soothsayers are women, and they claim lineage

that stretches back into the depths of prehistory. They are as much a part of Zingara as the famous grapes of the Zingg Valley. The women of the cult are selected and initiated upon their twelfth year. Once initiated, they remain members of the cult for life.

The cult does not have temples or chapter houses. Instead they meet at night in groves, many of which have been used since time immemorial. In Kordava, the most prominent members of the cult gather in a garden in the royal palace, for the queen is one of their most prominent of priestesses. In Zingara, tradition holds that the king must be wed to a soothsayer. Each king abides by this, shortly after his election marrying the bride chosen by the soothsayers, sanctifying his reign with a bond to the ancient traditions. If already married, the king is by custom required to temporarily forsake his wife before his coronation and then enter a "true" marriage to the chosen soothsayer, but in practice, accommodations are made.

The soothsayers are skilled at reading the stars and the weather. One of their important duties each year is to select the first day for planting. They are most known, though, for their reading of individual fortunes in the dregs of a tea cup. These readings are often conducted as part of elaborate rituals that involve brewing the tea, selecting the cup, and drinking the tea — culminating in the reading. The soothsayers are called on to give readings before most important events in Zingara. Spells commonly known by more learned soothsayers include *Atavistic Voyage*, *Favor of the Gods* (**Conan** corebook, pages 174 and 179), and *Weave of Fate* (see page 64).

> *"They have gone back into the still waters of the lakes, the quiet hearts of the hills, the gulfs beyond the stars. Gods are no more stable than men."*
>
> — "Iron Shadows in the Moon"

SEA HAGS

There is a loose cult of sorceresses found scattered through isolated places in the Baracha Isles, the Zingaran coast, and even the depths of the Pictish wilderness. These women practice a sorcery closely linked to the sea, and they have great knowledge and mastery of the winds, waves, and tides. "Sea hags" are how most pirates know them. Some call them "the witches of the wilds", and no one is certain what they call themselves in private. Others say they have no name and that there is no actual cult, but many small unrelated sects and covens. Regardless, they have much in common and their shared aspects point at some distant connection. Spells that a sea hag might learn include *Commune with the Wild*, *Form of a Beast*, *Fury of the Elements*, and *Venom on the Wind* (see **Conan** corebook, pages 175, 179, 181, and 187).

Many of their sorceries deal with transformation, and they are highly skilled in potions and petty enchantments, most infamously the black barnacle (see sidebar). An oft-told tale in along the northern coasts is that of the seal woman who comes to live with a lonely fisherman for a time before returning to the sea. Another tale features a witch that turns half of a ship's crew into pigs that she then encourages the rest of the crew to hunt and roast. These sorceresses often have wild animals as familiars and have been seen with eagles, wolves, wildcats, panthers, dolphins, and even vultures.

The sea hags normally dwell apart but, from time to time, they gather for rituals or celebrations where they dance along moonlit beaches or among the stones of ancient ruins.

THE BLACK BARNACLE

An enchantment with a fearsome reputation among sailors, particularly pirates. This is a special type of petty enchantment known only by sea hags. The black barnacle is an actual barnacle taken from the hull of a ship or some area washed by the tide. The magic of the sea hag stains the barnacle as dark as midnight. A sorceress then attempts to place the black barnacle in the hand of an enemy (resolved as a struggle pitting the sorceresses' Persuade or Thievery skills against the target's Insight).

Once grasped, the black barnacle adheres to the target's hand and begins to poison the target's blood. The target also cannot grasp anything with that hand so long as the barnacle remains affixed. Many sailors see the black barnacle as an ill omen and shun anyone with it. It is also widely adopted as a common token of ill fortune. One sailor may hand another a barnacle that has been painted black or dipped in tar as a sign of ill-will. Among pirates, such painted barnacles are often used as a sign of a lack of faith in a captain or officer and as a challenge to their authority.

When enchanting the black barnacle, the sorceress determines the virulence of the poison, how often it damages a target, by the Difficulty of the enchantment: Average (D1), once per day; Challenging (D2), once every 12 hours; Daunting (D3), once every 3 hours; Dire (D4), once every hour. The sorceress can remove the barnacle, and often she offers to do so only when some task is completed.

- **Difficulty:** Varies
- **Damage:** 2 ⚔
- **Effects:** Persistent, Piercing 2.

MYTH & MAGIC   63

SPELLS

FLAMES OF THE DEEP

Difficulty: Daunting (D3)
Prerequisite: *Sorcerer*
Duration: 1 hour
Cost to Learn/Cast: 2 Resolve

The sorcerer steps into a boat or a small ship and calls up smokeless blue flames from the depths of the sea to play about the boat and to carry it forward across the waves. The flames carry the boat at an average rowing pace.

> "There was a strange moaning in the wind, and the sea whimpered like a thing in fear, and then he came.
>
> …
>
> He came from the sea in a strange black boat with blue fire playing all about it, but there was no torch."
>
> — "The Black Stranger"

FLAMES OF THE DEEP MOMENTUM SPENDS		
Type	Momentum Cost	Effect
Enduring Flames	X	The flames last one extra hour for each Momentum spent.
Fast Flames	2	The flames now carry the boat as fast as a galley might travel with the crew rowing as hard as they can.
Lifting Flames	5	The flames will lift the craft, granting it flight and allowing the vessel to clear obstacles such as ice or branches without risk of damage.

WEAVE OF FATE

Difficulty: Daunting (D3) or higher
Duration: 1 scene
Cost to Learn/Cast: 2 Resolve

It is difficult to read the future. The strands of fate rarely run cleanly or clearly, and the fate of one individual can change as they bind themselves to others. Then, there is the difficulty of telling someone their fate. Most want to hear of riches, love, and greatness. Some are to die poor, alone, and unknown. When reading the *Weave of Fate*, a sorcerer must choose their words carefully.

When reading the Weave, a sorcerer might look at the palm of a hand, gaze into a fire, look into a moonlit basin, breathe in a hallucinatory smoke, read the entrails of sacrifice, interpret the flight of birds, cast runes, or employ some other technique. Before a reading, the sorcerer asks a question, either one of their own or one by the person requesting the reading. When successfully cast, the caster may bestow 1 Fortune point to the character they are reading for, if desired, or curse them with the Evil Eye (see below).

If the sorcerer grants the character 1 Fortune point, and that point is used during the duration of the scene, there is no additional cost for the sorcerer. If the Fortune point is retained beyond the duration of the spell, the sorcerer must either pay 3 Doom or use one of their own Fortune points to grant to the subject of the spell.

The Evil Eye is a unique Threaten action. Characters seeking to oppose the Evil Eye in a Struggle must make a Challenging (D3) Sorcery or a Dire (D4) Discipline test. Failing this test causes 4 mental damage, but the Evil Eye is otherwise a Threaten action, gaining bonus damage from Personality.

> ### LOOKING IN THE MIRROR
> A sorcerer using the *Weave of Fate* spell upon their own self almost certainly sees dire portents. A sorcerer casting the spell in this selfish fashion must pay 1 Doom for every d20 they roll on the test, regardless of the source of the die. This is in addition to any other cost, including Fortune points, Momentum, Doom, or offerings.

WEAVE OF FATE MOMENTUM SPENDS

Type	Momentum Cost	Effect
Binding Strands of Fate	1	The fate extends its reach and binds other characters into its web. The spell gains the Area Quality. All characters touched by the spell gain the Fortune point or suffer the *Evil Eye* (as picked by the sorcerer).
A Crossroads Awaits	1	The character gains insight into one challenge that awaits them and can ask the gamemaster one direct question about likely future events.
Cold Eyes of Bitter Truth	1	When used with the Evil Eye, the damage has the Vicious 1 Quality.
Doomed Fate	1+X	Every time the character gains any Momentum on any test, the gamemaster gains X Doom.
Lingering Fate	1	The Duration of the spell increases to one day.
True Fate	2	The Duration of the spell becomes effectively infinite, ending only when the next Fortune point is spent.

WEAVE OF FATE ALTERNATIVE USES

Type	Momentum Cost	Effect
A Dark Stranger	2	When the player character next meets a non-player character, this spell grants 1 bonus Momentum for the purposes of making a positive impression using a Personality-based skill. This need not be a romantic one, nor does the spell guarantee that the non-player character will even like the character; merely that the non-player character will be more favorable than normal.
Health and Prosperity	1	When the character next has make a Resistance test against illness, a Society test to make a payment, or a Survival test to find food and shelter, the character gains the effect of 1 bonus Momentum on the test. The sorcerer can spend up to 2 Momentum to grant an additional bonus success.

SHIPS OF THE DEAD

Sailors are generally brave and intrepid souls — they must be to risk the agonizing deaths which await any whose good fortune deserts them for even a moment — but even then, they must abide by the limitations of their crafts and the vagaries of the tides. This means that most sailing is carried out close to the shoreline, utilizing the currents and winds from both the sea from the land. To desert these well-known, well-sailed channels and embark on voyages on the open sea is a measure of defiance, recklessness, and courage which few possess. Of those few bold or stupid enough to leave land far behind, fewer still return, and even those that do, return changed. Most send no message back, no wreckage is recovered, and no bodies wash ashore.

And yet, there are tales... tales of ships whose crew never speak and whose faces retain only a single expression — a painful rictus grin. Some say that this permanent arrangement of flesh, muscle, and exposed teeth never abates, never gives even for a second — even as the exposure to salt-tinged wind strips away skin and muscle fiber. There are those who claim to have seen this ship, its crew mechanically carrying out their duties, bleached bone clearly visible beneath layers of excoriated flesh. But this is only one, lone example of the dozens of strange stories told of such vessels — ships manned by the dead, by phantoms and figments and shades of the netherworld; there are many others. Ships long lost, reappearing to bring desperate tidings, to beg for release from their immortal voyage... the many ports of the Western Sea abound with such strange tales.

GHOSTLY SLAVE (MINION)

ATTRIBUTES			
Awareness	Intelligence	Personality	Willpower
7	—	—	—
Agility	Brawn		Coordination
8	8 (2)		8

FIELDS OF EXPERTISE			
Combat	1	Movement	1
Fortitude	—	Senses	—
Knowledge	—	Social	—

STRESS AND SOAK
- **Stress:** Vigor 6, Resolve —
- **Soak:** Armor 5 (Insubstantial), Courage 5

SUMMONING A GHOST SLAVE
Should a sorcerer come across a corpse of someone who has died in bondage, they can attempt to use *Raise the Dead* to summon a ghost slave. The corpse must not at any point have been freed from its chains, and the key to the slave's freedom must be in the possession of the caster. The casting is an Epic (D5) casting, with Difficulty decreasing by one step for every decade that the corpse spent as a slave.

ATTACKS
- **Ghostly Fists (M):** Reach 1, 4 ☠, Vicious 1
- **Flung Object (R):** Reach 1, 2 ☠, Improvised
- **Terror of the Dead (T):** Range M, 3 ☠ mental, Area

SPECIAL ABILITIES
- **Enslaved for Eternity:** A ghostly slave cannot be killed by conventional weaponry. It can be beaten back by swords or other weapons, but this is temporary and lasts only for the scene. Permanently defeating the slave will require it to be claimed as booty. To do this, its captor must be defeated and the key that opens the slave's chains be claimed. Once claimed, the new captor can open the locks, at which point the ghostly slaves will be freed and vanish. A sorcerer can also use the *Placate the Dead* spell (**Conan** corebook, page 183) to put this shade to rest.
- Fear 1
- Incorporeal 5
- Inhuman Brawn 2
- Inured to Fear and Pain
- **Invisible:** Ghostly slaves gain 3 bonus Momentum on any Stealth test. While invisible, the shade doesn't have the Fear ability until it manifests. Slaves prefer to remain invisible and only manifest at the command of their captor.
- Mindless
- Unliving

DOOM SPENDS
- Doom Spends
- **Man the Oars:** If commanded to man the oars, a single ghostly slave is capable of moving any vessel as if it were fully crewed. This will cost the slave's captor 3 Doom for every scene the vessel moves under the power of that slave.

The Virago

Perhaps the most famous of those mythic ships, crewed by the damned, is the *Virago*. There is scarcely a tavern in Messantia, a sailor in Tortage, or a harlot in Kordava who doesn't have a story about that bewitched vessel. The *Virago* quickly became feared throughout the Western Sea for its ability to appear and disappear virtually at will, scything through wave and wood, wreaking bloody destruction on any ship unfortunate enough to draw within sight of the spotter, clinging to the upper mast. It was for good reason that those who sought profit and trade along the Western coastline began to refer to it as "the Widowmaker".

This respite was not to last long, however. Word of the *Virago*'s return spread through the merchant shipping routes with the same celerity as news of its disappearance had. Panic gave way to the grim conclusion that this had been a ruse — a ploy to ensure that fewer armed men were onboard each ship, that preparations were laxer. The merchants braced themselves for the inevitable butchery. But it never came... the sightings of the *Virago* continued, but there were no attacks. Instead, there were merely strange accounts of a ship at full sail, its crew screaming entreaties to those sailors who glimpsed them — shouting messages to be taken to family members, pleading for news of home, begging for intervention and relief.

Many insisted that the *Virago* itself bled into the sea; that the wood wept ichor, thick gobbets of viscera oozing from the timbers and dispersing in the salt water. At first, none would draw near to the *Virago*, fearing a trap, but soon, as the formerly fearsome ship's apparent impotence became more obvious, those captains whose curiosity superseded their talent for survival began to approach. It was in this way that the anguished shrieks of the *Virago*'s crew were heard and remembered. There is only one story recounted of any ships ever coming into direct, hull-to-hull contact with the *Virago* since its reappearance as a macabre ghost-ship. What was later found of this vessel and its crew, washed up on the Shemitish coast, has dissuaded any from making such an attempt since.

But what happened to the *Virago*? There are many permutations of this strange legend, though only a few are worth relating. The strangest claim is that the *Virago* was so saturated with the blood of its victims that Hell itself claimed the ship, dragging it into the uttermost deeps, along with all those onboard. The vessel is now but a memory, freshly escaped from Hell, and to set foot upon its hull is to touch the stuff of madness itself, twisting soul and flesh into hideous shapes. Others maintain that the screaming sailors aboard the *Virago* speak of a bargain which their captain made with a sea god; in exchange for the power to rule the seas uncontested for seven years, the captain would serve the god forever. He also included his ship and crew in the deal. When the god came to collect, the terms were not open to renegotiation.

Those of a more skeptical nature opine that the *Virago* was not torn from the oceans and consigned to the Outer Dark, but that the crew claimed one of the Baracha Isles for themselves and have built their own pirate kingdom, a new and better Tortage. Their secret, however, is preserved through the legend of the *Virago* — deploying tricks of the light, potions of peculiar alchemical composition, and ominous hints of a hideous fate awaiting any who draw too near.

Whatever the truth, the myth of the *Virago* only waxes stronger with time. Soon, it is certain, someone else will attempt to find out the truth concealed by the legend... and who can say what it is that they will find?

The Wreck of the Kerberos

Ship wrecks are common to the shores of the Western Sea. Hidden reefs and networks of submerged rock make landing a vessel a frequently deadly affair. Even bays and inlets that offer relative safety and are used as ports and harbors can still prove a lethal surprise to any crew that grows complacent. It is for this reason that, when the *Kerberos* ran aground on a long stretch of Zingaran beach where wrecks were rare, few amongst the local fishermen living nearby were surprised. Only after clambering aboard did they realize their mistake. Word was sent to the nearest city and a troop of Zingaran soldiers were dispatched to investigate the wreck and its cause.

MYTH & MAGIC

> *The ocean burst suddenly on his view, and in his swimming gaze floated the Wastrel, unharmed. Men tumbled into the boats htelter-skelter. Sancha fell into the bottom and lay there in a crumpled heap. Conan, though the blood thundered in his ears and the world swam red to his gaze, took an oar with the panting sailors.*
>
> — "The Pool of the Black One"

The ship, when the soldiers entered, most closely resembled an abattoir. The crew had been butchered, to a man — a few even having been dismembered, apparently, while still alive. There was nothing onboard the ship which might have carried out such frenzied attacks and, initially, it was thought that the crew had gone insane. Then, while inspecting the lower decks, a soldier glanced upwards to see the words, scrawled in blood above. The script, illegible at some points, meaningless at others, had been written with the fingers of its author — at least one fingernail stuck out from the thick, damp wood of the upper deck, torn off during frenzied scratching — and its words were almost unfathomable:

'the three-lobed burning eye... madness... the gem... puppets... so full, so fragile in its grip...'

At last, amongst the viscera which decorated the interior of the hull, the soldiers found the shattered fragments of an enormous crystal. It seemed to have been made of obsidian, but none could be certain of its true substance. Once their investigations had been concluded, the soldiers burnt the ship and all its contents. The ashes and anything which would not burn was collected and dumped in the sea. Even the records which referred to the *Kerberos* and the investigation in Zingara were expunged.

The story of the wreck and its hideous content has been pieced together by those who believe the ship held a great treasure — a treasure so great the crew mutinied and slaughtered one another to own — and from the whispered, terror-seized recollections of those soldiers who explored the charnel innards of that cursed ship, when drink has robbed them of the ability to mask their terror. Perhaps there was a treasure aboard the ship, now long-since confiscated by the Zingaran authorities and hidden away. And perhaps there is no truth to the tales told throughout the Zingaran coastlands and beyond, of a dark, sinuous creature which has preyed on isolated coastal villages for years, moving slowly inland and growing in strength as it seeks to fulfil some unknowable goal.

Perhaps it is only coincidence that, when asked to describe this creature, those who have glimpsed it draw a single image, their hands shaking as they do so... a three-lobed eye, alive with flame.

THE BARACHAN ORACLE

To those who must know such things, there are many available means of divining the future, many different forms of seeing beyond the limits of human comprehension, of witnessing events which have yet to transpire. Of course, such feats are beyond the capacities of normal people, and even those blessed (or cursed) with sorcerous gifts can rarely achieve knowledge of the future while retaining their sanity. Instead, sufficiently curious men and women turn to oracles, found throughout the many kingdoms.

There are as many oracles as there are questions to be asked of the future. Some depend for their prophetic power on interpreting the noise of rustling leaves in a sacred grove: the breath of a god caught for a fleeting moment. Others use the strange, mephitic vapors which seep from between the natural fissures in volcanic caves. These oracles are, however, mistrusted by those who recognize how easy it is to dupe the faithful; they rely, after all, on the intercession of a human being. Whether as the recipient of the message or as its interpreter, such a position is too ripe for abuse for such prophetic possibilities to be trusted.

That is why, for those who are wealthy and desperate enough, there is another option, one in which there is no need for a human interlocutor, no need for the message from beyond this world to be mediated: the Barachan oracle. Few know of it. Fewer still have ever visited it. The cost of an

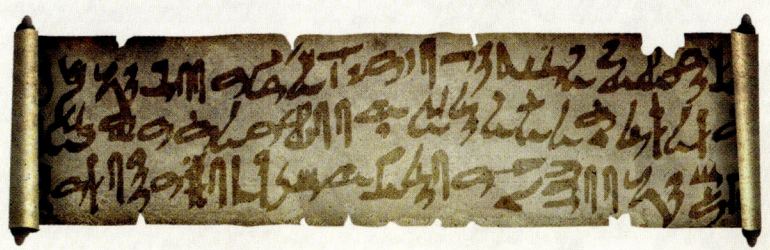

oracle there is high. It requires the sacrifice of something the supplicant truly loves, above their own self-interests — whether it is a family member, a treasure hoard, a weapon forged from the metal of a fallen star, or even a warrior's iron code; something must be offered up which cannot be returned. Only then can the Barachan oracle be approached and the question posed.

The oracle chamber is a room within a stone shack. The room is round and made from the raw stone of the island, hewed from the cliffs by the island's ancient residents and hauled to the desolate outcrop where the shack stands. There is little beyond the shack to keep one's attention; even the hardy scrub-grass of the islands does not grow. There is only stone, sea, and the shack. Within the shack, however, the stone of the walls is almost entirely effaced by salvaged wood — it is timber from a thousand broken, ruined ships, ships tempest-tossed against the island's stark cliffs, ships never finished but partly made when a merchant's finances finally failed, ships burned by crews pushed too far by tyrannical captains, and ships destroyed by captains whose crews proved impossible to control. The remnants of these different ships have been affixed to every wall, to every surface. After a few moments within the room, with the noise of the wind outside and the sound of the wood breathing softly, one might begin to believe you were in fact in the hold of some impossible vessel.

And the oracle itself waits in the center of the room — five long, beak-like protrusions: the prows of five ships which destroyed each other in a single, vicious sea battle. Each of these ships collided with the others, simultaneously. In doing so, those five rostra became a tangled mass of wood and iron and... something else. Those who have paid to visit it say that the rostra have attained some form of life, of animation. The structure moves, the ornamented tips of the individual beaks having gained some power of speech — a series of grinding voices that utter unerring prophecies, visions articulated in the groaning, rasping, creaking voice of wood. All who emerge from the Barachan oracle's chamber do so convinced that they have heard the future.

Is the oracle genuine? Is it instead an inspired front for an organization of pirate lords who use the legend of the rostra as a means of extorting riches and favors from those desperate enough to seek out promises of the future? Or did the long-forgotten sea battle which welded the five rostra together bind something else to them? Something strange and alien and capable of seeing things long before they happen? And who is willing to pay the price to gain admission to the Oracle and then disbelieve its message?

> *On through the blackness that preceded moonrise they drove, between banks that were solid palisades of darkness, whence came mysterious rustlings and stealthy footfalls, and the gleam of grim eyes. And once an inhuman voice was lifted in awful mockery of the cry of an ape, Bêlit said, adding that the souls of evil men were imprisoned in these man-like animals as punishment for past crimes.*
>
> — "Queen of the Black Coast"

CHAPTER 5
ENCOUNTERS

> *There were some seventy of them, a wild horde made up of men from many nations: Kothians, Zamorians, Brythunians, Corinthians, Shemites. Their features reflected the wildness of their natures. Many bore the scars of the lash or the branding-iron. There were cropped ears, slit noses, gaping eye-sockets, stumps of wrists — marks of the hangman as well as scars of battle. Most of them were half naked, but the garments they wore were fine; gold-braided jackets, satin girdles, silken breeches, tattered, stained with tar and blood, vied with pieces of silver-chased armor. Jewels glittered in nose-rings and ear-rings, and in the hilts of their daggers.*
>
> — The Red Brotherhood, "Iron Shadows in the Moon"

The following chapters describe a variety of foes, friends, and fearsome creatures suitable for pirate-based campaigns and encounters. Far more than mortal threats abound, as well, sending sailors and even entire ships into peril. They are divided into by human foes, wild beasts, supernatural creatures, and significant non-player characters of note. The gamemaster is encouraged to customize or modify these beings as desired.

A further section is dedicated to Bêlit's *Tigress* and its crew, the vessel Conan is associated with at this phase in his storied career.

SEA-DOGS AND HARDIES

Ships cannot, except for the hand of sorcery, sail unmanned, and thus the vessels that ply the waters of the Western Sea are filled with a myriad of humans. These mortal foes swell the ranks of those sailing upon the Western Sea, and present the most obvious challenges to any pirate player characters, whether as rivals, allies, or even prey.

MARINE (MINION) OR MARINE SERGEANT (TOUGHENED)

The troops carried by the warships of the nations that border the Western Sea are much like the pirates they often face, only the marines are usually better equipped and exhibit better discipline. A Squad of marines is usually led by a marine sergeant. The pirate captain (**Conan** corebook, page 113) can be used for this purpose.

The primary warship used by the nations along the Western Sea is the bireme, though a wide variety of other ships may be found in the open sea.

ATTRIBUTES					
Awareness	Intelligence		Personality		Willpower
8	7		7		7
Agility		Brawn		Coordination	
8		9		8	

FIELDS OF EXPERTISE				
Combat	1	Movement		2
Fortitude	1	Senses		1
Knowledge	—	Social		1

STRESS AND SOAK
- **Stress:** Vigor 5 or 9, Resolve 4 or 7
- **Soak:** Armor 1 (Quilted Hauberk), Courage 1

ATTACKS
- **Sea Bow (R):** Range C, 3 ☠, 2H, Volley
- **Shortsword (M):** Reach 1, 5 ☠, 1H, Parrying
- **Shield (M):** Reach 2, 3 ☠, 1H, Knockdown, Shield 2

Following are notes on distinguishing weapons and tactics employed by marines of various countries.

Argos
Argos maintains the largest navy of any of the seafaring nations. Its ships are mainly used for protecting traders, patrolling for pirates, and harassing the navies of Zingara, Shem, and Stygia. Argossean marines are identical to the generic marine described above.

Kush
Kush has the smallest navy along the Western Sea and its main warship is the giant war canoe. Its ships primarily patrol its coast to look for pirates and to guard against Stygia. Marines rarely wear armor, and are equipped as below.

ATTACKS
- **Sea Bow (R):** Range C, 3 ☠, 2H, Volley
- **Spear (M):** Reach 3, 5 ☠, Unbalanced, Piercing 1
- **Tower Shield (M):** Reach 2, 3 ☠, Unbalanced, Knockdown, Shield 4

Shem
Shem has a small navy, largely patrolling the waters around Asgalun. Her sailors are traditionally armed with metal caps (Armor 1; Head) in addition to the armor described above, and they use Shemite bows (Range L, 3 ☠, 2H, Piercing 1, Volley) to deadly effect.

Stygia
Stygia's black galleys appear ominous even when on the most routine trade missions. All Stygian ships are owned by its ruling caste, which is in turn ruled by the priesthood of Set. Thus, most Stygian ships encountered in other waters are on missions for the priests of Set. Only a few Stygian ships have sorcerers onboard, but sailors from other nations often give Stygian ships a wide berth out of suspicion. Stygia patrols its own waters to guard against pirates, intrusions from other nations, and any potential escapes by those from its enormous slave population.

Stygian ships sometimes enslave the crews of traders on the slightest pretext so that the vessel and cargo may be seized, but they leave slave traders unmolested, for fear of harming their access to such a commodity. For this reason, many Zingaran, Argossean, and Shemitish traders venturing through Stygian waters carry a complement of slaves as proof against their own enslavement.

Stygian marines differ from the standard marines above in the following aspects. They wear metal caps (Armor 2: Head) and their quilted hauberks are sleeveless.

ATTACKS
- **Stygian Short Bow (C):** Range C, 3 ☠, 2H, Volley

SPECIAL ABILITIES
- **In the Name of Set (T):** Range L, 3 ☠ mental, Area. A Stygian captain may invoke the authority of the Stygian ruling priesthood when commanding a ship to heave to so that it may be boarded and inspected.

Zingara
With a rich sailing tradition second only to that of Argos, the navies of Zingara are a proving ground for its hot-headed youths, enlisting to serve their country and seek fortune beyond what they might find in their proud-but-poor homeland.

DOOM SPENDS
- **Zingaran Drill:** Though Zingarans are reputed to be brash and individualistic, their infantry can be ruthlessly efficient in its military drills. For 1 Doom, the leader of a Squad receives 1 bonus Momentum for each Squad action for the remainder of the scene.

The men on the stockade gripped their bows or boar-spears and stared somberly at the carack which swung inshore, its brass work flashing in the sun. They could see the figures swarming on the deck, and hear the lusty yells of the seamen. Steel twinkled along the rail.

— "The Black Stranger"

PIRATE (MINION, TOUGHENED)

Pirates are described in **Conan**, page 319. Following are stats distinguishing between the various bands of pirates. In addition to a captain, each crew usually has a few officers — boatswain, mate, quartermaster, etc. — that are treated as Toughened foes.

Black Corsairs

Raiders of the Black Coast, many of whom come from the Southern Isles, the black corsairs favor short spears (javelins) and hide shields. They typically wear scant clothing, and little armor. As they close with an enemy, they hurl their spears and then take up another spear for boarding.

STRESS AND SOAK
- **Soak:** Armor —, Courage 1

ATTACKS
- **Javelin (M):** Reach 2, 3 ☠, 1H, Fragile, Piercing 1, Thrown
- **Shield (M):** Reach 2, 3 ☠, 1H, Knockdown, Shield 2

DOOM SPENDS
- **Battle Cry:** Prior to and during boarding actions, black corsairs let out a blood-curdling battle cry. For 1 Doom, a black corsair can add +1 ☠ to the mental damage of a Steely Glare attack.

Red Brotherhood

Based in the Baracha Isles, the pirates of the Red Brotherhood are mainly from Argos, but they have members from many lands.

ATTACKS
- **Sea Bow (R):** Range C, 3 ☠, 2H, Volley

SPECIAL ABILITIES
- **Band of Brothers:** In combat, if the pirate filling one of the crew roles is killed or disabled, another member of the Red Brotherhood immediately steps into his place.

DOOM SPENDS
- **Pirate of the Isles:** Members of the Red Brotherhood are skilled at using the currents, reefs, and rocks of the Baracha Isles to their advantage. The gamemaster can spend 1 Doom to gain +1d20 for all Sailing tests made by the Red Brotherhood when maneuvering in the waters of the Baracha Isles for the remainder of the scene.

Zingaran Freebooters

Privateers in times of war and pirates as they desire, the Freebooters are mainly Zingarans. They favor the leather doublets and long-bladed swords favored by their countrymen.

STRESS AND SOAK
- **Soak:** Armor 2 (Brigandine Armor), Courage 1

ATTACKS
- **Sword (M):** Reach 2, 5 ☠, Parrying
- **Sea Bow (C):** Range C, 3 ☠, 2H, Volley

DOOM SPENDS
- **Zingaran Drill:** Though Zingarans are reputed to be brash and individualistic, their infantry can be ruthlessly efficient in its military drills. The gamemaster can spend 1 Doom so that the leader of a Squad receives a bonus Momentum for each Squad action for the remainder of the scene.

VANIR RAIDER (TOUGHENED)

Out of the cold mists along the coast of Vanaheim, Vanir raiders strike south in their longships. The size of a raid can range from a single vessel, to a handful of ships, to a great fleet. Vanir frequently raid villages along the Pict coast, Zingaran towns, and the Baracha Isles. Most Vanir raids are brutally simple. They land and march overland to a village, surprise the villagers at dawn, and then return north with treasure and slaves, leaving a smoking ruin behind them. Statuesque, red-headed warriors, the Vanir fight with axes, swords, and shields.

A group of Vanir raiders may include one or more berserkers (**Conan** corebook, page 312).

ATTRIBUTES

Awareness	Intelligence	Personality	Willpower
9	6	7	7

Agility	Brawn	Coordination
9	10	9

FIELDS OF EXPERTISE

Combat	1	Movement	—
Fortitude	1	Senses	1
Knowledge	—	Social	—

STRESS AND SOAK
- **Stress:** Vigor 10, Resolve 7
- **Soak:** Armor 2 (Brigandine), Courage 1 (Savage)

ATTACKS

- **Battleaxe (M):** Reach 2, 6 🔱, Unbalanced, Intense, Vicious 1
- **Broadsword (M):** Reach 2, 7 🔱, 1H, Parrying
- **Shield (M):** Reach 2, 4 🔱, 1H, Knockdown, Shield 2

SPECIAL ABILITIES

- **Sea Raider:** The Difficulty of all Sailing tests made in the waters off Vanaheim is reduced by one step, to a minimum of Simple (D0). Additionally, the Difficulty of any Athletics test related to swimming is similarly reduced.
- **Strength from the Sea:** Vanir raiders are used to combat aboard ship and only suffer penalties in the fiercest of weather.

BEASTS FROM THE DEPTHS OF SEA

The sea is the vastest region of the world, and many are the natural creatures that call it home. Only the shallowest expanse of the sea is known to humans, and there are a hundred unknown species of fish or aquatic animals for every one familiar. This section covers some of those that pirates are most likely to encounter, for good or ill.

Suitable creatures from the **Conan** corebook are: crocodiles (page 325), native to Stygia, Kush, and the Black Coast; rat swarms (page 327) found in especially infested sea vessels; and all types of snakes (pages 328–330) common in Set, Kush, and the Black Coast.

DOLPHIN (MINION)

Dolphins are intelligent, marine mammals slightly larger than a man. They live in pods of up to a dozen individuals. Dolphins have been known to come to the aid of drowning sailors and to defend humans from sharks. Dolphins also have great enmity for the dwellers of the deep (**Conan** corebook, page 128), and villages of human-dweller hybrids frequently hunt dolphins. Dolphins can attack their foes by either bite or beak.

ATTRIBUTES

Awareness	Intelligence	Personality	Willpower
9	6	7	7
Agility	**Brawn**		**Coordination**
10	9		5

FIELDS OF EXPERTISE

Combat	1	Movement	2
Fortitude	—	Senses	2
Knowledge	—	Social	1

STRESS AND SOAK

- **Stress:** Vigor 4, Resolve 4
- **Soak:** Armor 1 (Hide), Courage —

ATTACKS

- **Bite (M):** Reach 1, 2 🔱
- **Nose Butt (M):** Reach 1, 3 🔱, Stun

SPECIAL ABILITIES

- **Keen Senses (Echolocation)**
- **Pod Hunter:** Dolphins work together to herd their prey, often driving it into shallow water or even onto land. A dolphin gains 1 bonus Momentum on any attack roll against a foe already attacked by an ally this round, and on Movement tests where the enemy can see one or more of the dolphin's allies.

GIANT CRAB (TOUGHENED)

Freakishly huge crabs that can be found in near-shore waters anywhere along the Western Sea. They range from the size of a large goat to the size of a bull. A giant crab will often attempt to grapple a foe and then drag it under water.

ATTRIBUTES

Awareness	Intelligence	Personality	Willpower
7	3	4	8
Agility	**Brawn**		**Coordination**
9	10		3

FIELDS OF EXPERTISE

Combat	2	Movement	1
Fortitude	2	Senses	—
Knowledge	—	Social	—

STRESS AND SOAK

- **Stress:** Vigor 10, Resolve 8
- **Soak:** Armor 2 (Shell), Courage 1

ATTACKS

- **Claw:** Reach 1, 4 🔱, Grappling

SPECIAL ABILITIES

- **Burrow:** A giant crab can hide by burrowing into mud or soft sand.

ENCOUNTERS

THINGS FROM THE BLACK COAST

On every hand I was ringed in by a strange and horrible throng. If you can imagine spider crabs larger than a horse — yet they were not true spider crabs, outside the difference in the size.

...

They sat up and looked at me. I remained motionless, uncertain just what to expect — and a cold fear began to steal over me. This was not caused by any especial fear of the brutes killing me, for I felt somehow that they would do that, and did not shrink from the thought. But their eyes bored in on me and turned my blood to ice. For in them I recognized an intelligence infinitely higher than mine, yet terribly different. This is hard to conceive, harder to explain. But as I looked into those frightful eyes, I knew that keen, powerful brains lurked behind them, brains which worked in a higher sphere, a different dimension than mine.

— "The People of the Black Coast"

Even more frightening than the normal, relatively unintelligent giant crabs are a peculiar species that has evolved an inhuman intelligence, paired with terrifyingly potent psychic abilities. These creatures can dominate lesser minds — casting them into fogs of despair and luring them to their death. They regard humankind as a gross, apish mistake, and will stalk and kill any humans they encounter. These crabs possess a culture and civilization altogether alien, and even build cities concealed high upon cliffsides, hidden from the sight of humans.

These crabs are equivalent to the normal giant crabs, but with Intelligence 12, Personality 10, Willpower 10, and a Knowledge Field of Expertise 3. Their psychic abilities manifest in a special Threaten attack, described below.

ATTACKS
- **Inhuman Regard (T):** Range C, 4 🗲 mental, Area, Stun, Vicious 1

SPECIAL ABILITIES
- **Cosmic Sorcery:** These ancient and terrible beings have an intuitive understanding of the laws of reality beyond the most advanced philosophers, scholars, or sorcerers of the Hyborian Age. They can spend Doom to achieve the following sorcery spell-like effects, though their actual practice relies on abstract manipulation of physical reality and powerful psychic influence versus supernatural intervention: *Enslave, Fury of the Elements, Haunt the Mind,* and *Venom on the Wind.*

Despite their immense intellect, these monstrously intelligent crustaceans have no interest in humankind whatsoever, and will not make any attempt to communicate, even if threatened. They will not listen to any entreaties for assistance, or even respond if threatened by superior might, other than to strike back or flee, depending on circumstances.

DOOM SPENDS
- **Crush:** A giant crab that has grappled an enemy may spend 1 Doom to close its claw, without having to make an attack, crushing its enemy for 6 🗲, Piercing 1, Vicious 2.

GIANT TURTLE (TOUGHENED)

When caught in a net, these great turtles often escape by eating the fisherman. Their shells are the size of large tables, and their heads are as large as a bull's. They are strong swimmers with a bite that can easily break a man's leg. They can easily upset small boats by surfacing below them or attempting to clamber onboard.

ATTRIBUTES

Awareness	Intelligence	Personality	Willpower
5	3	1	8
Agility	**Brawn**		**Coordination**
8	12		8

FIELDS OF EXPERTISE

Combat	1	Movement	—
Fortitude	2	Senses	1
Knowledge	—	Social	—

STRESS AND SOAK
- **Stress:** Vigor 12, Resolve 8
- **Soak:** Armor 3 (Carapace), Courage —

> *The Venturer, showing no lights, stole past the port in the night, and before dawn discovered her, anchored in a small bay a few miles south of the city. It was surrounded by marsh, a green tangle of mangroves, palms and lianas, swarming with crocodiles and serpents. Discovery was extremely unlikely. Conan knew the place of old; he had hidden there before, in his corsair days.*
>
> — The Hour of the Dragon

ATTACKS
- **Bite (M):** Reach 3, 5 🜲, Piercing 2, Vicious 2

SPECIAL ABILITIES
- **Sluggish Gait:** A giant turtle can haul itself out of the water, but it cannot move faster than the Adjust Action when out of the water.

DOOM SPENDS
- **Capsize:** A giant turtle can spend 2 Momentum to capsize a light craft. This takes one Standard Action.

MONKEY (MINION)

Small tree-dwelling primates, found mainly in the Black Kingdoms. Monkeys are popular with pirates and others as pets. Some sorcerers take monkeys as familiars.

ATTRIBUTES

Awareness	Intelligence	Personality	Willpower
6	3	1	8
Agility	**Brawn**		**Coordination**
10	6		10

FIELDS OF EXPERTISE

Combat	1	Movement	2
Fortitude	—	Senses	1
Knowledge	—	Social	—

STRESS AND SOAK
- **Stress:** Vigor 3, Resolve 4
- **Soak:** Armor —, Courage —

ATTACKS
- **Bite (M):** Reach 1, 2 🜲
- **Thrown Rock (R):** Range C, 1 🜲, 1H, Thrown
- **Howl (T):** Range C, 1 🜲 mental

SPECIAL ABILITIES
- **Brachiating:** Monkeys can move through trees with remarkable agility, swinging or leaping from branch to branch. A monkey may ignore all challenging terrain when moving through zones that include trees, and may re-roll any d20 that does not generate a success when making a Movement-related test when climbing or moving through trees.

NEW MONSTER QUALITY — IMMENSE

A step above the Monstrous Creature Quality (CONAN corebook, page 310), this indicates that the creature is vast in size, to a degree that normal combat with it becomes impractical, and generally requires either a group of characters or an incredible effort by a single individual. A creature with this Quality cannot move within spaces made for humans.

For every point of this Quality, the being:

- May absorb five additional Wounds before dying.

    For example, with Immense 2, a Minion can suffer 10 Wounds in additional to the normal before it is slain, a Toughened being can suffer 11 Wounds, and a Nemesis can suffer 15 Wounds.

- Ignores one step of Difficulty from Harms it has suffered.

- Has 1 additional point of Armor protection.

- Increases the Difficulty of any attempts at moving it by two steps, such as with the Knockdown Quality or some other attack type. If the Difficulty increases above Epic (D5), the creature cannot be moved against its will.

- Additionally, the creature can inflict additional structural damage against a structure or vessel at the rate of 1 per Effect rolled.

This is an extraordinarily potent Quality and should be applied only to huge beings, such as whales, dinosaurs, or titanic horrors of a scale beyond human understanding.

ENCOUNTERS

SHARK (TOUGHENED)

Notorious predators of the sea, sharks will prey on any creature that they can. Sharks are known for having powerful jaws filled with sharp teeth and for their triangular fins that cut through the water as they circle or approach their prey. On some of the islands along the coast of the Black Kingdoms, villagers see sharks as embodying the spirits of their ancestors. Many species are common in the Western Sea: the one described below is the great white shark.

ATTRIBUTES

Awareness	Intelligence	Personality	Willpower
6	3	1	8

Agility	Brawn	Coordination
10	12	6

FIELDS OF EXPERTISE

Combat	1	Movement	—
Fortitude	2	Senses	1
Knowledge	—	Social	—

STRESS AND SOAK
- **Stress:** Vigor 12, Resolve 8
- **Soak:** Armor 2 (Hide), Courage 2

ATTACKS
- **Bite (M):** Reach 1, 6 ⚡, Grappling, Unforgiving 2

SPECIAL ABILITIES
- **Blood in the Water:** The scent of blood in the water can both drive a shark into a frenzy and attract additional sharks. When a creature in the water has suffered a Harm, or otherwise when there is blood in the water, a shark will relentlessly and savagely attack both foes and friends. If one Effect is rolled on any attack, the shark will attack its target again. If two Effects are rolled, a shark will attack a friendly creature that is close.

WHALE (NEMESIS)

Normally docile mammals, whales can be aggressive when angered. Whales are capable of diving to great depths, and a slap from a whale's tail can smash or overturn a small boat. Many species of whale roam widely throughout the Western Sea: the specimen described below is the dwarf sperm whale, smallest of the various types at a mere ten yards from snout to tail-tip. Some species, such as the blue whale, are so great in size that they cannot be described as creatures and must be contended with as if forces of nature.

CHAPTER 5

MONSTROUS FOES

Humankind is not the only threat to safe passage upon the Western Sea — its waters conceal all manner of unnatural beings, horrible and sorcerous creatures that bring dismay and ruin to those they encounter. The following monsters are exceptional foes and should only be encountered under rare and specific circumstances, and in many cases their arrival will signal a turning point, perhaps the end of a vessel's existence.

From the **Conan** corebook, the children of Set (page 334) may be encountered in Stygia, and malign plants (page 340) flourish within the jungles of Kush and the Black Kingdoms. Winged apes (page 343) and winged ones (page 344) are found on islands and remote ruins along the Zarkheba River, and dwellers of the deep (pages 336–337) are found wherever there is water deep enough to hide within. These creatures have fostered human cults, filling their ranks with their half-amphibious, half-human progeny. To the south they are sometimes called "Akka", an ancient name that predates the Cataclysm.

BLACK OCTOPUS (TOUGHENED)

A beast said to lurk in coastal waters of Kush and the Black Kingdoms. Nearly as large as a man, it can haul itself out of water and travel across land to prey on children and small livestock. Some are said to specifically seek out women. They are also known to attack small boats by snatching oars, grabbing passengers, or overturning the boats. Some villagers attempt to placate them by leaving live sacrifices for them in primitive shrines near the shoreline. Like other octopi, the black octopus can squeeze its body through surprisingly small spaces.

ATTRIBUTES

Awareness	Intelligence	Personality	Willpower
10	5	5	8
Agility		Brawn	Coordination
10		9	6

FIELDS OF EXPERTISE

Combat	1	Movement	1
Fortitude	1	Senses	1
Knowledge	—	Social	—

STRESS AND SOAK

- **Stress:** Vigor 10, Resolve 8
- **Soak:** Armor 1 (Hide), Courage 1

ATTACKS

- **Tentacle Slam (M):** Reach 3, 4 🛡, Grappling

ATTRIBUTES

Awareness	Intelligence	Personality	Willpower
8	6	6	5
Agility		Brawn	Coordination
7		15 (5)	10

FIELDS OF EXPERTISE

Combat	—	Movement	2
Fortitude	5	Senses	1
Knowledge	—	Social	—

STRESS AND SOAK

- **Stress:** Vigor 25, Resolve 15
- **Soak:** Armor 6 (Hide), Courage 5

ATTACKS

- **Bite (M):** Reach 1, 8 🛡, Area, Fearsome, Grappling
- **Crushing Mass (M):** Reach 1, 12 🛡, Area, Fearsome

SPECIAL ABILITIES

- **Immense 3** (see sidebar)
- **Inhuman Brawn 5**
- **Ram:** The whale charges a ship, slamming its head into the ship. The whale causes 6 🛡 impact damage to a ship (see page 115 of *Chapter 8: Ship Combat* for more information). A small boat might be capsized.
- **Tail Smash:** The whale attacks a small boat, thrashing at it with its tail. The whale causes 6 🛡 impact damage to a light craft.

DOOM SPENDS

- **Swallow Whole:** When grappling a target, for 1 point of Doom the whale may swallow its target whole. Inside the whale's stomach, the victim will suffer 4 🛡 damage per round with the Persistent 2 Quality through a combination of the experience and the lack of air. Armor offers no protection against this. Cutting oneself free from a whale's stomach requires the character to inflict Wounds on the whale equal to the character's Brawn score.

SPECIAL ABILITIES

- **Amphibious:** A black octopus may not wander far from water, and when challenged while on land it will usually seek to return to water as soon as possible.
- **Bite (M):** The black octopus may pull a grabbed creature closer so that it may bite it. Two Standard Actions are required to pull the target in before it may be bitten on the octopus' next action. Reach 1, 3 🜲, Piercing 2, Vicious 2.
- **Camouflage:** When in water, the black octopus can take an action to change its coloring to match its surroundings.
- **Drowning:** When in water, if a black octopus successfully grabs its prey, the grabbed creature will begin to drown. See the **Conan** corebook, page 127 for details on drowning. This is in addition to any damage the octopus inflicts on the grabbed enemy.
- **Fear 1**
- **Sluggish Gait:** A black octopus may only take the Sprint Action when in water.

BLACK ONE (TOUGHENED)

Inhabiting a mysterious and unnamed island in the Western Sea far to the west of the Baracha Isles, the Black Ones are ancient creatures from long before the rise of humankind, a long-distant race more akin to demon than human. It may be that these are the last of this damned species, or they may inhabit more islands further afield, or lands uncharted at this time. These creatures are incredibly long-lived and possess the rudiments of their own culture. Though they are physically superior to humans, they are nonetheless a barbaric and cruel species, with nothing approaching a soul or conscience.

> *The superb symmetry of body and limbs was more impressive at close range. Under the ebon skin long, rounded muscles rippled, and Conan did not doubt that the monster could rend an ordinary man limb from limb. The nails of the fingers provided further weapons, for they were grown like the talons of a wild beast. The face was a carven ebony mask. The eyes were tawny, a vibrant gold that glowed and glittered. But the face was inhuman; each line, each feature was stamped with evil — evil transcending the mere evil of humanity. The thing was not a human — it could not be; it was a growth of Life from the pits of blasphemous creation — a perversion of evolutionary development.*
>
> — "The Pool of the Black Ones"

In the curious ruins they inhabit, the Black Ones worship a pool — or the thing dwelling within it — and exult in sacrificing humans to it, submerging them into its greenish depths. Through some diabolical process, the sacrifices they make are transformed into smallish statues, seemingly of bone, wrought in the semblance of the being sacrificed. They collect and display these relics alongside the green pool, their appearance giving evidence that the Black Ones have been at this for a very long time, as many of the victims depicted are from cultures long-vanished from the world.

ATTRIBUTES

Awareness	Intelligence	Personality	Willpower
9	9	10	10
Agility	Brawn		Coordination
10	12 (1)		8

FIELDS OF EXPERTISE

Combat	1	Movement	1
Fortitude	3	Senses	—
Knowledge	—	Social	—

STRESS AND SOAK

- **Stress:** Vigor 15, Resolve 13
- **Soak:** Armor —, Courage 3 (Horror)

ATTACKS

- **Claws (M):** Reach 1, 5 🜲, Grappling
- **Mocking Visage (T):** Range C, 4 🜲 mental, Stun
- **Strange Pipes (T):** Range M, 2 🜲 mental, Stun

SPECIAL ABILITIES

- **Fear 1**
- **Inhuman Brawn 1**
- **Servant of the Pool:** Black Ones are completely immune to any Threaten Action while they are adjacent to their pool.

DOOM SPENDS

- **Hypnotic Pipes:** The Black Ones often use strange golden pipes to lull their victims into a trance-like state, causing a frenzied dance, its purpose either entertainment or ritual in nature, perhaps both. When using these pipes, the Black Ones may spend three Doom to use the *Enslave* spell, as if they were sorcerers. With a successful Average (D1) Observation test, these strange pipes can be heard from a great distance, though hearing the pipes inflicts the damage described above.

BLACK STRANGER (NEMESIS)

This nameless being was summoned to serve at the whim of a Zingaran noble, put to grim purpose and left to roam the earth after its purpose was fulfilled. Appearing as a great tall man with night-black skin and clad all in black, the entity is demonic entity, a soulless waif of darkness summoned by a sorcerer from the outer gulfs of existence, clothed in the form of a man. However, it still casts an inhuman shadow with close-set horns, peaked ears, and a gaping mouth, and blue flame sometimes emanates around it.

> *She was still shaken with horror, though she could not decide just what there had been about that black figure etched against the red glow that had roused this frantic loathing in her soul. It was manlike in shape, but the outline was strangely alien — abnormal — though she could not clearly define that abnormality. But she knew that it was no human being that she had seen.*
>
> — "The Black Stranger"

The Black Stranger is obsessed with revenge against the one who had him brought into this world: Count Valenso. It seeks him throughout the world, having lost the Zingaran's trail when Valenso fled Korzetta Castle. Eventually the Black Stranger will find its prey, and have its vengeance. Should the player characters know Valenso or have any idea as to his whereabouts, they might encounter the Black Stranger on its implacable quest. None have heard it speak or interacted with it in any fashion, other than the sorcerer who summoned it, but might conceivably be able to communicate if desiring to.

ATTRIBUTES

Awareness	Intelligence	Personality	Willpower
10	8	8	10

Agility	Brawn	Coordination
10	15	10

FIELDS OF EXPERTISE

Combat	2	Movement	1
Fortitude	1	Senses	1
Knowledge	1	Social	—

STRESS AND SOAK

- **Stress:** Vigor 15, Resolve 8
- **Soak:** Armor 5 (Unnatural), Courage 2

ATTACKS

- **Pummel (M):** Reach 2, 6 🜨, Knockdown
- **Strangle (M):** Reach 1, 6 🜨, Vicious 2
- **Demonic Leer (T):** Range C, 4 🜨 mental, Stun, Vicious 1

SPECIAL ABILITIES

- **Dread Creature 2**
- **Fear 2**
- **Silver and Fire:** Like many demonic beings, the Black Stranger is vulnerable to silver and fire, and only has Armor 1 against those sources of harm.
- **Sorcery:** The Black Stranger is a powerful sorcerer able to cast many spells, including *Flames of the Deep* (page 63), *Commune with the Wild*, *Enslave*, *Haunt the Mind*, *Summon Horror*, and *Venom on the Wind*.

DOOM SPENDS

- **Shadow in the Night:** By spending 1 Doom, the Black Stranger can hide himself where no one can find him and can effortlessly move past guards and doors that have been barred and bolted.

GHOST SHIP SAILOR (MINION)

Out on the Western Sea, far from shore, sailors have claimed to see a ghostly galley with tattered sails. Always appearing at night, the spectral vessel often emerges from fog or rain. Shipwrecked sailors report climbing aboard the ship, glad for their safety, only to be horrified at the apparitions that man the decks. Its sailors are said to be gaunt, with pale skin that is almost translucent, staring eyes, and lank, sparse hair, though the ship's crew are also described as bloated and waterlogged corpses, desiccated, or even skeletal, depending who tells the tale.

The sailors of the ghost ship are always looking for new recruits, and if they cannot find volunteers, they will board ships and attempt to take people by force. The hell they inhabit may be eternal, but it need not be lonely.

ATTRIBUTES

Awareness	Intelligence	Personality	Willpower
7	5	6	8

Agility	Brawn	Coordination
5	10	5

FIELDS OF EXPERTISE

Combat	1	Movement	—
Fortitude	2	Senses	1
Knowledge	—	Social	—

ENCOUNTERS

STRESS AND SOAK
- **Stress:** Vigor 10, Resolve 8
- **Soak:** Armor 2 (Unearthly Flesh)

ATTACKS
- **Sword (M):** Reach 2, 4 🎲
- **Clawlike Hands (M):** Reach 1, 3 🎲, Grappling
- **Soulless Gaze (T):** Range C, 3 🎲 mental, Area, Stun

SPECIAL ABILITIES
- **Fear 1**
- **Strength from the Sea:** Ghost sailors seem to be part of the sea, and when aboard ships, they only suffer penalties for combat in the fiercest of weather.

DOOM SPENDS
- **Shadow in the Night:** By spending 1 Doom, the Black Stranger can hide himself where no one can find him and can effortlessly move past guards and doors that have been barred and bolted.

GIANT HYENA (TOUGHENED)

Savage beasts of surprising intelligence, normal giant hyenas once inhabited the savannahs and jungles of the Black Kingdoms, but were hunted to near-extinction wherever humankind dwells. They were pack animals and scavenging carnivores, through greatly preferring live prey to carrion.

> *And now from the shadows dark shapes came silently, swiftly, running low — twenty great spotted hyenas. Their slavering fangs flashed in the moonlight, their eyes blazed as no true beast's eyes ever blazed.*
>
> — "Queen of the Black Coast"

Some of these creatures, however, have origins far more sinister. They are said to be the descendants of a group of Stygian soldiers lost in the dense jungles of the south, transformed through sorcery by winged horrors into a great pack of spotted hyenas. Now these beasts inhabit an overgrown ruin in the dense jungle up the poisonous Zarkheba River, and slay and devour any who trespass. Unlike mortal hyenas, these killers are almost entirely silent, their only utterance a disturbingly human-like yelp when in extreme pain.

If slain, a great hyena will revert to its human form, that of a Stygian soldier, bearing the wound that slew it. Then, it will crumble to dust.

ATTRIBUTES
Awareness	Intelligence	Personality	Willpower
9	5	6	7
Agility	**Brawn**	**Coordination**	
10	10	10	

FIELDS OF EXPERTISE
Combat	1	Movement	2
Fortitude	1	Senses	2
Knowledge	—	Social	—

STRESS AND SOAK
- **Stress:** Vigor 10, Resolve 7
- **Soak:** Armor 1 (Hide), Courage 1

ATTACKS
- **Slavering Fangs (M):** Reach 1, 4 🎲, Vicious 1
- **Blazing Vampire Eyes (T):** Range C, 2 🎲 mental, Area

SPECIAL ABILITIES
- **Blasphemous Aura:** The great hyenas of the Zarkheba River ruins emanate a diabolical aura, almost palpable. A giant hyena can re-roll any 🎲 for a Threaten Attack that fails to yield a success, but must accept the second result.
- **Feed Upon Fear**

DOOM SPENDS
- **Call to the Master:** If in mortal danger, a giant hyena can call to its master, a winged one equivalent to the winged ape (*Conan* corebook, page 343). This desperate yelp costs 3 Doom, and the winged one will appear at the beginning of the next round.

KRAKEN (NEMESIS)

An immense species of giant squid, krakens are often large enough to bring down longships or even the masted ships of Argos or Zingara, and are more than a match for their most deadly natural enemy, the grey whale. Kraken can grow up to thirty yards in length from the tip of their longest tentacles to the top of their bloated heads. These leviathans are feared by any who traverse the northern waters, and are rarely hunted, though the substance of a kraken's horned beak is highly sought by armor makers and alchemists alike.

ATTRIBUTES

Awareness	Intelligence	Personality	Willpower
6	4	1	8

Agility	Brawn	Coordination
8	15 (2)	10

FIELDS OF EXPERTISE

Combat	2	Movement	1
Fortitude	2	Senses	1
Knowledge	—	Social	—

STRESS AND SOAK

- **Stress:** Vigor 17, Resolve 10
- **Soak:** Armor 2, Courage 2

ATTACKS

- **Tentacle Slam (M):** Reach 3, 8 , Grappling, Stun

SPECIAL ABILITIES

- **Fear 1**
- **Immense 3**
- **Inhuman Brawn 2**
- **Drowning:** When in water, if a kraken successfully grabs its prey, the grabbed creature will begin to drown (**Conan** corebook, page 127). This is in addition to any damage the kraken inflicts on the grabbed enemy.
- **Bind Boat:** The kraken wraps its tentacles about a ship, snapping oars and stopping its movement. Each following round, the kraken may begin to squeeze and torque the ship, inflicting 3 impact damage to the ship's hull (see page 115 of *Chapter 8: Ship Combat*).

DOOM SPENDS

- **Whirlpool:** At the cost of 5 Doom, the kraken can move through the water so fast that it can leave a whirlpool in its wake. The helmsman of any ship caught in its whirlpool must attempt a Daunting (D3) Sailing test to avoid being sucked under or capsized by the whirlpool.
- **Leviathan:** When introduced into an encounter, a kraken has a personal pool of 10 Doom it may draw from exclusively. This may not be shared by other foes — even if allied with the kraken — and these points are not replenished once spent

SARGASSO STRANGLER (NEMESIS)

Far out in the Western Sea, great mats of sargassum, a seaweed, float upon the surface of the water. These mats have been known to entangle all manner of creatures and ships. More disturbingly, some of the larger mats appear to have a malevolent intelligence. It is said that the "Sargasso Strangler" was first bred in times agone for some unknown, malevolent purpose. The Sargasso Strangler appears as a mounded mass floating on the water amid a large expanse of sargassum. The Great Sargasso (see page 38) is covered with this particularly terrible form of sea-weed.

The Sargasso Strangler works slowly to draw in its prey before striking. It is only when targets are near the being that they may sense that it is more than a mere mat of seaweed.

ATTRIBUTES

Awareness	Intelligence	Personality	Willpower
6	3	1	8

Agility	Brawn	Coordination
10	8	6

ENCOUNTERS

FIELDS OF EXPERTISE

Combat	1	Movement	—
Fortitude	2	Senses	1
Knowledge	—	Social	—

STRESS AND SOAK

- **Stress:** Vigor 10, Resolve 8
- **Soak:** Armor 2 (Dense, Ropey Fibers), Courage 2

ATTACKS

- **Tentacle (M):** 3 🗡, Grappling

SPECIAL ABILITIES

- **Drowning:** When in water, if a Sargasso Strangler successfully grabs its prey, the grabbed creature will begin to drown (**Conan** corebook, page 127).
- **Fear 1**
- **Thick Weed:** The waters surrounding the Strangler are filled with sargassum, so that swimming tests are increased in Difficulty as follows: Close, three additional steps of Difficulty; Medium, two additional steps; Long, one additional step.
- **Unstable Mat:** The sargassum close to the Strangler is thick enough and matted with enough debris that characters may stand on it and move across it at a Hindrance with a successful Average (D1) Acrobatics test. Characters that fail the Acrobatics test may either fall off the mat into the surrounding water (Medium range) or fall through the mat. An adventurer seeking to climb up through the mat must succeed at a Challenging (D2) Acrobatics test.

DOOM SPENDS

- **Entangling Sargassum:** The Strangler guides the sargassum that floats on the waters around it, all the way out to Extreme range, causing one of the following effects: fouling the rudder of a ship, grounding a small boat, or creating a new zone of Thick Weed (see above).
- **Fog:** The Strangler creates a fog above the sargassum, extending to Medium range. The fog acts as a Hindrance and as cover against ranged attacks. For 1 additional Doom, the fog cover can be extended to Long range.
- **Tentacle Strike:** Up to three times per combat round, the Stranger can spend 1 Doom to extend a tentacle from beneath the water's surface to strike a target at Medium range. The tentacle has no armor, no Vigor, and 1 Wound, and it can come from anywhere beneath the sargassum.

SEA SERPENT (NEMESIS)

Out in the vastness of the Western Sea dwell monstrous creatures from an earlier age, sea serpents that swim swiftly through the water, preying upon other monstrous creatures, as well as the occasional boat. Long-necked, with fierce snake-like heads full of pointed teeth, these creatures are often labeled as dragons. Surprisingly swift, these vicious predators occasionally even venture onto land for brief periods, and occasionally make their home in bodies of water there. They are sometimes found in some meres, lakes, and other bodies of water inland, and have even been spotted swimming in deep rivers.

ATTRIBUTES

Awareness	Intelligence	Personality	Willpower
6	3	1	8
Agility	Brawn		Coordination
10	10		10

FIELDS OF EXPERTISE

Combat	1	Movement	1
Fortitude	2	Senses	1
Knowledge	—	Social	—

STRESS AND SOAK

- **Stress:** Vigor 12, Resolve 10
- **Soak:** Armor 4 (Tough Scaled Hide), Courage 2

ATTACKS

- **Bite (M):** Reach 3, 6 🗡, Grappling, Piercing 2

SPECIAL ABILITIES

- **Drowning:** When in water, if a sea serpent successfully grabs its prey, the grabbed creature will begin to drown (**Conan** corebook, page 127).
- **Fear 1**

FAMOUS PIRATES AND OTHERS

The ports of the Western Sea are home to all manner of characters, heroes and villains. The following characters are among the most notorious pirates, freebooters, and buccaneers to have sailed the waters of the Hyborian Age. The other notable figures described in these pages are those caught in their wake, or guiding their destinies from the safety of the shore.

Another famous pirate, Valeria of the Red Brotherhood, appears in the **Conan** corebook on page 355.

DEMETRIO (TOUGHENED)

The master of the *Venturer*, an Argossean trade galley out of Messantia, Demetrio plies the coasts between Argos and Shem, typically dealing in high-value items such as mirrors, silk, fine weapons, and armor in return for copper and gold ore. Demetrio is a typical Argossean, stout and brown-bearded, and dresses in finery as befits his rank as captain. He is happily willing to dragoon or waylay civilians to swell the ranks of his crew, though he will allow such captives the right to work amongst the free sailors, rather than being chained with the slaves.

ATTRIBUTES

Awareness	Intelligence	Personality	Willpower
8	10	9	9
Agility		Brawn	Coordination
8		10	9

FIELDS OF EXPERTISE

Combat	2	Movement	1
Fortitude	1	Senses	1
Knowledge	1	Social	2

STRESS AND SOAK

- **Stress:** Vigor 10, Resolve 9
- **Soak:** Armor —, Courage 1

ATTACKS

- **Knife (M):** Reach 1, 5 ⚔, 1H, Hidden 1, Improvised, Unforgiving 1
- **Angry Bellow (T):** Range C, 3 ⚔ mental, Area, Vicious 1

SPECIAL ABILITIES

- **Strength from the Sea:** Demetrio is used to combat aboard ship and only suffers penalties in the fiercest of weather.

DOOM SPENDS

- **Call to the Sea-Dogs:** Demetrio can rally his crew, a hard-bitten lot of loyal sailors, to his side, at a cost of 1 Doom per crewmember. Each receives 1 Courage Soak against mental attacks until the engagement is over, or until Demetrio is incapacitated or dead, whichever comes first.

PUBLIO (TOUGHENED)

Publio owns a ramshackle shop that sits on the waterfront of Messantia in Argos. Smelling of fish and cheap wine, the shop sells goods for sailors, but its real stock in trade is illegal activities. Publio has no qualms with moving goods brought by all sorts of shady characters. He's quick to strike a deal which puts him ahead. His coterie of clients buy ivory, ostrich feathers, copper, skins, pearls, and hammered gold ornaments well below market value. They do not ask where he gets them, and he does not tell them how he avoids paying the inflated prices out of Stygia by dealing with corsairs.

Short in stature, Publio boasts a massive head and dark eyes. He is happy to lie, cheat, steal, and fight his way up from his poor situation to get ahead. He knows the underworld of Messantia intimately and runs a network of informants. At the same time, he manages to stay out of sight of the authorities and the well-to-do merchants in town, who see him as a young upstart. He is the man to go to when you have a risky proposition. He may be a crook, but he knows to keep his mouth shut.

ATTRIBUTES

Awareness	Intelligence	Personality	Willpower
10	11	11	8
Agility		Brawn	Coordination
8		7	8

FIELDS OF EXPERTISE

Combat	1	Movement	2
Fortitude	1	Senses	1
Knowledge	3	Social	2

STRESS AND SOAK

- **Stress:** Vigor 10, Resolve 9
- **Soak:** Armor 1 (Clothing), Courage 2

ATTACKS

- **Dagger (M):** Reach 1, 3 ⚔, Hidden 1, Parrying, Thrown

SPECIAL ABILITIES

- **Hidden Allies:** Publio knows people throughout Messantia and at a moment's notice can summon them to his defense. While in Messantia, with a successful Average (D1) Social test, Publio can produce one bystander per Momentum gained, of a type to be determined by the gamemaster. These can be neighbors, customers, guards, fellow merchants, or even friends.
- **Gift of Gab:** Publio can hold off an attack by offering all manner of bribes, with a keen ability to divine what the assailant truly wants. If he can make a successful Average (D1) Insight test, he can ascertain what his attackers are after, even if they may not know it themselves.

ENCOUNTERS

RED ORTHO (NEMESIS)

Red Ortho is a notorious Zingaran pirate, though not so famous as Zarono, Zaporavo, or Strom. Nonetheless, he enjoys a bit of infamy and will readily commit despicable acts to further his reputation. A rare red-haired Zingaran (likely due to Vanir ancestry), Ortho steers clear of the better-known pirates described above by focusing his efforts upon the southern coasts of Kush and the Black Kingdoms. His ship, the *Vagabond*, is a fine carrack of Zingaran make, and the device upon Ortho's flag is a skull-faced mermaid.

Red Ortho has a special hatred for Valeria (**Conan** corebook, page 355), borne out of her bitter rejection of him and her subsequent escape from his clutches. He is identical in all aspects to the pirate captain described on page 319 of the **Conan** corebook.

SANCHA OF KORDAVA (MINION)

The life of a noblewoman is not easy. If they do not live in the shadow of their fathers or brothers, often they must barter and parley their name or beauty for power and protection. Sancha, a victim of piracy and slavery, eventually found how to channel the lust men had for her into a method to control them. From a near-helpless victim onboard the *Wastrel*, she seduced her way up to being the mistress of its captain, Zaporavo, following him wherever his ambition and curiosity drives him.

> *No great length of time lay between her and the palaces of Kordava, but it was as if a world of change separated her from the life she had lived before Zaporavo tore her screaming from the flaming caravel his wolves had plundered. She, who had been the spoiled and petted daughter of the Duke of Kordava, learned what it was to be a buccaneer's plaything, and because she was supple enough to bend without breaking, she lived where other women had died, and because she was young and vibrant with life, she came to find pleasure in the existence.*
>
> — Sancha, "The Pool of the Black One"

Sancha is like to be encountered in close company of Zaporavo or another captain or noble she's found amenable to her will. She has little interest in returning to Zingara.

ATTRIBUTES

Awareness	Intelligence	Personality	Willpower
9	8	9	8
Agility	**Brawn**		**Coordination**
10	7		10

FIELDS OF EXPERTISE

Combat	—	Movement	1
Fortitude	—	Senses	1
Knowledge	1	Social	2

STRESS AND SOAK

- **Stress:** Vigor 4, Resolve 4
- **Soak:** Armor —, Courage —

ATTACKS

- **Stiletto (M):** Reach 1, 3 🜲, 1H, Hidden 1, Parrying, Thrown, Unforgiving 1
- **Admiring Glare (T):** Range C, 3 🜲 mental, Non-lethal

SPECIAL ABILITIES

- **Defenseless:** As a means of defense, Sancha has learned to present herself to others as if in need of assistance, using her allure to disarm potential allies and sway them to her side. Any attempt at such manipulation earns her an additional 1d20 for Personality-based tests.

SERGIUS OF KHROSHA (NEMESIS)

A Kothian pirate captain in the Red Brotherhood's branch on the Vilayet Sea, Sergius of Khrosha is known on the Western Sea, as well, one of the few pirate captains to ply his trade on both major bodies of water. Originally enlisting in the Argossean navy as a marine, he eventually rose to mutiny, taking control of his first posting and embarking on a long and outstanding career as a pirate of the Red Brotherhood, preying upon the coast of Argos and Shem. It was on this coast that he made an enemy of Conan of Cimmeria, who ran him aground off the coast of Shem.

Captured by the Shemites and ransomed to the King of Koth, Sergius was delivered to Khrosha for execution. However, he escaped and made his way eastward along the Zaporoska River, reaching the Vilayet Sea. There, he quickly threw in with the eastern branch of the Red Brotherhood, recruiting from within that despicable band of rogues and cutthroats. A short while later, he had a ship, the *Calypso*, and a band of escaped criminals and slaves to crew her. Now he preys upon the Vilayet's southern shores, his malignant reputation continuing to spread and darken.

ATTRIBUTES

Awareness	Intelligence	Personality	Willpower
9	8	10	9
Agility	Brawn		Coordination
9	11		10

FIELDS OF EXPERTISE

Combat	3	Movement	1
Fortitude	2	Senses	1
Knowledge	1	Social	1

STRESS AND SOAK

- **Stress:** Vigor 13, Resolve 11
- **Soak:** Armor —, Courage 2

ATTACKS

- **Sword (M):** Reach 2, 6💀, 1H, Parrying
- **Fierce Bellow (T):** Range C, 3💀 mental, Area, Stun

SPECIAL ABILITIES

- **Strength from the Sea:** Sergius is used to combat aboard ship and only suffers penalties in the fiercest of weather.
- **My Ship Is My Castle:** On his own vessel, Sergius always has Light Cover, with 2 Cover Soak against ranged weapons.

DOOM SPENDS

- **Fearsome Reputation:** At any point in an encounter, Sergius can spend one Doom (Repeatable) to add 1💀 to the mental damage of his *Fierce Bellow* attack.
- **Vengeful Right Hand:** If incapacitated, Sergius can spend 1 Doom for a Toughened pirate (page 71) to intervene to keep him alive, or, if he has been slain, to avenge him.

CAPTAIN STROM (NEMESIS)

Like many in the Red Brotherhood, Strom is from Argos, raised on the streets of Messantia. He went to sea to seek his fortune as a sailor and then found his way as a pirate among the Red Brotherhood. Though his gruff demeanor suggests frankness, his wide eyes are lit with the dancing lights of cruelty and treachery. His preference is always for quick, impulsive action.

Aboard his carack, the *Red Hand*, Strom has a crew of some 150 men. When ready for action, he unfurls his black flag emblazoned with a red skull. From the Baracha Isles, Strom and his crew harass ships and villages from Zingara to Shem, sometimes ranging north along the Pictish coast or south to Stygia and the Black Kingdoms. As with others of the Red Brotherhood, the crew of the *Red Hand* abides by the rules of the Trade, a code that governs the division of loot and holds the captain and officers accountable to the rest of the crew. Despite his brashness, Strom knows that if he strays from these articles the crew could elect some challenger as their new captain. When not at sea, Strom is often found at his fortified villa in Tortage.

Along with his greatest rival, Black Zarano (page 87), Strom is obsessed with the search for the long-lost treasure of the legendary pirate Tranicos. Like Zarano, he knows that only one of them can possess it.

ATTRIBUTES

Awareness	Intelligence	Personality	Willpower
9	8	10	9
Agility	Brawn		Coordination
9	10		9

FIELDS OF EXPERTISE

Combat	2	Movement	2
Fortitude	2	Senses	1
Knowledge	1	Social	1

STRESS AND SOAK

- **Stress:** Vigor 12, Resolve 11
- **Soak:** Armor 1 (Clothing), Courage 2

ENCOUNTERS

ATTACKS

- **Cutlass (M):** Reach 2, 6 ⚔, Unbalanced, Fearsome, Vicious
- **Dagger (M):** Reach 1, 5 ⚔, Hidden 1, Parrying, Thrown, Unforgiving 1
- **Mighty Name (T):** Range C, 4 ⚔, Area
- **Steely Glare (T):** Range C, 4 ⚔ mental, Stun

SPECIAL ABILITIES

- Blood on Steel
- No Mercy 2
- **Strength from the Sea:** Strom is used to combat aboard ship and only suffers penalties in the fiercest of weather.

DOOM SPENDS

- **Vengeful Retaliation:** When he thinks that he has been betrayed, Strom's wrath is unleashed. He can spend 2 Doom to gain an immediate Standard Action, which may only be used to attack.

> *Strom had halted just within good ear-shot. He was a big man, bare-headed, his tawny hair blowing in the wind. Of all the sea-rovers who haunted the Barachans, none was more famed for deviltry than he.*
>
> — "The Black Stranger"

TITO, SHIPMASTER OF THE ARGUS (TOUGHENED)

Born in a small fishing village, Tito, like all Argossean youths, dreamed of one day serving in the royal navy. He imagined great adventures bringing pirates to heel, defending the coast, and being admired by Argossean society as a mighty sea-captain. His youth, alas, was spent on his uncle's fishing trawler, visiting his nation's capital on market days.

When Argos went to war against Zingara, all youths with sailing experience were drafted to crew Argos' war galleons. Tito's romanticized view of the navy quickly cooled as he saw friends consumed by slaughter and fire, and he served his time dutifully, if with extreme caution.

Through skill, luck, and persistence, Tito served his duty and mustered out a licensed shipmaster, captaining the *Argus*, sailing a route up and down the Western Sea's coastline, from Argos to Kush. There, he plans to earn a small fortune trading in the exotic ports. After a few hard years, and with a bit of luck avoiding pirates, he hopes to retire to a happy and long life in his old fishing village.

ATTRIBUTES

Awareness	Intelligence	Personality	Willpower
9	9	9	8

Agility	Brawn	Coordination
8	10	9

FIELDS OF EXPERTISE

Combat	1	Movement	1
Fortitude	1	Senses	1
Knowledge	1	Social	1

STRESS AND SOAK

- **Stress:** Vigor 10, Resolve 8
- **Soak:** Armor —, Courage 1

ATTACKS

- **Long Knife (M):** Reach 1, 5 ⚔, 1H, Parrying, Unforgiving 1
- **Sea Bow (R):** Range C, 4 ⚔, 2H, Volley
- **Fierce Glare (T):** Range C, 3 ⚔ mental, Area, Non-lethal

SPECIAL ABILITIES

- **Careful Insight:** Tito is a good judge of people, and when attempting Insight tests, can re-roll any d20s that are unsuccessful, though he must accept the result of the second roll.
- **Master-shipman:** Tito has been licensed as a master-shipman, giving him access to Argos' merchant guilds and their resources. While in Argossean ports or those with trade ties to Argos, any successful Persuade or Society test relating to his license yields him an additional Momentum.

COUNT VALENSO (NEMESIS)

Count Valenso was born into Zingaran nobility where he was known as the "red falcon" of the Korzetta family. In his youth, Valenso had an enemy at the court in Kordava that stood between him and his ambition. He intrigued with a black magician to raise up a nameless being to slay his enemy: a fiend from the outer gulfs of existence, clad in human form. The magician bound this "black stranger", but it slipped those bonds. One day, the magician was found slain in his castle with the marks of the demon's fingers on his throat.

Certain that the demon would come for him next, Valenso sold his castle and lands, loaded a galleon with his remaining wealth, and sailed north to the uncharted coast of Pictland. There, in a bay along the wild Pictish coast, his galleon wrecked upon the rocks. He stripped his wrecked ship and rebuilt his estate in the inlet he has dubbed Korvela Bay, surrounding it with a stockade. Valenso lives like a noble in the wilderness, accompanied by his niece Belesa, his seneschal Galbro, and almost a hundred soldiers and servants.

Korvela Bay and Valenso's estate are described on pages 54–55.

ATTRIBUTES

Awareness	Intelligence	Personality	Willpower
8	11	10	9

Agility	Brawn	Coordination
9	10	9

FIELDS OF EXPERTISE

Combat	2	Movement	1
Fortitude	—	Senses	—
Knowledge	1	Social	2

STRESS AND SOAK

- **Stress:** Vigor 10, Resolve 9
- **Soak:** Armor 1 (Clothing), Courage 1

ATTACKS

- **Sword (M):** Reach 2, 6 ⚜, Parrying
- **Steely Glare (T):** Range C, 4 ⚜ mental, Stun

SPECIAL ABILITIES

- **Man of his Word:** Count Valenso has a reputation as a man of honor. When he makes a pledge, he gains an extra d20 on any Persuade test related to that oath.
- **Haunted:** The Count lives in fear of the Black Stranger (see page 78), and the mere suggestion that the Stranger may be nearby forces Valenso to attempt a Discipline test to avoid suffering 4 ⚜ mental damage. No one else alive knows of the Black Stranger, or his connection to that entity.
- **Scribe**

DOOM SPENDS

- **Politically Savvy:** Count Valenso can spend 1 Doom as if it were a Fortune point when making Society tests, while dealing with the affairs of Zingaran royalty or nobility. His ability is adaptable enough that he can still score one automatic success per Doom point when dealing with nobles and royalty from other western kingdoms.

CAPTAIN ZAPORAVO (NEMESIS)

A Zingaran grandee of no great title, Zaporavo had little to inherit other than a share in a small merchant vessel. His true interest was the sword, and he was as deadly with a blade as any of his caste. When drafted into war against Argos, he and his crew became sailors and marines, fighting for Zingara's honor. When that vessel was lost, Zaporavo served aboard a carrack called the *Wastrel*, eventually rising to become the ship's mate, then leading a mutiny and taking the captaincy for his own. Since then, he and his crew have become Freebooters, distinguishing themselves — in name only — from the Barachan pirates, whom they despise.

Zaporavo is known as "the Hawk" for his features, as well as his viciousness while hunting prey upon the open sea. He is bold and intelligent, though preoccupied with goals of something grander than mere piracy. Unlike others of his ilk, Zaporavo places great stock in books and learning, and has pored over the pages of that cursed tome, the *Book of Skelos*. His greatest wish is to claim one of the lost treasures alluded to in that work, a forgotten hoard of some ancient culture, waiting to be plundered and worth enough to enrich him beyond mortal imagination.

As some point in his piracy, Zaporavo seized a caravel upon which was Sancha (page 83), daughter of the Duke of Kordava. Rather than ransom her, he found that she was amenable to his interests, and became his mistress. Now she sails with Zaporavo and his crew on the *Wastrel* as he seeks his destiny.

ATTRIBUTES

Awareness	Intelligence	Personality	Willpower
9	10	10	10

Agility	Brawn	Coordination
10	9	11

FIELDS OF EXPERTISE

Combat	4	Movement	3
Fortitude	3	Senses	3
Knowledge	3	Social	2

STRESS AND SOAK

- **Stress:** Vigor 11, Resolve 12
- **Soak:** Armor 3 (Clothing and Chain Hauberk, Steel Helmet), Courage 2

ATTACKS

- **Sword (M):** Reach 2, 5 ⚜, 1H, Parrying
- **Resentful Snarl (T):** Range C, 4 ⚜ mental, Non-lethal

SPECIAL ABILITIES

- Adaptable Combatant
- Deflection
- Deft Blade
- No Mercy
- Riposte

DOOM SPENDS

- **Secretive:** So great is his tendency towards secrecy and his distrust of anyone, Zaporavo must spend an additional point of Doom per Toughened or Minion pirate he summons to his aid.
- **Blind Ambition:** Zaporavo's obsession leads him to overlook the obvious. He must spend 1 Doom when making any Insight test against another, or must suffer one step of Difficulty.
- **Fearsome Reputation:** At any point in an encounter, Zaporavo can spend 1 Doom (Repeatable) to add 1 ☯ to the mental damage of a Threaten Attack.

> *Strom had halted just within good ear-shot. He was a big man, bare-headed, his tawny hair blowing in the wind. Of all the sea-rovers who haunted the Barachans, none was more famed for deviltry than he.*
>
> — "The Black Stranger"

BLACK ZARONO (NEMESIS)

Zarono rose from humble origins to become a familiar figure at the royal court in Kordava. But, he fell into political disfavor and so went to sea and became one of the Zingaran Freebooters. As Black Zarono, he harried shipping and coastal villages from Argos and the Barachan Isles to as far south as Stygia. He sails aboard a carrack with some 170 crew. Zarono still affects the demeanor of a courtier, in clothing and manners. He continues to desire a life of noble comfort and privilege and seeks a way to acquire it, whether in Zingara or elsewhere. Despite his past with the court, Zarono flies the royal golden flag of Zingara while indulging in acts of piracy, though that may merely be a ruse or open act of defiance.

Zarono has been obsessively searching for the fabled treasure of Tranicos. As told in the famous tale, Tranicos vanished into the Pictish wilderness with a fabulous treasure seized from a Stygian prince. In a town on the Zingaran coast, Zarono once saw a map drawn by the sole survivor of Tranicos' last voyage that showed where the treasure was hidden. Zarono was with his rival Strom (see page 84, a Freebooter named Zingelito, and a third Nemedian who sailed with the Red Brotherhood when he saw the map. They all only got a brief glimpse of the map before someone knocked over the lamp and disappeared in the dark, leaving the miser who owned the map with a dirk in his heart. Since then, Zarono watches Strom for any sign that the pirate knows where the treasure is hidden.

ATTRIBUTES

Awareness	Intelligence	Personality	Willpower
9	10	11	9
Agility	Brawn		Coordination
9	9		9

FIELDS OF EXPERTISE

Combat	1	Movement	2
Fortitude	2	Senses	1
Knowledge	1	Social	2

STRESS AND SOAK

- **Stress:** Vigor 11, Resolve 11
- **Soak:** Armor 1 (Clothing), Courage 2

ATTACKS

- **Sword (M):** Reach 2, 5 ☯, Parrying
- **Dagger (M):** Reach 1, 5 ☯, Hidden 1, Parrying, Thrown, Unforgiving 1
- **Steely Glare (T):** Range C, 4 ☯ mental, Stun

SPECIAL ABILITIES

- Deflection
- **Experienced Captain:** When leading a crew of Freebooters, Zarono can roll an additional d20 on all tests required for his command.
- Riposte
- **Strength from the Sea:** Freebooters are used to combat aboard ship and only suffer penalties in the fiercest of weather.

DOOM SPENDS

- **Fearsome Reputation:** At any point in an encounter, Zarono may spend 1 Doom (Repeatable) to add 1 ☯ to the mental damage of a Steely Glare attack.

THE TIGRESS

It was just at sunrise when the lookout shouted a warning. Around the long point of an island off the starboard bow glided a long lethal shape, a slender serpentine galley, with a raised deck that ran from stem to stern. Forty oars on each side drove her swiftly through the water, and the low rail swarmed with naked blacks that chanted and clashed spears on oval shields. From the masthead floated a long crimson pennon.

— "Queen of the Black Coast"

Though Conan's career spanned the Western Sea as well as the Vilayet Sea, there is one vessel he is most associated with: his beloved Bêlit's *Tigress*. He sailed for several years alongside Bêlit and her crew of black corsairs and in this time his reputation grew, spreading up and down the coastline. As the lover of the proclaimed Queen of the Black Coast, Conan existed outside the command structure of the vessel, accepted by its crew as one of their own and respected for his battle-prowess and the devotion of their captain.

Bêlit's own reputation was well-established long before Conan crossed her path, and if encountered before that fateful rendezvous, she will be accompanied by a full complement of 80 black corsairs (see page 71), including the notable characters described below. If the player characters cross paths with Bêlit while she is accompanied by Conan, they will find him at her side, as deadly and implacable a foe — or as loyal an ally — as they have ever met.

Bêlit is described on page 354 of the CONAN corebook, and the *Tigress* is a long galley of Black Kingdoms craftsmanship, as described on page 124.

N'GORA, CHIEF OF THE BLACK CORSAIRS (TOUGHENED)

He no longer doubted the visions of the black lotus. He understood that while waiting for him in the glade, N'Gora and his comrades had been terror-stricken by the winged monster swooping upon them from the sky, and fleeing in blind panic, had fallen over the cliff, all except their chief, who had somehow escaped their fate, though not madness.

— "Queen of the Black Coast"

All his life N'Gora's ambition was to be a man of importance. From a young age, he hunted and shared his kills with the tribe to win glory. In the internecine wars, it was N'Gora who collected the most heads and took the most slaves. As his skill and reputation in warfare grew, there came those that would shackle their fate to his rising star.

In time, N'Gora would challenge the fat fool who called himself chief. It had been years since the lazy bastard had been on a raid, or hunted game to feed the village. It disgusted N'Gora how everyone paid tribute, how young women were bartered by their families for his favor. By N'Gora's hand, this waste of skin would be put to better use. There was enough of him to make a fine rucksack.

Before N'Gora could set his coup in motion, a ship visited his village. Onboard was a goddess who had come looking for warriors to earn glory on the sea. Her beauty was mesmerizing, and N'Gora would follow her to the ends of the earth. Boarding the *Tigress*, N'Gora and his followers were blessed and reborn as Bêlit's black corsairs. In short time, N'Gora would earn enough glory to be chief among them, serving their Queen of the Black Coast to fortune and glory.

Continued on next page...

ENCOUNTERS

...continued from previous page.

ATTRIBUTES

Awareness	Intelligence	Personality	Willpower
9	9	9	8
Agility	Brawn		Coordination
10	12		8

FIELDS OF EXPERTISE

Combat	2	Movement	1
Fortitude	2	Senses	1
Knowledge	—	Social	—

STRESS AND SOAK

- **Stress:** Vigor 12, Resolve 8
- **Soak:** Armor —, Courage 2

ATTACKS

- **Javelin (M):** Reach 2, 3 🔥, 1H, Fragile, Piercing 1, Thrown
- **Shield (M):** Reach 2, 3 🔥, 1H, Knockdown, Shield 2
- **Steely Glare (T):** Range C, 2 🔥 mental, Stun

SPECIAL ABILITIES

- **Captain**
- **Strength from the Sea:** Black corsairs are used to combat aboard ship and only suffer penalties in the fiercest of weather.

DOOM SPENDS

- **Battle Cry:** Prior to and during boarding actions, black corsairs let out a blood-curdling battle cry. For 1 Doom, N'Gora can add +1 🔥 to the mental damage of a Steely Glare attack.

N'YAGA, SHAMAN OF THE TIGRESS (TOUGHENED)

N'Yaga is a shaman in service to Bêlit, captain of the *Tigress* and Queen of the Black Coast. He has sailed with Bêlit since she gathered her first crew, a witness to the beginning of her great and terrible glory. He offers her counsel and wisdom, which is often ignored, but follows his ivory goddess despite his better judgment. N'Yaga is skilled in the healing arts, divination, and some small magic. Many years raiding aboard the *Tigress* has taught him seamanship skills and practical knowledge of the sea and its ways.

ATTRIBUTES

Awareness	Intelligence	Personality	Willpower
11	11	10	9
Agility	Brawn		Coordination
7	8		8

FIELDS OF EXPERTISE

Combat	—	Movement	—
Fortitude	—	Senses	2
Knowledge	2	Social	1

STRESS AND SOAK

- **Stress:** Vigor 8, Resolve 9
- **Soak:** Armor —, Courage —

ATTACKS

- **Knife (M):** Reach 1, 4 🔥, 1H, Hidden 1, Improvised, Unforgiving 1
- **Dire Premonition (T):** Range C, 4 🔥 mental, Area, Non-lethal

SPECIAL ABILITIES

- **Alchemist**
- **Dabbler**

DOOM SPENDS

- **Physicker:** N'Yaga's knowledge of plants, herbs, and healing techniques is beyond that of many chirurgeons and healers. He possesses the Healing talents *Bind Wounds*, *A Little to Ease the Pain*, and *This Will Hurt* (**Conan** corebook, pages 66–67), and can spend Doom in place of Momentum, receiving an additional point of Momentum when making a successful Knowledge test.

Continued on next page...

...continued from previous page.

SAKUMBE, KING OF TOMBALKU (NEMESIS)

Sakumbe, once a man of remarkable courage, vitality and statescraft, had degenerated into a mountainous mass of fat, caring for nothing except women and wine.

— *Untitled Synopsis*

Sakumbe, a Suba from the Black Coast, was recruited by Bêlit during one of her many expeditions to the Black Kingdoms to replenish her crew. Throughout his life, he was often lucky at the expense of others — always seeming to choose a path that led to fortune, while those who took a different route often met great misfortune or calamity. Sakumbe is possessed of a powerful selfish streak, and a greed for both gold and power. His time onboard the *Tigress* overlapped Conan's by several months, before he struck out on his own.

After his service on the *Tigress*, Sakumbe spent several years providing mercenary work to whomever would hire him, and in this way, he traveled throughout Shem, Stygia, and the Black Kingdoms. Somewhere along the way, he encountered the wizard Askia, and their wanderings ended in Tombalku. There, their combination of unconventional dark magic and conventional skullduggery fostered Sakumbe's rise to becoming one of the two kings of Tombalku. He has become bloated and indulgent, but drink and food have not dulled his shrewd sense of self-preservation.

ATTRIBUTES

Awareness	Intelligence	Personality	Willpower
10	9	10	7

Agility	Brawn	Coordination
7	11	9

FIELDS OF EXPERTISE

Combat	1	Movement	1
Fortitude	1	Senses	2
Knowledge	1	Social	2

STRESS AND SOAK

- **Stress:** Vigor 13, Resolve 8
- **Soak:** Armor —, Courage 1

ATTACKS

- **Shortsword (M):** Reach 1, 6 💀, 1H, Parrying
- **Javelin (M):** Reach 2, 5 💀, 1H, Fragile, Piercing 1, Thrown
- **Tower Shield (M):** Reach 2, 4 💀, Unbalanced, Knockdown, Shield 4
- **Fierce Glare (T):** Range C, 4 💀 mental, Stun

SPECIAL ABILITIES

- Captain
- Inspiring Leader
- A Modicum of Comfort
- Garrulous
- Reputation

DOOM SPENDS

- **Self-Preservation:** At any time when Sakumbe's life is endangered, the gamemaster may spend 1 Doom to let him make an Average (D1) Insight test. If successful, Sakumbe gets a clear sense of the danger and its nature, and can act accordingly.

CHAPTER 6
HITHER CAME CONAN…

> *He saw a tall powerfully built figure in a black scale-mail hauberk, burnished greaves and a blue-steel helmet from which jutted bull's horns highly polished. From the mailed shoulders fell the scarlet cloak, blowing in the sea-wind. A broad shagreen belt with a golden buckle held the scabbard of the broadsword he bore. Under the horned helmet a square-cut black mane contrasted with smoldering blue eyes.*
>
> — "Queen of the Black Coast"

An unlikely pirate, Conan nonetheless spent several years in this phase of his career, even returning to it later in his life, and here his legend began to grow. His origin and first exploits were chronicled in *Conan the Barbarian*, his early career as a thief in *Conan the Thief*, and his time as a sell-sword in *Conan the Mercenary*. It is after the period described in that latter work that the Cimmerian makes his way westward, arriving eventually in Argos.

QUEEN OF THE BLACK COAST

Conan's career as a professional sell-sword comes to a rapid halt in the city of Messantia, in Argos, when he is forced to flee after a dispute with a local magistrate. Pursued by the city's guard onto the docks, Conan leaps onboard the *Argus*, a departing merchant vessel, narrowly escaping the law. He is grudgingly accepted by the ship's captain, Tito, and volunteers to accompany the *Argus* on its trade voyage southward, to Kush.

As the *Argus* travels down the coast, past Shem and Stygia, it has the misfortune to attract the attention of one of the most notorious pirates of the age, Bêlit, and her ship, the *Tigress*, crewed with fanatically loyal black corsairs. Conan fights fiercely to defend the *Argus*, even after Tito's death, and leaps onto the *Tigress*, ready to die in battle. He is spared by Bêlit, impressed by his prowess and his exotic appearance, and she pledges herself to him. Her corsairs accept him as one of their own, and thus Conan enters the world of piracy, becoming Bêlit's deadly right hand and partner.

Conan spends several years with Bêlit and her crew, raiding up and down the coasts of the Black Kingdoms, Kush, Stygia, and even to Shem. His reputation grows in that time, despite the long shadow cast by his lover, and he earns the title "Amra", the Lion.

> *The Tigress ranged the sea, and the black villages shuddered. Tom-toms beat in the night, with a tale that the she-devil of the sea had found a mate, an iron man whose wrath was as that of a wounded lion. And survivors of butchered Stygian ships named Bêlit with curse, and a white warrior with fierce blue eyes; so the Stygian princes remembered this man long and long, and their memory was a bitter tree which bore crimson fruit in the years to come.*
>
> — "Queen of the Black Coast"

This period of violent bliss ends when Bêlit urges Conan and her crew on to a treasure hunt, seeking a mythical lost

CHAPTER 6

CONAN THE PIRATE

Here we see Conan in his mid-to-late-20s, coming into the height of his prowess and establishing himself as one of the deadliest and most capable pirates of the Hyborian Age. Though his exploits are beginning to be famed and though he has traveled widely, his wanderlust is barely piqued. He has earned and spent thousands of experience points, broadening and improving his talents and his skills, learning a few new languages, and increasing his attributes and skills. Though considerable wealth passes through Conan's hands as Bêlit's partner in piracy, he holds on to little, and emerges from this period with nothing more than what he can carry.

city located upstream on the poisonous, dreaded Zarkheba River. There, in an ancient temple built by inhuman hands, they find wealth unimaginable, but the treasure comes at the cost of the lives of Bêlit and all her crew. Conan avenges her, exterminating her killers, an ancient race of winged demons.

At that point, he turns away from the sea for many years, making his way up northward and westward, a period to be addressed in *Conan the Brigand*. Conan's later experiences as a pirate and pirate captain in the Red Brotherhood are featured in that sourcebook, covering his adventures in and around the Vilayet Sea.

> *The stranger was dark, with a lean, predatory face, and a thin black mustache. A bunch of lace was gathered at his throat, and there was lace on his wrists.*
>
> *"I know you," said Valenso slowly. "You are Black Zarono, the buccaneer."*
>
> *Again the stranger bowed with a stately elegance.*
>
> *"And none could fail to recognize the red falcon of the Korzettas!"*
>
> *"It seems this coast has become the rendezvous of all the rogues of the southern seas," growled Valenso.*
>
> — *"The Black Stranger"*

CONAN THE PIRATE

AGILITY	10	
Skill	TN	Focus
Acrobatics	14	4
Melee	15	5
Stealth	13	3

AWARENESS	9	
Skill	TN	Focus
Insight	10	—
Observation	11	1
Survival	12	3
Thievery	11	2

BRAWN	13	
Skill	TN	Focus
Athletics	16	3
Resistance	15	2

COORDINATION	11	
Skill	TN	Focus
Parry	15	4
Ranged Weapons	13	1
Sailing	14	3

INTELLIGENCE	9	
Skill	TN	Focus
Alchemy	9	—
Craft	9	—
Healing	10	1
Linguistics	13	2
Lore	10	1
Warfare	11	1

PERSONALITY	8	
Skill	TN	Focus
Animal Handling	9	1
Command	10	2
Counsel	11	1
Persuade	10	2
Society	9	—

WILLPOWER	9	
Skill	TN	Focus
Discipline	13	3
Sorcery	9	—

BACKGROUND

- **Homeland:** Cimmeria
- **Caste:** Barbaric
- **Caste Talents:** Savage Dignity, Uncivilized
- **Story:** Born on a Battlefield
- **Trait:** Born to Battle
- **Archetype:** Barbarian
- **Nature:** Proud
- **Education:** Educated on the Battlefield
- **War Story:** Defeated a Savage Beast
- **Languages:** Cimmerian, Nordheimer, Aquilonian, Hyperborean, Nemedian, Zamorian, Kothic, Shemitish, Stygian, Turanian, Argossean, Kushite

SOAK
Soak	3 (Mail Corselet, Horned Helmet)
Courage	3

FORTUNE POINTS

STRESS
Vigor	
Resolve	

HARMS
Wounds	
Trauma	

ATTACKS
- **Broadsword (M):** Reach 2, 8⚔, Unb, Parrying
- **Dagger (M):** Reach 1, 6⚔, 1H, Hidden 1, Parrying, Thrown, Unforgiving 1
- **Shemite Bow (R):** Range L, 4⚔, Piercing 1, Volley
- **Brawl (M):** Reach 1, 5⚔, 1H, Improvised, Stun
- **Steely Glare (T):** Range C, 3⚔ mental, Stun

SOCIAL
Social Standing	2
Renown	6
Gold	12+

TALENTS
- **A Born Leader:** Conan can, once per battle, re-roll any failed Command test.
- **Ancient Bloodline — Atlantean**
- **Animal Magnetism:** Most women (GM's discretion) take a one step penalty when trying to resist Conan's Persuade.
- **Agile**
- **Command**
- **Courageous**
- **Deflection**
- **Deft Blade**
- **Dodge**
- **Hardy**
- **Healthy Superstition**
- **Human Spider**
- **Knack for Survival:** Conan may spend 1 Fortune point to survive the most seemingly inescapable death.
- **Master Thief**
- **Might**
- **No Mercy**
- **Savage Dignity:** Conan may roll an additional d20 for any test to resist being intimidated, persuaded, or impressed by a "civilized" person.
- **Savage Instincts**
- **Strong Back**
- **Thief**
- **Traveler's Tongue**
- **Uncivilized:** Conan suffers one step of Difficulty in social tests when dealing with people from more civilized countries. However, his Upkeep is reduced by 2 Gold.

OTHER BELONGINGS
- Broadsword
- Dagger
- Chain Hauberk and Horned Helmet
- Red Cloak

CHAPTER 7
THE WAY OF THE PIRATE

> "Come with us, warrior! The sea road is good for wanderers and landless men. There is quenching of thirst on the grey paths of the winds, and the flying clouds to still the sting of lost dreams."
> — King Harold, "The Road of Azrael"

Many sail upon the sea roads in search of adventure, profit, and fame, and still others seek a refuge from troubles incurred upon land. The life of piracy, however violent, can seem the only sane place to be in the world, where duties are straightforward and one's choice of path is narrowed to that of hunter or prey. The latter role is reserved for the timid and foolhardy, to set forth seeking wealth through trade or transport upon the most dangerous of modes of travel. For those, the sea's only protection is its vastness, and sea-captains all put forth with one hope: to stay clear of pirates.

For those who would choose to be hunters, the way of the pirate is a glorious one: free from responsibility to any other than captain and crew, their worth measured by the strength and speed of their sword-arm and their sea-craft, and life truly lived on the ocean's limitless frontier. This chapter addresses the many aspects that make up the Trade, its groups and subcultures, its customs, and the rewards that might be had.

PIRATE ORGANIZATIONS

Most pirate vessels are solitary endeavors, captained by a single strong figure presiding over a more democratic assembly of crewmembers. Some particularly influential or successful pirate captains control more than one ship. That said, there are organizations greater than any single captain, alliances across multiple captains, each with their own traditions and customs.

However, a pirate organization is not like a land-based trade guild or even a mercenary group such as the Free Companies. They are generally not for hire, sharing of wealth and knowledge is rare and non-compulsory, and pirate captains are just as likely to have rivals within their organization as outside it. These affiliations exist for one primary purpose: reputation. Any other benefit, such as a shared meeting place, or customs of behavior towards one another, is utterly secondary.

The reputation of a pirate organization is far greater and more widespread than the individual members. Rival pirates are generally wary of attacking ships of one of these alliances, as they fear reprisal, and merchants and traders are more likely to have heard of one of these organizations than any individual pirate within it.

THE RED BROTHERHOOD

Following are descriptions of two of the greatest pirate organizations of the Hyborian Age: the Red Brotherhood and the Zingaran Freebooters, both feared wherever their flags are displayed.

THE RED BROTHERHOOD

The Red Brotherhood of the Baracha Isles has members from many nations, but most are from Argos. They live by a code that ensures their liberty and equality, and binds them together as sea-dogs. Though the codes vary from crew to crew, most provide for the election of the captain by the crew, define a fair division of plunder, set the rules for life aboard ship, and describe the punishments for those who break the rules. In some ships, it is the crew rather than the captain that decides where a ship voyages. Each ship also has its own flag, usually in red or black. The Red Brotherhood is mainly based out of Tortage in the Baracha Isles, but they roam widely, raiding all along the coast of the Western Sea like a fickle hurricane, having spread even as far across the continent as the Vilayet Sea.

As the Red Brotherhood is composed mainly of sailors from Argos, their membership tends to grow when Argos is at peace and decline when Argos is at war, as the sailors move from military service to piracy. Members of the Red Brotherhood are sometimes loath to attack Argossean vessels out of fraternity, but others disdain this reluctance and prey upon their fellows with gusto. Bold and unscrupulous traders from Argos sometimes visit the Baracha Isles, giving members of the Brotherhood a chance to sell their plunder and to purchase ships stores, wine, and other supplies, though such trade is considered illegal in Argos.

The Red Brotherhood is known for its rivalry with the Zingaran Freebooters, an unsurprising stance, as Zingaran shipping lanes and coastal towns are some of the favorite targets for the Red Brotherhood's raids. Other than a handful of absolute thieves and renegades, few Zingarans can be found among its members.

ZINGARAN FREEBOOTERS

The Zingaran Freebooters are a loose collection of privateers and renegades turned to rude piracy. Whether captains are privateers or pirates usually depends on whether they are in favor at court. As such, the Freebooters are typically led by captains from the Zingaran nobility, usually disenfranchised or without inheritance. Many second sons of Zingara go to sea as Freebooters to make names for themselves.

When they are in favor and working as privateers, the Freebooters have access to Kordava and other harbors in Zingara. When they are out of favor, they must seek refuge on one of the isolated islands off the coast of Zingara or north along the Pictish coast. There they set up camps

---

PIRATES, PRIVATEERS, AND FREEBOOTERS

Little love was lost between Zingaran renegades and the outlaws who infested the Baracha Islands…They raided the shipping, and harried the Zingaran coast towns, just as the Zingaran buccaneers did, but these dignified their profession by calling themselves Freebooters, while they dubbed the Barachans pirates. They were neither the first nor the last to gild the name of thief.

— "The Pool of the Black One"

These terms are usually interchangeable when referring to the thieves and looters of the high seas, but sometimes a more specific description is needed for these sea-dogs.

- **BUCCANEER:** A pirate by yet another name, the Zingarans often define themselves as buccaneers, as a means of distinction from common pirates.

- **CORSAIR:** Pirates generally equipped with a fast ship well versed in chasing down merchant vessels. To the south off the shores of Kush and the Black Kingdoms, the black corsairs ply their trade, striking northward into Stygia and even as far away as Shem.

- **FREEBOOTER:** One in search of plunder or free booty, but merely a pirate by another name. Some pirates define a freebooter as an experienced pirate who has served on many ships, while others use the term exclusively for the Zingaran Freebooters.

- **PIRATE:** A general term for any who rob and commit illegal violence at sea or on the shore.

- **PRIVATEER:** A privately owned ship (or the captain and crew) that operates against enemies of one kingdom, usually with a commission or license issued by that government. It is not necessary for privateers to be from the country they serve. Essentially, privateers practice sanctioned piracy.

- **REAVER:** A term reserved exclusively for the Vanir raiders that harry their own coasts and occasionally venture southward, to raid Pictish coastal villages or even Zingaran towns.

The terms are further confused as they sometimes refer to the vessel as well as its crew, and a ship might be a pirate vessel in some waters and a freebooter in others, or even trading as merchants and raiding as pirates, as the opportunity presents itself.

where they can rest and repair their ships. These camps are usually temporary affairs with tents, lean-tos, and other simple shelters.

> [D]ark-faced men in flaming silk and polished steel, with scarfs bound about their heads and gold hoops in their ears.
>
> — "The Black Stranger"

The camps off the Zingaran coast are often visited by fishermen, prostitutes, and merchants bringing food, wine, news, and other supplies. The merchants also seek to trade with the captains and crews, providing the Freebooters with an opportunity to exchange their plunder for other goods. These camps often feature drinking, singing, and gambling around great bonfires that last well into the night.

The camps along the wind-swept beaches of the Pictish Wilderness are, by necessity, more sparse affairs. There, the Freebooters must rely on what they can forage for themselves or trade with the ever-wary Picts. The Picts, though, are ever changeable, and even if one tribe in the area is willing to make peace and trade with a ship's crew, the other tribes may be waiting to strike. In exchange for these dangers and deprivations, the beaches along the Pict coast offer privacy and access to needed timber and seals that are hunted for their hides and their meat.

The one thing that binds the Freebooters together is their enmity and rivalry with the Red Brotherhood of the Baracha Islands. As privateers, the Freebooters are primarily charged with defending the ships traveling along the coast of Zingara from Barachan raids. The royal court in Kordava offers a special bounty for members of the Red Brotherhood brought into port for trial. Pirate captains and other leaders are usually executed. Common sailors are sold as slaves, usually to work in quarries throughout Zingara.

As the Freebooters are usually led by Zingaran nobles, their crews function more like mercenary companies or naval vessels than the more democratic companies among the Red Brotherhood. As such, the Freebooters usually fly a flag with some variation of the coat of arms from the captain's family. Before battle, they often raise below it a red or black flag as a sign that no quarter will be given.

A captain among the Zingaran Freebooters has responsibilities to his crew, ensuring that they are well-equipped and rewarded. But there is no question as to who is the master and who is the servant. A Freebooter crew that loses faith in its captain is more likely to desert and seek to join a more successful band of Freebooters than to mutiny.

ALL THE SEA'S WEALTH

Freebooters, buccaneers, corsairs, and all manner of pirates freely roam the waters during the Hyborian Age, from the Western Sea to the Vilayet Sea. Pirates come from all walks of life and can include bored farmers, dissolute nobles, bankrupt traders, and unsuccessful fishermen. Most pirates, though, are sailors. Some turn to piracy when they mutiny against their captain. Many choose to join a pirate crew when their ship is seized. Many just see it as an opportunity for freedom at sea.

> "Well," said Tito hardily, "the courts have fleeced me too often in suits with rich merchants for me to owe them any love. I'll have questions to answer if I ever anchor in that port again, but I can prove I acted under compulsion."
>
> — "Queen of the Black Coast"

THE SHIPPING LANES

All countries bordering the Western Sea send ships to sea for fishing and trade. The main shipping lanes, though, run from Zingara to Kush, from Kordava to Abombi. This area includes the major cities on the Western Sea, and here is where most of the merchant ships sail on trading ventures between the cities. Pirates, whether they are based in the Baracha Isles, Zingara, the Black Coast, or elsewhere, come to the shipping lanes in search of fat merchants to plunder. For that reason, many merchants stay close to the coast, where there is more traffic, where there are ports they might run to for refuge, and where they might find the occasional navy patrol. It is also true that many captains are such poor navigators that they need to stay in sight of land.

PILLAGE

Pirates pillage to keep their ships supplied and their crews happy. A pirate crew has a hierarchy of needs that runs from food to supplies to treasure. Thus, pirates are as likely to raid a coastal village or town for food and supplies as to seek out a ripe merchant vessel. In many cases, a successful raid is one that gains food, sails, and rope.

When carrying out their raids, pirates prefer to rely on two things: surprise and superior numbers. To gain surprise, a pirate will engage in trickery so that they can come upon a target unguarded. To aid in this, pirates often keep a chest filled with various flags so that they might present their vessel as a merchant from a friendly country. Frequently, a pirate crew will remain out of sight below-decks until the last moment, then surge forth when an unsuspecting vessel pulls alongside. When attacking a village or town, a pirate crew may land at a nearby cove and then march overland to attack the village at dawn, catching them by surprise when the villagers are wary against sea-raiders.

While surprise can be unpredictable, superior numbers are reliable. Whenever possible, pirates prefer to overwhelm a target with a force of numbers, intimidating them into surrender. For this reason, most pirate ships have two to three times as many crew, if not more, as might be found on a similar merchant ship. For a merchant vessel, keeping the crew to a minimum boosts the profit margin, while more pirates mean a more likely success while raiding. A merchant ship with less than ten crew may surrender when overtaken by a ship with thirty or more ruthless, armed pirates. Despite this, a smaller number of pirates can also strike effectively against larger merchant crews, as the latter are generally unwilling to die for their goods and pirates are all-too-happy to indulge in wanton slaughter.

When possible, pirates will also attempt to operate with multiple ships to better out-maneuver their targets or even to drive them into a trap, or run them aground. They can also obtain superior numbers by using small boats. Particularly when raiding a village, a pirate ship might have several canoes and small boats tied to its rails and towed after so that the pirates may easily approach their target through shallow water. In the Baracha Isles and other island areas frequented by pirates, several small boats may surprise a merchant by darting out from behind a point of land, seeking to surround their target.

Once they have seized a prize, pirates will quickly search the ship and interrogate the crew, seeking any valuables that might be hidden aboard. The pirates may also offer merchant sailors a chance to join their crew. Skilled crewmembers such as a carpenter or boatswain might be kidnapped and forced to join the pirates. The pirates will attempt to move on as soon as possible before another ship might come to aid their target. Along the coast of the Western Sea, a port or a fishing village is almost always a short sail away.

Once done with a ship, a pirate may sail away, or they might choose to take the ship, either in exchange for their ship or to increase their flotilla. The captain and crew of the target may then either be marooned on an island or set afloat in a small boat.

WOLVES BY ANY NAME

For all the talk of the romance of the way of the pirate, the freedom it affords, the adventure of such a path, and the rewards that may be heaped at the feet of the bold, it is nonetheless a life marked by murder and theft, preying upon the weak or defenseless, and in many cases, wanton butchery and merciless depravity. Pirates are, like bandits and thieves, criminals by another name, and even those who take on the title of privateer or corsair are nonetheless considered evil by most civilized societies in the Hyborian Age. Only a few kingdoms support such endeavors as lawful, and for those cultures where sea-raiding is considered normal, it is only when it is employed against enemies. Vanir may choose to reave their icy fjords and raid up and down the Pictish coastline, but they are only heroes to the people of their village, just as the black corsairs are lionized amongst their own folk but hated and feared by their neighbors and those they prey upon.

Embarking upon a life of piracy is to live outside the rules, and to subject oneself to the scorn of those that have suffered at pirate hands. It is also to forsake the protections that come with living within societies governed by laws. Once outside the protection of civilization — such that it is — life is dangerous and subject to the depredations of even one's fellow pirates. Rivalries between pirates are legendary, and when pirates deal with one another, they show each other much less mercy than they do their victims.

PLUNDER

What a pirate is really looking for in a raid is plunder. The following tables provide a method for generating plunder for pirates to gain from seizing vessels and raiding villages. To generate plunder, the gamemaster should roll a d20 and consult the *Plunder* table (on the next page). Each entry has a description that is then expanded on by rolling on subsequent tables as described.

> *For example, Valeria of the Red Brotherhood and her crew seize a Stygian galley. A roll of a 12 on the Plunder table indicates that it is a "Handsome" haul. Four rolls are then made on the Basic Cargo table: 4, Livestock (the gamemaster decides that these are goats); 11, Rope; 16, Food (the gamemaster says it is dried fruit); and 18, Sails. One roll is made on the Exotic Goods table: 20, Sorcerer's Goods. A roll is then made on the Sorcerer's Goods table: 8, yielding Alchemy ingredients.*

When raiding villages and other targets onshore, roll 2d20 and keep the lower result.

Stealing sorcerers' goods is generally avoided, if possible, and pirates are loath to involve themselves in sorcery. Most sorcerers don't like people who take their things, and they often have the means and motivation to track down the people that steal from them. For descriptions of alchemical items, see the relevant descriptions in *Chapter 6: Equipment* and *Chapter 7: Sorcery* of the **Conan** corebook.

A ROAD OF SLAUGHTER

Though piracy is merely thievery by another name and in a different context, everything depends on that context. What might seem squalid or cowardly on land becomes tinged with a greater sense of liberty, of romance on the high seas. Perhaps this is a result of the increased risk and difficulties pirates face when compared to their landlubber colleagues. The violence of storm and wave arrayed against them, the tyranny of cruel captains, and the deprivation of shipboard life as fresh water runs low and food with anything resembling taste or flavor is quickly consumed by weevils. Those weevils may very well end up being the closest thing a pirate comes to fresh meat in weeks.

Such is the life of the pirate, like the waves themselves, heights when the spoils are more than one can indulge in, and lows when life onboard grows desperate and bleak.

MAKING ONE'S MARK

What kind of pirates are the player characters going to be? Are they unabashed sea-dogs, cutlasses in one hand and rigging in the other, loyal only to the sea, their ship, and whatever plunder they can wrest from the holds of their enemies? Do they prefer to think of themselves as more honest seafarers, perhaps licensed to pursue those corsairs that prey on merchants, making their profits from payment for each pirate they bring to justice and the booty they seize from them? Both are perfectly valid options — though there is no guarantee that the player character's self-characterization will be one observed and believed by others. To a pirate, a privateer or freebooter is simply a pirate with an overactive conscience.

The third option for player characters is to be as Conan was... a pirate by circumstance and by inclination. After all, when aboard the *Argus*, owned by the merchant captain Tito, Conan was content to observe the more prosaic pastimes of that class of sailor. However, when given the chance for slaughter and riches aboard the *Tigress*, Conan seized upon them delightedly, though his alternative was to die fighting.

THE WAY OF THE PIRATE

PLUNDER

Result	Description	Plunder
1–2	Miserly	Basic cargo, roll two times on *Basic Cargo* table.
3–4	Meager	Basic cargo, roll three times on *Basic Cargo* table.
5–9	Average	Basic cargo, roll five times on *Basic Cargo* table.
10–14	Handsome	Basic cargo, roll four times on *Basic Cargo* table. Exotic goods, roll once on *Exotic Goods* table.
15–18	Generous	Basic cargo, roll four times on *Basic Cargo* table. Exotic goods, roll twice on *Exotic Goods* table.
19–20	Rich	Basic cargo, roll four times on *Basic Cargo* table. Exotic goods, roll four times on *Exotic Goods* table.

BASIC CARGO

Result	Description
1	Navigation charts or log
2	Metals
3	Building stone
4–5	Livestock
6	Slaves
7	Hides
8–9	Cloth
10–11	Rope
12	Wine
13–14	Grain
15–17	Food
18–19	Sails
20	Carpenter's tools
18	Perfume
19	Incense
20	Sorcerer's goods (roll on *Sorcerous Goods* table)

EXOTIC GOODS

Result	Description
1–2	Wool rugs or tapestries
3–4	Noble passenger (may be ransomed)
5–6	Spices
7–8	Weapons and armor
9	Live beasts (livestock, exotic animals, horses, etc.)
10	Silk or fine cloth
11	Treasure (roll on *Treasure* table)
12	Feathers
13	Statuary
14	Flowers or other live plants
15	Glassware
16	Fine pottery
17	Mining equipment
18	Perfume
19	Incense
20	Sorcerer's goods (roll on *Sorcerous Goods* table)

TREASURE

Result	Description
1–6	Small chest with silver coins or bars
7–9	Large chest with silver coins or bars
10	Two large chests with silver coins or bars
11–13	Small chest with gold coins or bars
14–15	Large chest with gold coins or bars
16–17	Small chest with jewels and gold coins or bars
18–19	Large chest with jewels and gold coins or bars
20	Two large chests with jewels and gold coins or bars

SORCEROUS GOODS

Result	Description
1–3	Lore, personal library
4–6	Alchemy, personal library
7–9	Alchemy reagents
10–11	Alchemy, field laboratory
12	Erotica, personal library
13–14	Sorcery, personal library
15	Mummy
16	Exploding powder
17	Blinding powder
18	Burning liquids
19	Exotic beast preserved in salt
20	Lotus flower

> "I have a ship and a fighting crew and a girl with lips like wine, and that's all I ever asked."
>
> — Conan, "The Pool of the Black One"

Borrowing this route into piracy for a Conan campaign is a perfect way of quickly ensuring that the player characters are thrust into the action, but also that they have an exit. Should they tire of their fates and fortune being so dependent on the whims of the sea, they can easily leave. An exciting and sudden beginning to a career of piracy is perfectly suited to a sword-and-sorcery game, and it can be easily adapted to suit the needs of the game.

Are the player characters seeking to escape imprisonment as Conan was? Perhaps they leap aboard a ship leaving port, as the Cimmerian himself did, only to discover that this *is* a pirate vessel, disguised while in dock but about to engage in looting up and down the Black Coast. Alternatively, perhaps the player characters, recognizing that the merchant vessel they are on is captained by a brutal maniac and that the crew are poor and desperate, organize a mutiny and point the newly liberated vessel toward the path of piracy.

Perhaps, during a particularly intensive binge to celebrate a triumphant heist or the conclusion of a mercenary expedition, the player characters are bought a round of drinks by a friendly man at the bar. He, too, is battle-scarred and weathered. He toasts the player characters' courage as companions-in-arms, and in blood. When the player characters wake up after their indulgence of the night before, they find themselves on a ship with an angry quartermaster screaming at them to awake…

They may also have been taken while incapacitated, such as when Conan was brought aboard the *Venturer*, having been found unconscious on a beach. The player characters may awaken from some sort of mishap, perhaps a side effect of an adventure near the shore, find themselves below-deck on a pirate vessel, their options limited to "join or die".

PIRATE CODES

Pirates form their own, strange sub-cultures. It is inevitable — just as the thieves of Zamora and Shadizar have developed their own lexicon and signals, their own practices and protocols when it comes to the division of loot, so too do pirates. How else to stop the festering resentments and jealousies which infest a ship, long out to sea, from

THE WAY OF THE PIRATE

swelling into something more noxious and invidious to survival — after all, when being hunted by the Argossean privateers, a means of ensuring that the crew will not turn on each other is vital.

Thus, the pirate code, sometimes called "the laws of the Trade", has flourished. Some older pirates, beards graying and minds long ago pickled in rum and salt air, claim that this was once a codified set of laws, etched into vellum by a great pirate king, while others claim it is a mere consensus, barely consistent from ship to ship.

> *"Then if I am one of the Brotherhood," he grunted, "the laws of the Trade apply to me; and since I killed your chief in fair fight, then I am your captain!"*
>
> — Conan, "Iron Shadows in the Moon"

The code itself is an amorphous thing, with very few truly fixed laws. Most are dependent on the circumstances in which the ship finds itself and the captain and crew's memory of regulations and statutes they were told by friends and former shipmates many years ago.

Those laws which all agree on, however, are these:

- Mutiny is never permissible and is punishable by death. Unless it succeeds, in which case most tend to turn a blind eye to it and swear to the new captain.

- Murdering a crewmate is not allowed while on ship and is punishable by death, unless said killing was committed as a means of entering the crew, or as a fair duel. Captains, on the other hand, can kill as they see fit.

- All disputes, regarding money, rations, deck duties, gambling, and other disagreements are to be arbitrated by the captain, whose decision is final.

- To disobey the captain of the vessel is punishable by flogging — the precise number of lashes is left to the captain to determine.

- A crew-member can challenge the captain to a duel for the captaincy. Such duels are inevitably to the death, and quarter is not given: it would be folly to let the loser live.

The code also covers shares in treasure recovered: each full member of the crew receives a single share; all newcomers receive a half share; the captain receives two shares; and the captain's mates receive a share and a half. Recompense is owed to the crew should captains be unable to meet their obligations to those under their command. This final tenet chiefly consists of guidance on how much extra money the captain needs to pay to his crew should their share not be available, or if additional hardship is endured due to the captain's poor leadership.

The code's nebulosity is what makes it such an enduring part of the strange fabric of pirate life. It changes to suit the needs of those invoking it. Calling upon the code is something the player characters can do, whenever it suits them. They should be aware, however, that they will be called upon to defend the provenance of the law they are stating and their interpretation of it. While the code itself may be half-forgotten and half-invented, that does not stop pirates from becoming impressively litigious about its use.

FINDING THE PLUMB LINE

Once player characters are onboard — in both senses — and at sail, the pace becomes vitally important. It can often be the case that travel upon the ocean, whether for trade or raiding, is a slow, tortuous travelogue with stretch of sea replaced by stretch of sea. The gamemaster should avoid this at all cost, using such periods of inactivity only as a setup for later adventure. However, in saying that, variation of pace is also important — there are periods of time onboard a ship in which nothing is happening, there are no ships on the horizon, and there is no treasure-strewn island just out of sight.

This can also be reflected during an adventure, if only to show how a ship is its own enclosed environment. Piratical carousing can take place *during* an adventure, in a way which it can't in other forms of the game. Sometimes, there simply isn't anything else to do. For this reason, player characters who are pirates have access to an extra carousing table. There is the standard *Carousing Events* table (found on page 295 of the **Conan** corebook), the *Shore-Leave Carousing Events* table (see page 107 of this book), and the following *Doldrums Carousing Events* table. As the names of these two unique carousing events indicate, these tables should be rolled upon when the player characters are on shore (in place of rolling on the standard *Carousing Events* table) and when at sea.

The doldrums, in this instance, is a period of being becalmed due to climatic conditions or, more figuratively, in which the ship is sailing towards its next encounter — deliberately or not. After a major encounter, roll a d20 on the *Doldrums Carousing* table, as part of the usual carousing activities process.

The above is a good means of bringing in a sense of temporal flow in pirate-themed adventures that, at the same time, avoids having to narrate each minor mishap or fraying knot that might be encountered. Even Conan endured a few weeks of relative peacefulness aboard Tito's ship, before becoming involved with the remarkable Bêlit. Conan's adventures as a pirate are almost unique in this

DOLDRUMS CAROUSING EVENTS

Result	Event	Description
1–2	Mutiny!	The ship's crew, sick of intolerable conditions, has taken command of the vessel. Trying to prevent the mutiny, in favor of preserving the current captain, requires a successful Dire (D4) Persuasion test. Securing a place in the new regime and continuing your current course requires an Average (D2) Persuade test. A failure results in the new captain and mates turning the ship towards their home port.
3–4	Sprung a Leak	Damage to the hull is causing an influx of water at a perturbing rate. Bailing the ship out is going to take a lot of hard work to achieve. Any Wound recovery is halved, as time which might have been spent relaxing is instead spent scooping out brine and sealing up splits in slowly rotting wood.
5–6	An Ill Wind	The wind is wild and willful. It seems to change direction from one moment to the next, making its harnessing virtually impossible. What is going on? Have the player characters happened into strange latitudes? Or is the enemy they pursue instead trying to turn the tables — using sorcery to hamper their progress? There is no answer to be found yet, though the player characters may wish to exercise greater caution as they continue their travels.
7–8	Sickness	Illness is rife onboard a ship; with men and women cooped up in unbearably close quarters, it is only a matter of time until sickness takes hold. It is, for those who make their living at sea, a professional hazard. This time, however, it is worse. This may even be plague — though that is far from certain. The player characters must succeed in Challenging (D3) Resistance tests or suffer an immediate point of Fatigue. This cannot be recovered until the next down period.
9–10	Man Overboard!	Whether drunk, careless, unlucky, or all three, a member of the crew has fallen overboard. What do the player characters do? Is a search launched? Was the lost sailor murdered? The sailor's possessions will need to be shared out… what can be found amongst them and what will the player characters do with them?
11–12	Dubious Cargo	Examining the contents of the hold — whether filled with plunder from a recent raid or only with a dwindling food supply and barrels of increasingly stagnant water — the player characters find a strange amulet or idol. What it is and where it came from, no one is too sure, but the superstitious crew is frightened and afraid. Are the player characters being pursued by a ship they previously robbed, intent upon reclaiming this token? Is the icon itself cursed or malignant? Does it belong to a dangerous cultist onboard ship, waiting for a chance to betray her crewmates and avenge some past slight? Finding out might be a dangerous affair.
13–14	Storm!	The weather has turned and, quite suddenly, the ship is wracked by storm and tempest. All player characters should make a Challenging (D3) Agility test to maintain their stability and composure, even as the vessel shifts violently from side to side. A failure causes 4 💀 damage as they are pitched to the deck or into the rigging.
15–16	Cursed Pirates	Gambling is a common pastime onboard ship, though each pirate onboard has already dedicated their life to the acquisition of wealth through dishonest means. This wouldn't be too much of a problem if it weren't for the fact that the player characters are now in deep with at least one member of the crew. Have they been cheated? How are they going to pay off their debt? Are they willing to go to war with the whole ship either way?
17–18	Cabin Fever	Claustrophobia, boredom, and strong drink can have a dangerous effect when combined in sufficient quantities. That's what's happened and now there are fights erupting between former bosom friends, some are singing songs to themselves hiding away in dark corners, and others are filing their teeth to points, claiming to be the children of sharks. Cabin fever has hit. What are the player characters doing to relieve the symptoms? What are they suffering? Hallucinations, perhaps? And what dangers approach while the crew threatens to tear itself apart?
19–20	Plain Sailing	The weather is fine; better than fine, even. The wind is consistent, the seas calm, and the sun bright. Progress is swift and easy; the player characters can recover 1 bonus Harm due to the speed and simplicity of the voyage.

sense, as we gain a fuller sense of him as part of a crew, even if only briefly, than anywhere else. In Bêlit's heart and bed he was no longer obliged to fulfil the duties of a sailor, but while part of Tito's crew he did just that.

This sort of activity is an interesting way of allowing players to flesh out their characters, to engage in pursuits other than killing and looting. This interlude should only be brief — but striking a balance so that such moments can be had, amongst the tumult of battle and foul sorcery, can be a great deal of fun.

CUTTHROATS, CUTLASSES, AND CLASHES AT SEA

The ship combat rules found within *Chapter 8: Ship Combat* give a gamemaster the means of simulating the devastating impacts of triremes smashing into one another, of splintering wood, and the soft, panicked gurglings of lungs filling with blood and sea water that is ship-to-ship combat. Some ships are equipped with long-range weaponry such as ballistae or catapults, but, for the most part, the primary means of inflicting catastrophic damage on a ship itself is through collision, or by setting the ship afire with flame-tipped arrows or fiery catapults.

However, capturing a ship via hand-to-hand combat is just as common — it means that anything worth having onboard the foe's ships could be looted and that the most ambitious of pirates could begin to build their own fleet. Those members of the former crew who survived the ferocity of the boarding assault might be offered the opportunity to join the pirates. Or they'd be thrown into the sea. Either way, when the pirate player characters are about to go to war, it is worth bearing a few things in mind.

Firstly, how are they getting from ship to ship? Are they swinging across, using ropes tied to the yard arm? This is a little less likely, given the design of Hyborian Age vessels such as triremes and larger ships, but what's the point of being a pirate if one can't swing across the raging sea beneath with a knife clenched between teeth? The second means of getting from one ship to an enemy's (and vice versa) is the *corvus*, a be-toothed length of reinforced wood. This simple but ingenious piece of technology offers pirates a means of swarming over the railings. The teeth hook into the side-rail or deck of the opponent's vessel, providing a path across the water which cannot be easily dislodged. The pointed teeth of the corvus hook make shifting it, especially with armed pirates rushing across it, extremely difficult. With two or three of these in place, the enemy vessel becomes stuck and the bloody, deck-to-deck combat can begin in earnest.

The second aspect of ship combat to consider is space. Things are tight onboard a ship. Even the largest and most impressive of craft can suddenly feel incredibly small once the fighting starts. Room for impressive dueling flourishes is limited; what matters in such claustrophobic, cramped combat is efficiency — short swords and knives, used in unison with cutlasses are far more effective than great swords or two-handed axes.

This is a great way of delineating the difference between fights on the ocean and those on land: introduce penalties for the use of large weapons or bulky shields. The gamemaster should emphasize the ecstasy of fumbling which such fighting results in, hands clutching at throats and scrambling for a spare knife, at the belt, after one has slipped from bloodied fingers.

Several methods of introducing this sense of chaos and panic are listed below. However, none of these is a substitute for games mastering which really accentuates the sensation of a chaotic maelstrom of gore and flashing steel!

The gamemaster is, of course, free to utilize these rules or ignore them, as they see fit. In fact, if the gamemaster desires to make them harsher and ship combat even more frenetic, these disadvantages can be increased or magnified with the rules for uncertain footing in environments (see *Movement and Terrain* on pages 111–112 of the **Conan** corebook). These rules are entirely optional and are designed to evoke a different feeling to that which combat in Conan typically conveys — still fast and exciting, but bloodier, more febrile, and prizing different strategies.

Fire

Fire arrows, and other ranged weapons with fire involved somewhere, are an extremely attractive option in ship-based combat. With wood being the material from which ships are made, fire is a weapon of truly devastating potential. However, it should also be a risk to those using it. Setting an enemy ship alight is an effective tactic, yes, but what happens if the wind changes and *your* ship gets set alight?

While the player characters should, of course, be free to explore any approach to a situation they choose, it is perhaps wise for them to remember that things can go quickly and disastrously wrong where only partially controlled elements are concerned. The gamemaster can of course use this to their advantage. Perhaps an overly confident, brash group of adventurers think to set a foe's ship on fire… only to have their own ship erupt into conflagration as the burning vessel crashes into them.

Finding One's Sea Legs

As anyone who has been on a boat can attest, the sea doesn't stay still. It is in a constant state of motion, undulating, shifting, currents pulling and pushing at the ships trying to ride the swells. It takes a degree of time and experience to truly become used to this rolling and pitching, to compensate for the sudden changes in gradient and move swiftly and surely along the deck. This is particularly true amid combat.

Another optional means of introducing the chaotic, messy nature of naval combat into your pirate games is to call for periodic Athletics tests, as the boat heaves from one side to another suddenly. These tests can be made as regularly,

PIRATE COMBAT VARIATIONS

Weapon	Advantage or Disadvantage / Result
Broadsword	**Advantage/Disadvantage:** Its size and weight, so useful on the battlefield, here makes it unwieldy and a danger to those around you. Using a broadsword in a vicious, ship-constrained melee is going to take remarkable skill. **Result:** When using a broadsword aboard a ship, the wielder must spend double any desired Momentum spends (see *Momentum Spends* on page 118 of the **Conan** corebook). This does not count for defensive effects such as Parrying.
Battleaxe	**Advantage/Disadvantage:** The power and terror which the battleaxe can inflict on the foe is entirely nullified here. The freedom and space needed to use such a weapon at its murderous best is simply not available. **Result:** Should a player character wielding a battleaxe onboard a ship inflict damage, any fellow player fighting in the same zone as anyone wielding a battleaxe must spend one Momentum or suffer 2 🔥 damage as their ally's weapon flies dangerously close. This Momentum must be spent whenever the player character with the axe misses an attack or has it parried successfully.
Spears, Pikes	**Advantage/Disadvantage:** These weapons are, depending on the circumstances, a distinct boon to those fighting onboard ship and a pronounced disadvantage. When attacking those still in the foe's ship from your own craft, they are lethal. Once battle is joined in earnest, they are a liability. **Result:** When fighting between two ships — that is, the player character is based in a zone aboard one ship and the opponent is in a zone upon another ship — the spear functions as normal, except that it does +1 🔥 damage, reflecting the difficulty of escaping from the spear's Reach. If fighting an opponent within the same zone as the player character, the spear does 2 🔥 and requires an additional Effect to trigger the Piercing effect — the space is too confined to easily generate the thrust required to truly drive the spear home.
Shields	**Advantage/Disadvantage:** Shields are always useful in combat and, while it is true that their capacity for defense is undiminished, the lack of room means that the ability to use the shield as a club is somewhat impaired. **Result:** The shield can still be used to Knockdown an enemy, but delivers only 1 🔥 in doing so.
Shortswords, Daggers, etc.	**Advantage/Disadvantage:** These weapons are almost perfectly designed for use in the cramped confines of the ships decks. **Result:** All 1H Reach 1 weapons generate +1 additional point of Momentum per Momentum generated.
Cutlasses	**Advantage/Disadvantage:** Cutlasses are immensely practical weapons for shipboard use, as well as in combat. **Result:** A cutlass can be used to reduce the Difficulty of any Sailing or related test by one step, when appropriate (gamemaster's approval), due to its general usefulness as a tool as well as a weapon.

or rarely, as the gamemaster chooses and are only worth doing so as long as it enhances the tension and excitement of the game. The *Sailing Weather* table (below) can help give an idea of the severity of the test required to act normally as the ship is subjected to the sea's tempestuousness.

WEATHERING THE SEAS

Sailing is, in nearly every sense, contingent on the weather. While the bireme and trireme ships are designed to be fast and maneuverable even when the wind is low, even a breeze can make operating a ship much easier. Similarly, a sudden squall can disrupt an entire voyage, utterly. It can send boats miles off course, irrevocably delay a pursuing foe or leave a group of adventurers wrecked and abandoned on an island without so much as a skin of water, let alone a map. On page 106 is a table of potential weather conditions.

The gamemaster can roll on this prior to a session beginning, to gain an idea of the prevailing weather conditions. Alternatively, the players can do so — often an excellent way of ensuring that the focus returns to events at the table, should distractions elsewhere have proven to be just that. These weather conditions will make life on ship more difficult, rendering the most mundane of tasks a risky business of sliding across sodden decks, trying to untie a saturated rope, or attempting to keep cargo from sliding into the hungry water below.

The gamemaster might want to introduce other weather categories, or tweak the severity of the effects mentioned above. The conditions and effects are designed to be broad and to offer new story avenues and plot points, new twists and difficulties to overcome, not to make things miserable.

GOING TO LAND

Even pirates must go to port sometimes. It may be brief — should they be forced to dock in a salubrious place, where the rule of law is enforced — or, should they moor themselves at a free-port, it may be considerably longer. Either way, a crew long confined to ship, the company of only each other, and the highly limited entertainment (and hygiene) which that betokens are likely to indulge their various appetites as thoroughly as possible.

The *Shore Carousing Events* table (page 107) is for pirates who have finally reached port and intend to squander as much of their illegally obtained gold and silver as they can, in as short a time as possible. The following table can be used in place of the *Carousing Events* table featured in the **Conan** corebook, if desired.

SEA WEATHER

Roll	Details
1–4	**Weather:** Thunder, lightning, the raging of the heavens. The sea is furious, the waves smash into the hull, sending freezing sheets of water swirling over the decks. **Voyage:** Steering the ship is harder and holding a course takes substantially greater strength than before. The player characters are likely to fall behind any opponent they are chasing. If they are being chased, however, it is likely that they will be able to elude their pursuer. **Crew:** Moving from one zone to another during combat, requires a Challenging (D3) Athletics test. Failure requires that the player characters remain where they are for that round and take 3 ♦ mental damage, from the cold and the panic caused by nearly slipping into the wild waters. The gamemaster may also add Vigor loss, to reflect a fall caused by the failed attempt.
5–7	**Weather:** Choppy waters — while not as severe as a storm, the waters beneath the ship are disturbed and roil with anger. Movement is far from impossible, but the effect of the ship's rolling and plunging is disorienting. **Voyage:** This makes the going a little slower, as the ship does not move along quite as smoothly or reliably as would be ideal. If pursuing a quarry, the player characters will fall a little behind and, if attempting to evade an enemy, they will draw a little ahead. **Crew:** Movement and combat can take place as normal, however, a fumble will now occur on a 19 or a 20, rather than just a 20 as is usual.
8–11	**Weather:** Wild and windy, the sails scarcely able to contain the gale swirling about the ship. The sails are straining at the ropes lashing them to the mast and the mast itself strains to rip itself free from its moorings. **Voyage:** Controlling the ship becomes a significant issue with this weather effect. While the speed of the ship is increased, it may veer off at any time and, if the player characters are not careful with their manipulation of the sails, they might damage them irreparably, leaving the ship a sitting duck for any pirates nearby. **Crew:** Movement and Melee combat are unaffected by this weather condition; however, all attacks made using ranged weapons are made at one step higher Difficulty than would have otherwise have been the case.
12–16	**Weather:** Fog coats everything; the surface of the water, the deck of the ship. It hangs in thick tendrils from the shoulders of the player characters and their fellow crewmembers. Almost nothing can be seen, either to fore or aft, and what lurks beyond the wreaths of opalescent mist does so silently, waiting… **Voyage:** Going is slow. It must be. Rocks, reefs, maelstrom… all might be concealed by the fog. It is not enough that sight is restricted either. The smothering layer of fog also deadens sound… an arrow might be nocked, string taut and pointed at your neck and you'd never know. The benefit is that any ship you are pursuing can be surprised in the fog. The issue is that they might be looking to do the same thing to you. **Crew:** Fog does not affect the movement of player characters from one zone to another. However, all Melee combat is conducted at one Difficulty level higher than would otherwise be the case. All Ranged weapon attacks are done so at three steps of Difficulty higher.
17–20	**Weather:** The weather is almost perfect for sailing — the sea smooth and undisturbed, the wind high enough to offer assistance, but not so much that it makes the vessel difficult to control. These are the days when the gods of the sea have truly smiled on those who trust their livelihood to the waves. **Voyage:** This is the ideal circumstances for the player characters to catch up with their foe, or else escape pursuit — at least until they are equipped and ready for the encounter. Things are easy, land hoves into view, the depredations of the maritime life seem less onerous. **Crew:** All successful movement related tests automatically generate +1 additional Momentum. All combat takes place as it would normally.

THE WAY OF THE PIRATE

	SHORE CAROUSING EVENTS	
Result	Event	Description
1–2	A Hearty Welcome!	The tavern you have stumbled into is filled with old crewmates, comrades-in-arms, and drinking friends who, too, have just disembarked. Stories are traded, as are rumored details of rich, poorly defended merchant fleets ripe for the taking. While the player characters' heads might not immediately feel like it, this experience will significantly enhance their recovery. The player characters may recover an additional point of Vigor or Stress.
3–4	The Black Spot	Some slight has been committed, some liberty has been taken, some tenet of piratical code breached. Word has been issued, action taken. The Black Spot — the piratical death sentence — has been handed down. Pressed into the hands of one of the player characters, this scrap of paper or crumpled playing card contains the titular spot and an ominous threat. Retribution will soon be handed down. What infraction the player characters have committed, what form the vengeance will take, and how to free themselves from the doom creeping up on them, they'll have to find out for themselves…
5–6	Bad Nights in the Bordello	While you all conducted yourselves as well as might be expected in a house of ill-repute, and the owners and residents of the place have no complaints, they also have lax security. Your gold, clothes, and weapons have all been taken (as have most of the valuables in the bordello itself) and your next half an hour is likely to be taken up with sprinting across town wearing nothing but a grimace. Finding those thieves who took your stuff might have to wait a little while.
7–8	A Tempting Offer	A captain, well-known and well-liked, approaches you in the bar where you are toasting the relief of not being stuck out at sea. She mentions that she has a proposition for you; it's dangerous but the rewards are great — robbing one of the most well-defended merchant fleets in Zingaran seas. She has someone on the flagship, waiting for the signal to start a mutiny. She wants your skills for the job. Are you in?
9–10	A New and Unexpected Berth	The chains on your hands and feet weren't there when you fell asleep… or passed out (to be more truthful). Now, however, you and your friends are chained together within a small, stinking jail cell, and the obese, gloating guard gleefully informs you that you are about to become the crew of the *Vitellus* — the captain of which is renowned as being amongst the most cruel and sadistic on the waves. Good luck!
11–12	Recognized!	Of all the ports, in all the world… you are recognized and immediately arrested; whether this is because you came to a legal port, convinced you'd never be noticed for the pirate you are, or because you crossed a member of the pirate brethren some time ago and they've just found the perfect way to pay you back, who can say? What can be said is that getting out of this predicament is going to cost you 2 Gold. That or you can wait for trial, which will likely lead to your execution.
13–14	Old Debts, Old Foes	Even as you raise the first tankard to your lips, you can feel him standing at your shoulder. Sallow, unkempt, and with a smile as cold as a Cimmerian's grave, he quietly reminds you of the debts you incurred to his master last time you were in port. They were… extensive. And now is the time to reimburse those debts. Whether you truly owe as much as he is claiming is debatable, but you did borrow some money that time. You must pay 3 Gold to clear your debts. That or be prepared to take on a criminal underworld.

_____SHORE CAROUSING EVENTS (CONT.)_____		
Result	Event	Description
15–16	Extra Shares	Stumbling down the street, you trip and nearly fall over a former shipmate. She has been significantly less fortunate than you, as the large knife protruding from the base of her neck indicates. However, she does not appear to have been relieved of all her hard-earned cash. Taking these extra shares earns you 2 additional Gold; however, the thieves may still be nearby, and while not against the pirate code, some other former shipmates might not take kindly to the idea that you killed a friend of theirs, however erroneous that view might be.
17–18	A Helping Hand	Luck continues to smile on you. Gambling finally pays off and that firm, sensible investment you made with the Gold from your latest voyage (putting it all on a well-made roll of the dice) has earned you an extra 3 Gold. Enjoy it, for the next time the dice are unlikely to be as kind.
19–20	"X" Marks the Spot	A stranger fumbles at your hand, blood leaking from the corners of his mouth and tracing a thin, crimson path down his throat. He thrusts a ragged chart into your hands and, with a last, ragged gulp of air, dies. But what he has given you almost takes your breath from your lungs, too. It is a treasure map. And it's a treasure you've heard tell of — a vast deposit of jewels just waiting to be acquired. But who murdered the stranger and why was it you he entrusted the map to? There is great wealth to be found, but there's likely to be some equally great danger along the way.

DEAD MEN TELL NO TALES

All the above provide a veritable pirate's hoard of potential tools and ideas which a gamemaster can draw on in order to invest pirate-themed games with the right mixture of brio, buccaneering, and brutality to capture the essence of one of Conan's adventures. This is far from exhaustive, however. When running a pirate campaign, the gamemaster isn't limited by geography — if the player characters decide to push beyond the horizons of the Hyborian Age charts, to leave behind the Thurian Continent, an entirely new and different world might be waiting for them. Lost continents, forgotten civilizations, and threats as deadly as they are ancient all wait to be found — the dreaming west and the mysterious east of Conan's world are not limits… but challenges.

> *The dullest was struck by the contrast between the harsh, taciturn, gloomy commander, and the pirate whose laugh was gusty and ready, who roared ribald songs in a dozen languages, guzzled ale like a toper, and — apparently — had no thought for the morrow.*
>
> — "The Pool of the Black One"

The gamemaster should keep in mind that a pirate-themed campaign will push things further, extending the parameters of the known world, incorporating new, strange ideas into play. Conan's own sojourns into pirate adventure were often into the unknown, rather than on the shores of the familiar. Who knows what Conan confronted out there, on the fickle tides? Ancient ruins full of slumbering monstrous gods? Degenerate rituals conducted by fallen races of half-men, preying upon hapless mortals? Something even stranger and more perilous?

Even safely ensconced within the Western Seas and Black Coast, where Conan plied his piratical trade, there are many more stories to tell and exciting ideas to explore: far more, indeed, than there is room to detail in these pages. Is there a pirate council, somewhere in the southern tip of the continent, slowly amassing a fleet which will allow them to take the seas for themselves entirely? Are the pirates of the Western Sea being hunted and claimed for sinister purposes by some bizarre, sea-dwelling creatures? Pirate campaigns allow the gamemaster to be completely unfettered, a place where player characters can forge themselves a legend vaster than anywhere else. Let the exploration be as remarkable as the combat is vicious.

Hoist anchor, raise the sails, and sharpen cutlasses. There are seas to be roamed, and blood to be spilt!

THE WESTERN CONTINENT

The major Thurian continent encompasses the whole of the known world, stretching from the Western Sea to the shores of distant Khitai in the east. But sailors whisper of a continent far to the west, many weeks across the Western Sea and beyond the reach of any but the most daring — or foolhardiest — captains and crew. Scholars find references to this continent in the scraps of knowledge retained from the days prior to the Cataclysm, but most view the existence of such a land as apocryphal, or even impossible, and stories about this unnamed western continent are outlandish and fanciful.

Into the Unknown

An attempt at navigating across the Western Sea to land upon the shores of such a continent — whether backed by a monarch, explorer, or pirate — seeking to discover such a place, would attract the bravest and most resolute, but the potential for adventure, fame, and wealth is beyond imagination. A gamemaster could fashion an entire campaign around such a grand endeavor, allowing player characters to encounter a world undescribed by Robert E. Howard, perhaps even unvisited by his most famous creation, Conan of Cimmeria.

The Northern Bridge

Rumors from the unassailable reaches of Nordheim speak of an occasional bridge of ice, its origins northward even of Vanaheim and the Arctic Circle, that connects to this continent in its own northern expanse, and skalds of Nordheim speak of bands of their kin who ventured across that bridge in search of a new land to colonize, making their way southward and into obscurity. How these stories returned to Nordheim, it is not said, and thus little stock is put in such tales. Despite this, every few years, an ambitious jarl of Vanaheim or an Æsir jarl seeking a new land to conquer tries to rally enough of their people for an expedition along the northern coasts (in the case of Vanaheim) or northward by foot (for the Æsir), and meets with little success.

> *We were the travelling of years from our northern homeland. Lands and seas lay between. Oh, that long, long trek! No drift of people, not even of my own people, whose drifts have been epic, has ever equaled it. It had led us around the world — down from the snowy north into rolling plains, and mountain valleys tilled by peaceful brown folk — into hot breathless jungles, reeking with rot and teeming with spawning life — through eastern lands flaming with raw primitive colors under the waving palm-trees, where ancient races lived in cities of carven stone — up again into the ice and snow and across a frozen arm of the sea — then down through the snow-clad wastes, where squat blubber-eating men fled squalling from our swords; southward and eastward through gigantic mountains and titanic forest, lonely and gigantic and desolate as Eden, after man was cast forth — over searing desert sands and boundless plains, until at last, beyond the silent black city, we saw the sea once more.*
>
> — "Marchers of Valhalla"

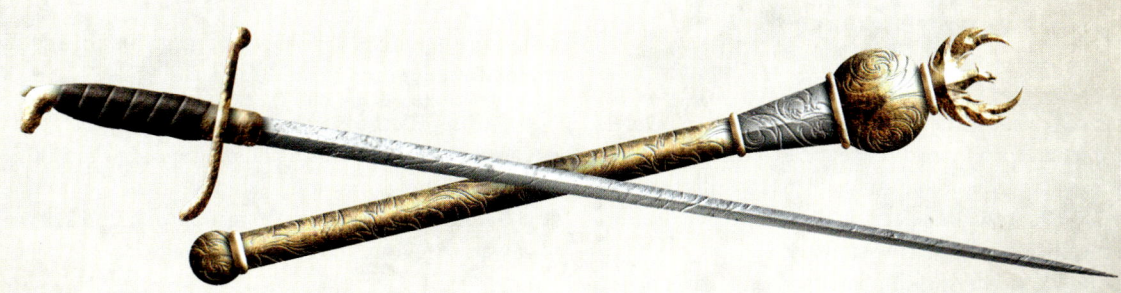

CHAPTER 8
SHIP COMBAT

> *With no one at the sweep, the Argus rolled broadside, and the steel-beaked prow of the raider crashed into her amidships. Grappling-irons crunched into the side. From the lofty gunwales, the black pirates drove down a volley of shafts that tore through the quilted jackets of the doomed sailormen, then sprang down spear in hand to complete the slaughter.*
>
> — "Queen of the Black Coast"

While some ships surrender at the sight of a black flag snapping in the wind, many more stand their stations and prepare to defend. From crashing prows to boardings atop blood-washed decks, the pirate must always be ready to kill. Whether hunter or prey, freebooters make their life through the red eye of battle and the threat thereof. While some quarter might be given to prisoners, a pirate cannot expect any in return. Such is the life of pirates, chased by great navies seeking to string them from the gibbets on the coast as warning to others of their ilk.

lines are thrown to bind the ships together. Then, combat becomes a melee between two floating platforms. In this instance, each ship is treated as one zone. Larger ships may have multiple zones, such as for aft, or stern castles, or areas below deck.

Rowed galleys offer more maneuverability, but they are also at risk of having their oars sheared off or broken if the other ship passes close along one side before the crew can bring in its oars. War galleys also usually have rams mounted on their prows which they can use to damage and upset an enemy ship so that it may be boarded.

BORNE ON THE WAVES

Sailing the waves is the life of a pirate, but it also involves many hazards of a more direct nature — that of one ship against the other. Ship combat functions basically the same as personal combat. As a result, this section deals more with the differences than the similarities.

In the Hyborian Age, combat at sea is mostly a matter of maneuvering, usually with one ship trying to get away. As they close, ships exchange volleys of arrows, spears, slings, or other missiles. Grappling hooks bite wood as

SHIP MOVEMENT

Ship movement is described in terms of **Sailing Range** and **Maneuver**:

- **Sailing Range** is a measure of how long a ship may remain at sea. Instead of listing speeds, the Sailing Range shows how long a ship can travel continuously before stopping ashore to resupply its stores of food, water, rigging, and other essentials.

- **Maneuver** is measured using abstract range categories, as with ranges for personal combat. Ships typically do not travel at their full speed during combat due to their need to maneuver for position. A

SHIP COMBAT

ship's Maneuver rating determines how quickly and easily the ship can change its heading to maneuver around obstacles or to close with an enemy ship. The Maneuver rating is a value between 0 and 3, and it is also the number of bonus d20s granted on Sailing tests for maneuvering.

SHIP QUALITIES

The following common Qualities are found on numerous ships of varying types and are collected here for convenience.

- **Agile:** These craft can accelerate and decelerate quickly, allowing them to maneuver swiftly in the battle zone. The craft can move one additional zone with any Movement action it takes.

- **Deep Draft:** A ship with a deep draft can carry more cargo and take rough seas, but can potentially run aground when in shallow waters or in crossing reefs. This increases the Difficulty of such maneuvers by one step when in shallows or when close to shore.

- **Galley:** A vessel propelled primarily by one or more banks of oars. Most galleys have a sail for use when the wind is favorable. Prior to combat, the crew of a galley usually takes down and stows the mast and sail.

- **Light Craft:** These small vessels include skiffs, fishing boats, canoes, and other small boats. All Light Craft have a Shallow Draft (see below) and need only one or two crewmembers. Additionally, they have only a single level of damage and a single hit location.

- **Ponderous:** The craft is so massive and bulky that it cannot move quickly. A Ponderous ship cannot take the normal Minor Action move, and can only move to an adjacent zone as a Standard Action.

- **Portage:** The vessel is capable of being carried or moved overland via rollers or planks for short distances; such as over river cataracts; from one river to another; or past rapids, shallows, or to bypass waterfalls. Generally, portaging requires the full crew complement and requires the vessel's cargo be emptied.

- **Ram:** On war galleys, a ram is a reinforced spur that extends from the prow of a ship at or below the waterline that is used to damage an enemy vessel in a collision. A ram adds +2 ⚡ to a ship's impact damage when ramming.

> *The bearded rowers grunted, heaved at the oars, while their muscles coiled and knotted, and sweat started out on their hides. The timbers of the stout little galley creaked and groaned as the men fairly ripped her through the water. The wind had fallen; the sail hung limp. Nearer crept the inexorable raiders, and they were still a good mile from the surf when one of the steersmen fell gagging across the sweep, a long arrow through his neck.*
>
> — *"Queen of the Black Coast"*

- **Rugged:** Sturdily built from strong timbers and well rigged, Rugged ships are easy to repair, saving time and resources, and allowing them to be put back into use far more swiftly. A successful Craft test to repair a ship with the Rugged Quality gains 2 bonus Momentum.
- **Shallow Draft:** A craft that floats lightly on the water and that may have a flat bottom. Shallow Draft craft are ideal for use on rivers and in coastal waters where the water is not deep. However, Shallow Draft craft do not do well in rough seas where the pilot may suffer increased Difficulty for Sailing tests.
- **Ship:** Ships are large-scale craft, capable of carrying an assortment of crew and cargo. A ship typically has a non-player character crew that can bolster the effectiveness of player character actions, at the gamemaster's discretion.

MOVING AT SEA

Movement in sea combat is identical to ground combat. Ships in combat at sea, though, are in near constant motion. A ship must take exactly one Movement action each turn — no more, and no less.

Just as in personal combat, ship combat uses zones to determine range and movement. Though combats can take place on the open sea, ships often engage in combat near shore or on rivers where reefs, rocks, shallows, islands, piers, and other man-made structures are present. These can serve as potentially hazardous terrain. Most tests to move through or around difficult terrain are Sailing tests taken by the pilot, but some situations may allow other characters to provide aid. For example, a player character may attempt an Observation test by taking soundings with a pole or weighed rope to determine whether a ship could safely cross through shifting sand bars.

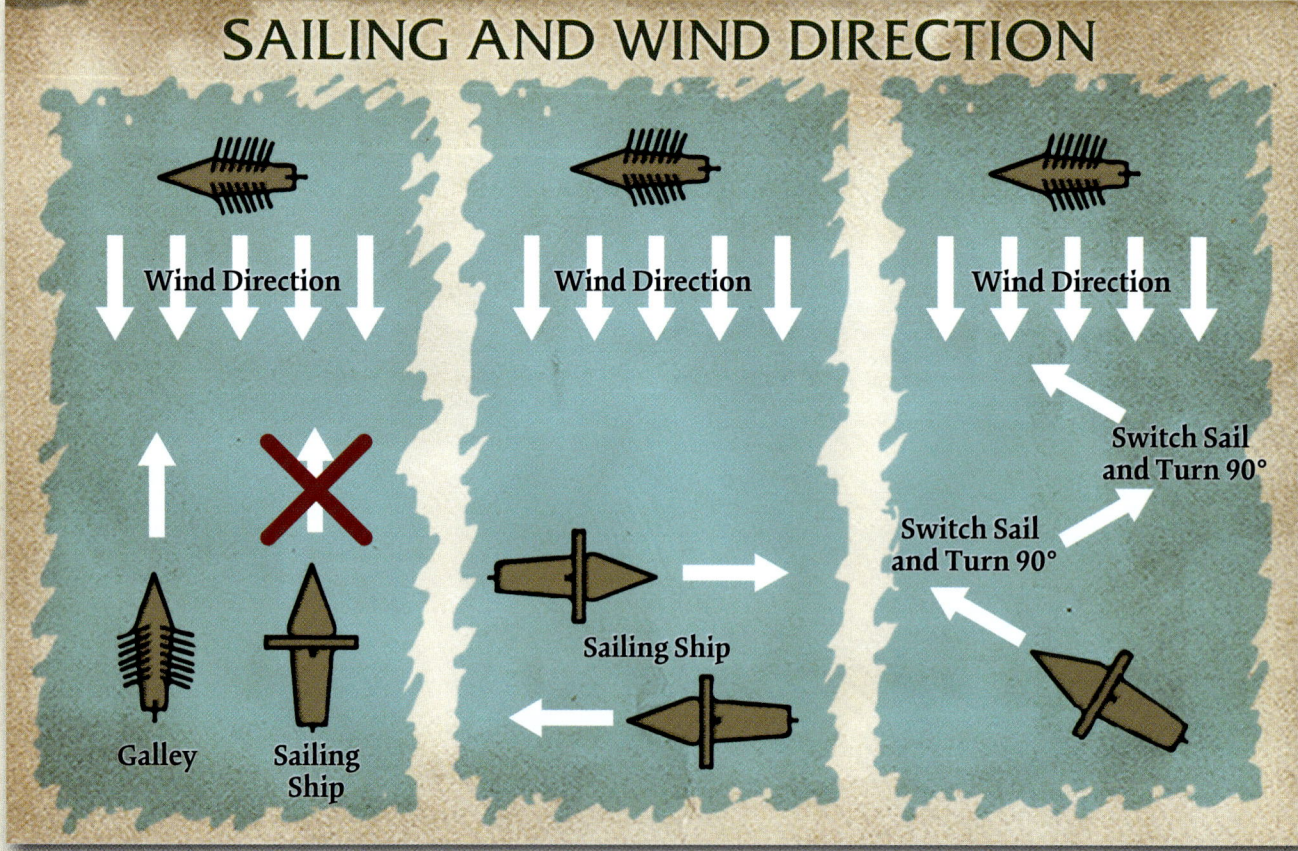

SAILING AND WIND DIRECTION

SHIP COMBAT

Ship Scale

When operating on ship scale, Reach covers any situation where the vessels are within a few yards, or in physical contact (as when bound together or after ramming). It is possible for a character to move between two ships within Reach, although an Acrobatics or Athletics test (player's choice) may be required.

- Close range covers any other objects and vessels in the same zone, which are close enough to be clearly seen and that can be hailed or targeted by a Ranged attack.
- Medium range covers objects and vessels in adjacent zones, which are too far away to be hailed or attacked.
- Long range covers any further zone.
- Extreme range is a special case, used only when a ship is barely seen on the horizon or at cloaked by twilight.

Weather Gauge

At sea, a ship that is upwind of another is said to have the weather gauge and to have an advantage in combat. A character making Sailing tests upon a ship with the weather gauge receives an additional d20 when attempting to outmaneuver an enemy vessel. At the start of an encounter at sea, the gamemaster may either determine the wind direction by the circumstances of the adventure or personal choice.

Against the Wind

It is difficult for a ship to sail into the wind. Ships can easily sail downwind or on a beam reach perpendicular to the wind, with the wind coming directly across the ship's port (left) or starboard (right) rail. To maneuver upwind, a ship must sail on a tack at an angle to the wind. At the end of a certain distance, a Reach, the ship must tack or come about, turning 90 degrees and shifting the sail to the other side of the ship, to continue moving up wind. A galley can always row directly upwind on a desired heading.

WOODEN SHIPS AND IRON MEN

Ships have multiple crew roles. During combat, each ship receives a single turn. During that turn, the craft receives a single action per crewmember, with the available actions defined by the role for each of the crew. The roles and the number possible are as follows: **commander** (one), **lookout** (one), **helmsman** (one), **marine** (one or more), and on a galley, a **piper** (one).

Smaller vessels — skiffs and other Light Craft — do not have sufficient space to fill all the roles with different characters, and a character can take on multiple roles. Each crewmember still only gets one action, no matter how many roles they fill.

- A character in the **commander** role can take actions from any other role, but only receives one Standard Action, so ships with multiple characters can achieve more. This consideration is for ships with smaller crews, where the commander may also be the pilot, or a small boat where one person must do everything. Commanders also have actions to benefit the performance of other characters, using the Command skill.
- The **lookout** may make Observation tests to track other vessels or to spot debris or other hazards in the water.
- **Helmsmen** can take actions to move the vehicle more quickly or through difficult environments. These actions require the Sailing skill.
- **Marines** can make Ranged attacks against other vessels at Close range, command a Squad of archers, and lead boarding actions.
- On a galley, a **piper** commands the rowers, coordinating and timing their movements. This can alternately be a drummer, a singer, chanter, or some other role charged with keeping and communicating the correct tempo.

Multiple actions from multiple crewmembers make larger ships more powerful than smaller ones. Further, the presence of non-player character crews bolsters the effectiveness of the main crewmember in each role, making large vessels much more potent than smaller ones.

General Actions

General actions can be performed by any members of the crew.

- **Damage Control:** Standard Action. Make an Average (D1) Craft test; restore one Surface Damage, +1 per Momentum spent. Alternatively, remove one status effect currently afflicting the ship.

Commander Actions

Commander actions bolster the effectiveness of other crewmembers, making them work as a coherent whole rather than as disparate individuals. Where a test is required, use the Command skill. A commander can take any action from any of the other roles. Performing any helmsman action requires that the commander have access to the vessel's helm, but the vessel cannot take more than one Movement action during a turn, from any source.

- **Coordinate:** Standard Action. The commander directs his subordinates to bolster their effectiveness. This is an Average (D1) Command test, which adds Momentum directly to the group Momentum pool.
- **Assign Crew:** Standard Action. The commander assigns one or more of his Crew Support to increase another role's Crew Support for this turn. This is an Average (D1) Command test, with each point of Momentum allowing you to assign crew to an additional role during that action.

Lookout Actions

Lookout actions all involve tracking the movements of an enemy vessel and watching out for hazards in the water. Where a test is required, use the Observation skill. The Sailing skill may also be used to identify the origin of an enemy vessel or other specific facts about the craft.

- **Heading:** Standard Action. The lookout reports to the commander and helmsman on the direction and speed of the enemy vessel. This is an Average (D1) Observation test, which adds Momentum directly to the group's Momentum pool.
- **Target of Opportunity:** Standard Action. The lookout points the marine to the commander or another crewmember on the enemy ship. This is an Average (D1) Observation test, which adds Momentum directly to the marine's Ranged attack.

Helmsman Actions

Helmsman actions all involve movement. Where a test is required, use the Sailing skill.

- **Standard Motion:** Minor Action move. The vessel moves anywhere within its current zone (including into Reach of another vessel), or into an adjacent zone. If it moves to an adjacent zone, it cannot move into Reach of another vessel.
- **Full Sail:** Standard Action move. The vessel moves to any zone in Long range, but all attacks made by the ship increase their Difficulty by two steps.
- **Half Sail:** Standard Action move. The vessel moves anywhere within its current zone (including into Reach of another vessel), or into an adjacent zone. If it moves to an adjacent zone, it cannot move into Reach of another vessel. Until the beginning of its next turn, all attacks against the vessel, as well as all attacks made by its crew, increase their Difficulty by one step.
- **On Target:** Standard Action move. The vessel moves anywhere within its current zone (including into Reach of another vessel), or into an adjacent zone. If it moves to an adjacent zone, it cannot move into Reach of another vessel. In addition, the helmsman must attempt an Average (D1) Sailing test. If successful, the pilot's Momentum is added to the group Momentum pool — the action is purely to assist another character's action.
- **Ramming Speed:** Standard Action move and attack. The vessel moves into Reach of any other vessel within Medium range, and slams into it. Make an Average (D1) Sailing test as a Melee attack, inflicting the vessel's impact damage, and, unless the vessel is equipped with a ram, suffering the target's impact damage in return. After ramming, the crew may attempt to board the enemy vessel. Against an enemy galley, the helmsman may choose to instead pass closely along one side of the enemy ship to shear off its oars. A successful ram that shears off the oars inflicts 1 Break and increases the Difficulty of movement tests until the oars are repaired.
- **Evasive Action:** Reaction. If the vessel is targeted by a ranged or ramming attack, the pilot may take this action to turn that attack into an opposed test.

Marine Actions

Marine actions coordinate attacks against an enemy vessel.

- **Boarding:** Standard Action move and attack. The marine leads a Squad over the rail to board the enemy vessel and engage its crew in melee. This is a Struggle between the marine's Command skill and the enemy marine's Command skill. If in the previous round the marine has used a Grapple Action (see below) on the other vessel, the marine's Difficulty is reduced to Simple (D0) for the attempt. Otherwise both parties make Average (D1) tests. Success inflicts 5 ⚔ non-lethal damage against the rival vessel. While blood is spilt aplenty and many lives are lost, the opposing vessel seldom founders due to their dead.
- **Bow Shot:** Standard Action. The marine makes a Ranged attack against an individual crewmember on the enemy vessel. Enemy must be at Close range or nearer. This is a normal attack, as per the Squad rules, and inflicts damage on a specific target, not the ship.
- **Fire Arrows:** Standard Action. The marine leads a Squad in firing a volley of flaming arrows at the sails of the enemy vessel. Each Effect rolled indicates a point where the sails have caught fire and begun to burn. For information on fire as a hazard, see page 274 of the **Conan** corebook. Otherwise this is a normal

SHIP COMBAT

attack as per squad rules, inflicting 4🦅 damage to the enemy ship.

- **Grapple:** Standard Action attack and move. The marine hurls a grappling hook to snare the enemy ship so that the two vessels may be pulled together for a boarding action. This requires a Challenging (D2) Ranged Weapons test.
- **Repel Boarders:** Standard Action. The marine leads a Squad to repel an enemy's attempt to board the ship. This is a Struggle between the marine's Command skill and the enemy's Sailing skill. Success inflicts 5🦅 non-lethal damage against the rival vessel.

Piper Actions

The piper directs the rowers of a galley, ensuring that they stay in rhythm.

- **Beat Time:** Standard Action. The piper calls out the time, efficiently directing the rowers through their strokes. This is an Average (D1) Command test, which adds Momentum to the helmsman's next action.
- **Ship Oars:** Reaction. The piper orders that the oars be pulled in to prepare for boarding or avoid having them be sheared off by an attacker. This is an Average (D1) Command test.

ATTACKING SHIPS

Attacking a ship is fundamentally the same as attacking a creature. The biggest differences are that most vessels function on a different scale than creatures — personal weapons cannot generally harm a ship — and ships track damage suffered slightly differently.

As pirates are out to seize a ship and its cargo, they usually don't want to damage the ship itself. Most attacks are with Ranged weapons, leading to boarding and then a fight on the blood-slicked decks. Warships hunting pirates are less concerned about causing damage to a ship. The exception to this is ramming, where the ships are deliberately slammed together.

DAMAGING SHIPS

Ships, in a similar manner to creatures, can take differing amounts of damage. Larger ones have multiple levels of injury. However, while the damage suffered by a ship is determined in essentially the same way as damage suffered by a creature, the means of tracking that damage, and determining the effects it causes, are different. Vessels use **Structure** instead of Vigor and suffer **Breaks** instead of wounds (see the **Conan** corebook, page 121). They do not recover lost Structure the way living beings do Vigor.

Damage and Soak

Most ships, by merit of being stoutly built for the rigors of sea, have a Soak value which reduces damage exactly as it does for creatures and characters. Larger craft and military vessels are likely to have much higher Soak values than Light Craft, but the specifics of working out how much damage is inflicted to a vessel are identical to damaging a creature with one small difference. Unless noted vessels are explicitly immune from the intense and knockdown qualities.

Damage

Damage between vessels is handled normally, for the most part, with a few exceptions. Most vessels larger than Light Craft are functionally immune to regular melee attacks, though at the gamemaster's discretion attacks from Sorcery may impact a vessel normally. Vessels are Toughened foes and can suffer a number of Breaks instead of two Harms. The gamemaster may choose to designate any warship or special vessel as a Nemeses, or can classify any smaller craft such a canoe or raft as a Minion.

SHIP COMPLICATIONS	
Complications	**Ship Complication**
1	**Scrape:** The vessel does not respond quite as desired and briefly collides with some obstacle. The vessel suffers a hit, dealing its own impact damage.
1	**Running on Empty:** The ship's water stores sour, leak, or otherwise run dry. The ship must stop and send a party ashore in search of water.
1	**Fight:** A simmering feud between two of the crew boils over into a fight on deck. The captain must restore discipline.
1	**Fouled:** Barnacles and other growths have gathered on the hull, slowing the ship. All Sailing tests are increased by one step of Difficulty until the ship is careened and scraped.
1	**Man Overboard:** One of the crew falls overboard and must be rescued.
1	**Becalmed:** The wind dies, and the water looks like glass. The ship must either wait for the wind to return or find another way to continue on its way.
1	**Grounded:** The ship has been caught by a falling tide or run aground on a reef, rock, or sandbar. The crew may have to wait for a change in the tide or find another way to float the ship.
2	**Mutiny:** Discontent grows within the crew, and they begin to plot against the captain.
2	**Storm:** A sudden and severe storm blows in. If there isn't a nearby port, bay, or other sheltered water that the ship might run to, requiring a Challenging (D2) Sailing test, the ship will be blown off course, possibly heading into uncharted waters.

COMPLICATIONS AT SEA

Ships can become impaired through methods other than being attacked. Any time a character attempting a test to control or operate a ship suffers a Complication, there is the possibility, some part of the craft malfunctions. This normally occurs with Sailing tests. At the gamemaster's discretion, a Ship Complications could occur (see table above). The gamemaster should choose the one most relevant to the current situation, as determined by the number of Complications generated

REPAIRS AT SEA

Permanent repairs are a time-consuming process, taking hours or even days of work to restore damaged rigging and other components. It is not the kind of thing achieved during battle. Combat repairs are a different matter, and far more temporary.

Light Craft, having only a small number of Structure and Breaks, cannot effectively be repaired while at sea. For the purposes of repairs only, any damage to a Light Craft are considered as Breaks.

Repairing Structure damage requires a successful Average (D1) Craft or Sailing test and a Standard Action. Tools and parts can be used as normal and a successful test restores 2 Structure damage +1 for each point of Momentum spent. If the vehicle has suffered Breaks, those Breaks will increase the Difficulty of the test one step per Break.

Breaks can be patched or repaired outside combat. Patching a Break is identical to treating a wound in that if another Break occurs, all the patched Breaks immediately affect the vessel again. Repairing a Break is a much harder proposition. The Difficulty for patching a Break is equal to the number of Breaks taken +1. Each Break being repaired takes a full day and while the repair is undertaken the ship can only move at the Standard Movement speed. At the end of a full day's work, the engineer makes a Daunting (D3) Craft test. If successful, the engineer fully repairs 1 Break +1 Break for every 2 Momentum spent. Making repairs in a harbor or dry-dock is much easier, with the Difficulty reduced by one step, in addition to any potential modifiers from facilities or specialists that might help with the repair.

SHIP COMBAT WEAPONS

Though the age is known for its savagery, ingenious weapons of war exist. Many of these are dedicated to sieges, but pirates, professional navies, and guarded merchant vessels use some few ship combat weapons while on the seas. Some of these devices are so clever as to be near-legend, while others are repurposed versions of more familiar land-bound war engines.

No great siege towers top giant ships — at least not since the Cataclysm — and ship-to-ship combat is still largely a matter of trying to ram, then board, an enemy vessel. However, proper use of the following devices can turn the

SHIP COMBAT

odds in favor of a battered crew or, more likely, reinforce the might of one of the great sea powers of the day.

Argossean Fire

A storied weapon that some sailors do not believe exists, only the Argossean navy knows this recipe of liquid fire and the means to launch it. While it is a formidable weapon, it can pose a danger to crew and vessel. After all, one does not long play with fire without being burned. At the gamemaster's discretion, any Complication rolled can backfire on the crew of the device, setting them aflame or merely breaking the weapon for the rest of the battle.

However, when Argossean fire works, it is a terror. Siphons of bronze, often decorated like dragon's heads, shoot a jelly-like substance. The jelly sticks and burns at such temperatures that flesh falls away from bone and wood combusts like an explosion. Water is not very effective at dousing these flames either. Only full immersion in the sea is like to cause someone to cease to burn. Bailing water upon the flames can mitigate the fire somewhat, but the viscosity of the fire proves hard to wash away. Depriving the fire of oxygen is the only sure way to stop this blaze, and Argossean vessels keep damp tarpaulins ready to throw upon the would-be conflagrations inflicted by Argossean Fire.

> ### A NOTE ON TACTICS
> By and large, the Hyborian Age tactics used today would be recognizable to early Hyborians and even to the Commorians and Valusians before them. While there are levels of technological development as evidenced in the machines above, naval warfare has changed very little over the ages.
>
> At its heart, sea combat is still mostly a matter of getting close to another vessel (ramming it or pulling up alongside it), then boarding it to capture or destroy the ship. Formations of varying degrees of sophistication aside, great naval commanders tend to be less master tacticians and more masters of improvisation.
>
> Even rowed galleys are slow and unreliable to maneuver, and so the commander who wins the day is the one who can rally troops and think on their feet, howsoever a deck might toss them. Once two forces meet, battle at sea becomes a free-for-all where careful reserves, flanking, and the like play much less a role than on land. Perhaps, that is why the above devices are so effective — they give options to a kind of warfare inherently limited in such.

NAVAL ARTILLERY							
Weapon	Reach	Damage*	Size	Qualities	Availability	Cost	Encumbrance
Argossean Fire	M	6 🔱	Crew 3	Area, Fearsome 2, Incendiary 2, Intense, Spread 2	7	10	Crewed
Ballista	L	4 🔱	Crew 2	Vicious 2, Intense (Bolt); Area, Knockdown, Stun (Stones) One step Difficulty penalty to all attacks due to inaccuracy.	3	6	Crewed
Cheiroballistra	2	5 🔱	Crew 1	Vicious 2, Intense (Bolt); Area, Knockdown, Stun (Stones) No penalty to attack.	7	7	Crewed
Corvus	1	4 🔱	Crew 2	Piercing 1	4	5	Crewed
Grapnel	2	2 🔱	Crew 2 + winchers	Special	2	2	Crewed
Iron Claw	2	2 🔱 or 10 🔱**	Crew 5	Grappling (effects increase efficacy. None needed to grapple a ship.), Knockdown (applies to crew on deck)	3	5	Crewed

* These weapons affect vessels at full force.
** When the ship is dropped.

Only alchemists of considerable skill can concoct Argossean fire, and only engineers of skill can make the bronze tubes and strange hoses required for its delivery system. Finally, the nature of the weapon and the damage it does to the human body is such that even the most stalwart cutthroats go pale and dive headlong into the water at the sight of a comrade consumed by this dire machine.

> *[A] serpent-prowed gondola shot from behind a castellated point of land, and naked dusky women, with great red blossoms in their hair, stood and called to his sailors and posed and postured brazenly.*
>
> — "Queen of the Black Coast"

Ballista

A ballista aboard a ship relies on smaller rocks or more frequent volleys to inflict damage and loss of morale against troops. It is unlikely to inflict substantive Structure damage with such a siege engine at sea, while the waves roll and pitch. Instead, the machine becomes entirely anti-personnel in its nature, more of a morale-breaker than a lethal weapon. It is simply too hard to aim a device of this size onto a shipboard target.

However, a hail of deadly stones or bolts causes an instinctive search for cover in even the most steadfast mariner. Delay and suppression are important tactics in determining who boards who first and in what numbers. The *cheiroballistra*, listed below, is a more accurate weapon at sea.

In any event, no foe wants to see an enemy ship armed with any sort of engine of war. Merely possessing one indicates a high level of training and professionalism in a ship's crew, and few freebooters will wish to engage such competent foes.

Cheiroballistra

An innovation, which dates to pre-Cataclysmic times, the *cheiroballistra*, is a portable version of the well-known ballista. However, while the *cheiroballistra* is not as unwieldy as its larger counterpart, it cannot be accurately crewed by a single soldier unless mounted, such as on a ship.

Instead, the weapon is mounted at the fore and aft of the ship as well as along the sides. Its extreme power drops rival mariners with ease and rend sails with their iron bolts.

Corvus

A simple yet ingenious invention, the corvus formalizes the chaotic process in which boardings occur. Rather than using hooks and rope to pull the two ships into a deadly embrace, the corvus is itself a long bridge spiked at the bottom end. Its weight causes the spike to plunge and fix within the deck of the opposing ship, while the bridge is thick, sturdy, with some even equipped with handrails.

Grapnel, Catapult or Ballista-propelled

Reputedly, this weapon was invented during a battle, though which battle has been lost to time. Both the Argosseans and the Zingarans claim ownership. Whatever the case, the propelled grapnel is essentially a giant harpoon with a grappling hook end. The steel bolt at the end can penetrate the hull or the weapon can fly in a parabolic arc and latch onto the deck.

The power of being launched by machine makes the embedded hook much harder to remove by human hands. Once a grapnel finds its mark, it is nearly impossible to dislodge in the heat of battle. Once it's fixed in an enemy vessel, the crew — often assisted by a crank attached to the machine — literally reels the ship in, like fish out of the water. A well-crewed grapnel team can winch a similar-sized vessel one zone per turn and boarding actions decrease the difficulty of their attack as if they had Grappled the ship last round (See *Marine Actions* on page 114).

Iron Claw

Said to be taken from inscriptions dating a time before the Cataclysm, the iron claw is an ancient weapon brought to terrible new use. The device itself is very complicated, and only an ingenious mind could have conceived of, let alone executed, it. The engine proper is a crane, either freestanding or topping walls or towers. It is never aboard a ship, being far too unwieldy for that. Thus, its role is that of defense.

From the crane dangles an enormous, articulated metal claw. The claw is maneuvered by the crew above, whose goal is to grab a ship below and pull is from the water as if by the hand of irate god itself. The crew then either winches the ship higher and drops it to calamitous effect, or simply keeps it so trapped as to remove it from the battle.

The selfsame inscriptions that render the device show it being used to scoop and smash ships, targeting one ship after another. These pictures show them atop mighty walls in battles so huge the mind can scarcely grasp the world's fleets marshaling in such number.

However, it is extraordinarily finicky and difficult to maintain, and one Complication is enough to cause it to lock and be inoperable until a Daunting (D3) Craft roll may be made to repair it, taking three full combat rounds to complete, and two Complications when using it causes it to lock until it can be disassembled and repaired, outside of combat.

SHIP COMBAT

AN EXAMPLE OF SHIP COMBAT

High seas combat has all the thrill of its bloody, land-bound cover and more of the danger. Not only must a mariner contend with their opponent, but the vagaries of the sea, shifting decks, and great waves all might assail them.

The Kraken vs. the Petrel

The *Kraken*, a pirate war galley, has just caught up with the *Petrel*, a guarded merchant bireme, off the coast of Shem. The stakes are obvious: the reavers take the day and the loot, the merchants hold their own against them, or the *Petrel* and her crew escapes with their lives. We join them shortly after the battle has been initiated and opening maneuvers have placed them almost next to one another.

On the *Kraken*, flat hands slap on the taught drum, the skin that of a pirate captain two years dead. The rowers time to the beat, muscles coiled, arms sheathed in sweat as the pirate galley pulls forward against the larger, slower *Petrel*. The war galley catches the merchant vessel using a Minor Move Action in the same zone to come within Reach, and is now considered in range. Due to careful maneuvering by the merchant captain, the *Kraken* has yet been unable to ram the *Petrel*.

The *Kraken*'s lookout directs the missile fire of the pirates. He attempts a Challenging (D2) Observation to help identify where the bireme's captain is at, hoping to take him out of the fight early, and gains 3 Momentum. The *Petrel* attempts an Evasive Action, but fails. The pirates on the *Kraken* use a Standard Action to make a Bow Shot, using the Momentum gained from the lookout, to pepper the merchant vessel with black arrows, many finding their marks within the bodies of the opposing crew and injuring the captain.

The pirates are close enough to lower their corvus, whose spike thunks satisfyingly into the deck of the *Petrel*. Now, the pirates are ready for a Boarding Action, and in double file pour down the corvus onto the merchant vessel. This is an easy attack with an Average (D1) Difficulty, the two ships are side-by-side.

The pirates follow this up with a Boarding Action, pitting their Sailing against the opposing crew's Command. The opposing crew loses the opposed roll, and with a spectacular effort, the pirates slay most of the deckhands, inflicting a Break upon the vessel. Boarders are met by counter-boarders as the pirate captain orders flame arrows to be fired into the rigging. While the *Kraken* suffers a Break from all the casualties, the *Petrel* suffers 4 Breaks (2 of them non-lethal) and is subdued.

The reavers clean their blades and demand the survivors join them or die. At this point, they are about to celebrate when the lookout on the *Kraken* spies a quickly approaching Argossean naval warship. It seems the Argossean ship laid in wait for the infamous *Kraken* just behind a small island, letting them lock themselves into place with the merchant vessel. This longer trireme, crewed by more rowers than the *Kraken*, seems likely to quickly close the distance. The Argossean naval vessel makes two Move Actions toward the Kraken, coming within one zone by the time the pirates return to defend their ship, freeing it from the distressingly empty *Petrel*.

The pirate captain succeeds in a Maneuver test, and the Argossean warship misses a chance to ram the smaller vessel. The pirates' cheers quickly fall silent, though, as they see a dragon's breath of fire spurt froth from the front of the Argossean ship. Damage is rolled, and another Break inflicted.

The last thing the pirates at the fore feel is pain as the liquid fire sticks to them, melting their skin and all dreams of further conquest. As for the rest, the pirate captain must rally what crew remains after witnessing the horrific demise of their sea-brothers. Including the deaths from fire, the *Kraken* now has 2 Breaks and thus suffers a two step increase in Difficulty applied to all actions.

The battle is all but lost for the *Kraken*.

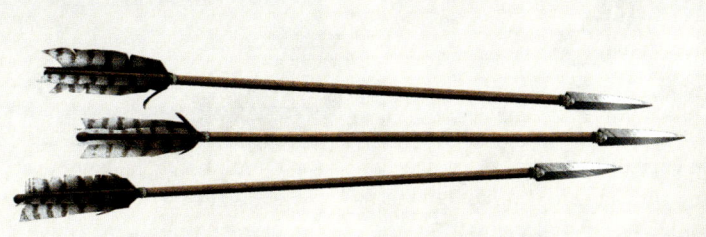

SHIPS OF THE HYBORIAN AGE

Many and varied are the ships that ply the waters up and down the coast of the Western Sea, and nearly every type has been turned to use in piracy. Pages 138–140 of the *Conan* corebook present a wide range of watercraft, and *Conan the Barbarian* provides additional varieties of ship types used along the shore of Vanaheim. The vessels in this section are intended to flesh out that roster, as well as providing additional rules for ships, ship-handling, and ship-to-ship combat not included in those sources.

These entries expand upon those provided in the *Conan* corebook, and the *Updated BarbarianShips* sidebar on page 122 updates those and the *Conan the Barbarian* entries, providing missing information from those sources.

Availability & Costs

Availability differs wildly based on location, and should be adjusted by the gamemaster as required, based on common sense. A fishing village may only have canoes available, whereas the port cities of Argos or Zingara will have a variety of fine vessels to choose from.

Costs are approximate, and generally reflect a used but serviceable example of the ship type, without any but the most basic of furnishings. At the gamemaster's discretion, the price may increase dramatically for a newly-made vessel, or one more richly appointed.

Similarly, crew and their wages must be determined with the gamemaster, and can be modified by availability of crew, locale, method of recruitment, division of loot (if any), role in the crew, reputation of the crewmember and the captain, potential hazards, or other factors.

Stowage

Stowage entries are provided for those with limited space: if the value is a "—", the amount of Stowage is so large, or so well-distributed throughout the ship, that it has no effect on the ship's ability to operate. Generally, any vessel with the *Ship* Quality has enough storage to accommodate any reasonable amount of cargo.

BIREME

Availability: 5
Cost: 25+

A galley with two banks of oars and a large, square sail. Biremes come in a wide variety of sizes, but typically they are about 80 feet long with a beam width of ten feet. Primarily used as warships by the Stygian navies, they are also somewhat common in Shem and considered greatly outdated in Argos.

ATTRIBUTES	
Sailing Range	Crew (+ Passengers)
5 days	120–130 (10+)
Impact Damage	Maneuver
4 ⚡	1

STRESS AND SOAK		
Soak	Structure	Breaks
3	12	3

QUALITIES AND NOTES
- **Qualities:** Agile, Galley, Ram, Ship.
- **Stowage:** —

CANOE

Availability: 2
Cost: 5

These lightweight, narrow boats are designed to be paddled or poled, and can range in length from eight to 15 feet. Most are made by hollowing out a tree trunk, and some are sealed with tree sap or even bound in tightly-stretched leather. Larger canoes are treated as longboats. Canoes can be found anywhere there are people to make them, from the southernmost reaches of the Black Coast to the uttermost frozen northern shores of Vanaheim, and along any river bank where trees grow, though they are most common amongst barbaric or tribal people. Pictish and Black Kingdoms canoes are often carved and painted brightly with symbols relating to the tribes they belong to, whereas those of the folk of the Westermarck are more functional.

ATTRIBUTES	
Sailing Range	Crew (+ Passengers)
1 day	1+ (1+)
Impact Damage	Maneuver
1 ⚡	1

STRESS AND SOAK		
Soak	Structure	Breaks
—	3	1

QUALITIES AND NOTES
- **Qualities:** Agile, Light Craft, Portage.
- **Stowage:** 50.
- **Notes:** A canoe may have a sail.

SHIP COMBAT

SHIPS OF THE HYBORIAN AGE

CANOE, WAR

Availability: 4
Cost: 20+

Ranging up to 80 feet long and hosting almost a hundred warriors, the war canoe is a sign of status amongst the war-chiefs of the various tribes of the Black Coast. Often constructed of a single tree trunk, the war canoe is narrow, seating only a few crew-members per bench, each expected to row. Due to their shallow draft, they are quite practical when navigating on wide rivers, and are often constructed so that the rowers can merely turn around to reverse direction.

ATTRIBUTES	
Sailing Range	Crew (+ Passengers)
3 days	40+ (40+)
Impact Damage	Maneuver
2 🅆	1

STRESS AND SOAK		
Soak	Structure	Breaks
3	3	8

QUALITIES AND NOTES
■ **Qualities:** Galley, Rugged, Shallow Draft, Ship.
■ **Stowage:** —

CARAVEL

Availability: 5
Cost: 30–35+

The caravel is a smaller, sleeker version of the three-masted merchant ship, with lateen sails (i.e., fore-and aft-rigged), often used for shorter coastal voyages. This craft is much more maneuverable and shallow-drafted than her larger counterparts, and can even navigate up larger, deeper rivers. Caravels might also be used as personal vessels for nobles and royalty. A caravel might be anywhere from 50–60 tons, 40–60 feet long, with a beam of 15 feet. Unlike larger three-masted merchant ships, caravels are also common upon the Vilayet Sea.

ATTRIBUTES	
Sailing Range	Crew (+ Passengers)
10–14 days	18–25+ (12+)
Impact Damage	Maneuver
3 🅆	1

STRESS AND SOAK		
Soak	Structure	Breaks
2	6	3

QUALITIES AND NOTES
■ **Qualities:** Agile, Shallow Draft, Ship.
■ **Stowage:** 100

CARRACK

Availability: 5
Cost: 30+ (Small), 35+ (Large)

An oceangoing ship with a high, rounded stern and a steering rudder. A carrack has both a high stern castle and high forecastle with multiple decks within them. A carrack has three masts, with the foremast and mainmast being rigged with square sails hung from yardarms and a mizzenmast rigged with a triangular sail with an additional sail flown from the bowsprit. A carrack could have up to three decks below the weather deck. A small carrack might have a length of 58 feet and a beam of 16 feet, with larger ones having a length of 90 feet and beam of 28 feet. The carrack is almost exclusively Zingaran in use.

UPDATED BARBARIAN SHIPS

Conan the Barbarian provides a variety of ships for player character and gamemaster use. As presented there, some information relating to ship-to-ship combat is missing from their writeups, and is included here for reference.

UPDATED SHIPS	
Ship	Notes
Drakkar	**Qualities:** *Agile, Galley, Shallow Draft, Ship*; **Sailing Range:** 10 days; **Maneuver:** 1; **Crew:** 30+; **Soak:** 3; **Structure:** 12; **Breaks:** 6; **Impact Damage:** 6 🅆; **Notes:** May be portaged.
Faering	**Qualities:** *Light Craft, Shallow Draft*; **Sailing Range:** 2 days; **Maneuver:** —; **Crew:** 1+; **Soak:** —; **Structure:** 6; **Breaks:** 2; **Impact Damage:** —.
Karvi	**Qualities:** *Agile, Galley, Portage, Shallow Draft*; **Sailing Range:** 6 days; **Maneuver:** 1; **Crew:** 4+ (20+); **Soak:** 3; **Structure:** 8; **Breaks:** 4; **Impact Damage:** 3 🅆.
Knarr	**Qualities:** *Galley, Portage*; **Sailing Range:** 12 days; **Maneuver:** 1; **Crew:** 4+ (20+); **Soak:** 3; **Structure:** 8; **Breaks:** 4; **Impact Damage:** 4 🅆.
Skeid	**Qualities:** *Galley, Shallow Draft, Ship*; **Sailing Range:** 12 days; **Maneuver:** —; **Crew:** 28+; **Soak:** 4; **Structure:** 10; **Breaks:** 6; **Impact Damage:** 3 🅆.
Snekka	Equivalent to the longship (page 125).

SHIP COMBAT

ATTRIBUTES

Sailing Range	Crew (+ Passengers)
10 days	30+ (30+)
Impact Damage	**Maneuver**
3 💀	—

STRESS AND SOAK

Soak	Structure	Breaks
2	8 (10)	4

QUALITIES AND NOTES

- **Qualities:** Deep Draft, Ponderous, Ship.
- **Stowage:** —

COG

Availability: 5
Cost: 25+

A merchant ship with a single mast. A cog may have fore and stern castles, particularly when used as a warship. It may be an open boat or have a single deck. A cog may be rowed or poled for a short distance. A small one may have a length of 50 feet and a beam of 16 feet. A large one may have a length of 80 feet and a beam of 26 feet. Cogs are used primarily in Zingara and Argos, though they are becoming more common on the coasts of Shem.

ATTRIBUTES

Sailing Range	Crew (+ Passengers)
8 days	10+ (20+)
Impact Damage	**Maneuver**
2 💀	—

STRESS AND SOAK

Soak	Structure	Breaks
2	10	4

QUALITIES AND NOTES

- **Qualities:** Deep Draft, Ship.
- **Stowage:** —

> *It was long and narrow, a typical trading-ship of the southern coasts, high of poop and stern, with cabins at either extremity.*
>
> — The Hour of the Dragon

DHOW

Availability: 4
Cost: 25+

Usually featuring one or more masts, *dhow* are mid-sized sailing vessels used along the coast of Kush in the Western Sea, and Turan in the Vilayet. Their hulls are light and flexible, the long boards often bound by rope rather than nailed. Traditionally fashioned for the transport of goods, *dhow* can also be fitted for war.

ATTRIBUTES

Sailing Range	Crew (+ Passengers)
12 days	12+ (18+)
Impact Damage	**Maneuver**
3 💀	1

STRESS AND SOAK

Soak	Structure	Breaks
2	10	4

QUALITIES AND NOTES

- **Qualities:** Portage, Shallow Draft, Ship.
- **Stowage:** —

GALLEON

Availability: 5
Cost: 50+

The greatest achievement of Hyborian Age shipwrights, the galleon is a three-masted sea vessel with multiple decks, one or more banks of oars, wider and with greater stowage than any other vessel on the Western or Vilayet seas. Galleons are expensive, the prize of any navy, and are coveted by pirate captains as a sign of prosperity, as well as for the more pragmatic reasons of cargo capacity and the ability to host a large crew.

Such a vessel requires the efforts of hundreds of craftsmen and laborers over months to make a single seaworthy vessel, and as such, they are beyond the reach of any but royalty, the wealthiest merchants, or those bold and capable enough to take them. Galleons are uniquely Zingaran in construction, though the shipwrights of Argos are attempting to outdo these fine craft. Though the galleon's initial role was for trade, some are fitted for war, and feature prominently in the Zingaran navy.

It is said that the emperor and warlords of Khitai have galleons of a scale far beyond even those of Zingara, elaborately carved, brightly painted and gilded, but such talk is regarded as mere hyperbole and exaggeration.

ATTRIBUTES	
Sailing Range	Crew (+ Passengers)
20+ days	60+ (40+)
Impact Damage	Maneuver
2 ♆	—

STRESS AND SOAK		
Soak	Structure	Breaks
2	10	4

QUALITIES AND NOTES
■ **Qualities:** Deep Draft, Galley, Ponderous, Ship.
■ **Stowage:** —

GALLEY

Availability: 4
Cost: 25+

A ship that is primarily propelled by rowing, though most have a triangular or square sail for traveling offshore. A large galley may have two masts. Galleys are particularly useful in waters near shore and rivers. A war galley may also be referred to as a *dromon*. They are common in Argos, Shem, Stygia, Kush, southward along the Black Coast, and even in the Vilayet Sea.

ATTRIBUTES	
Sailing Range	Crew (+ Passengers)
5+ days	60+ (40+)
Impact Damage	Maneuver
3 ♆	—

STRESS AND SOAK		
Soak	Structure	Breaks
2	10	4

QUALITIES AND NOTES
■ **Qualities:** Galley, Shallow Draft, Ship.
■ **Stowage:** —
■ **Notes:** A war galley has a ram.

GONDOLA

Availability: 2
Cost: 5+

A slender, flat-bottomed boat of about 20 feet in length that is rowed with a single oar from the stern in a sculling motion. Gondolas are primarily used as water taxis. Some may have a framed or tented enclosure for the privacy of passengers. Mostly used in Shem and Stygia, though variants exist elsewhere.

ATTRIBUTES	
Sailing Range	Crew (+ Passengers)
1+ days	1+ (2+)
Impact Damage	Maneuver
2 ♆	—

STRESS AND SOAK		
Soak	Structure	Breaks
—	3	1

QUALITIES AND NOTES
■ **Qualities:** Light Craft, Portage.
■ **Stowage:** 50

KAYAK

Availability: 3
Cost: 5+

A small, narrow boat that is propelled with a double-bladed paddle most often used on inland and coastal waters. A kayak is made by stretching and sewing sealskins over a wooden frame. Mostly reserved to Pictland and remote parts of Vanaheim.

ATTRIBUTES	
Sailing Range	Crew (+ Passengers)
1 day	1+ (0)
Impact Damage	Maneuver
1 ♆	2

STRESS AND SOAK		
Soak	Structure	Breaks
—	4	2

QUALITIES AND NOTES
■ **Qualities:** Agile, Light Craft, Portage.
■ **Stowage:** 20

LONGBOAT

Availability: 2
Cost: 10+

An open, rowed boat 18 or more feet in length and with a beam of five feet. Longboats are often used in harbors to row passengers and cargoes between larger ships and the shore. Also includes large canoes and some fishing boats. Most common in the south, and not to be confused with the longship (below).

SHIP COMBAT

ATTRIBUTES

Sailing Range	Crew (+ Passengers)
12 days	8+ (20)
Impact Damage	**Maneuver**
1 ⚡	2

STRESS AND SOAK

Soak	Structure	Breaks
2	8	2

QUALITIES AND NOTES

- **Qualities:** Agile, Galley, Portage, Shallow Draft.
- **Stowage:** 100

LONGSHIP

Availability: 4
Cost: 20+ (small), 25+ (large)

Long, narrow ships with graceful lines used by the Vanir. Longships are noted for their high prows that can be fitted during times of war with fearsome images of dragons and other beasts. Longships have both oars and a single, square sail. Instead of benches, the rowers sit on sea chests that hold cargo or personal possessions. Smaller longships are light enough to easily be portaged around waterfalls or rapids. The smallest longships are some 65 feet in length with a beam of 15 feet and 26 rowers. Larger longships can be up to 100 feet long with a beam of 15 feet and 80 rowers.

ATTRIBUTES

Sailing Range	Crew (+ Passengers)
8 days	27+ (20+)
Impact Damage	**Maneuver**
1 ⚡	1

STRESS AND SOAK

Soak	Structure	Breaks
3	8	4

QUALITIES AND NOTES

- **Qualities:** Agile, Galley, Portage, Shallow Draft, Ship.
- **Stowage:** —

RAFT

Availability: 1
Cost: —

More an assemblage of logs, barrels, or similar materials bound together with rope than a proper boat. Rafts are typically poled, with a flat top and possibly a simple structure or tent. They are most often used in harbors, as ferries, and to carry goods downstream as they have only a slight ability to move against the wind or current. A raft can be as small as a few small logs or it could be a large assemblage of logs that woodcutters transport downstream. Following a shipwreck, survivors have been known to construct a raft from the remaining debris. Rafts are used anywhere there is water and the means to fashion one.

ATTRIBUTES

Sailing Range	Crew (+ Passengers)
1 day	1+ (2+)
Impact Damage	**Maneuver**
1 ⚡	—

STRESS AND SOAK

Soak	Structure	Breaks
1	4	1

QUALITIES AND NOTES

- **Qualities:** Ponderous, Portage, Shallow Draft.
- **Stowage:** 20

SHIP

Availability: 5
Cost: 35–40+

Most merchant vessels are simply called "ships": triple-masted square-riggers with ample room for cargo, capable of being sailed by a small crew. Most merchant ships in the Western Ocean are three-masters like this: ranging from 50–300 tons, 60–100 feet in length, and with a beam of 20–25 feet. Pirates and navies sometimes use ships such as these, adding large complements of marines or raiders to overwhelm their prey during boarding parties or other naval engagements.

ATTRIBUTES

Sailing Range	Crew (+ Passengers)
14–21 day	20–30 (20+)
Impact Damage	**Maneuver**
3 ⚡	—

STRESS AND SOAK

Soak	Structure	Breaks
2	8	4

QUALITIES AND NOTES

- **Qualities:** Deep Draft, Ship.
- **Stowage:** —

CHAPTER 9
A PIRATE OF THE AGE

The sailors who caught and understood the burden of that awesome shout paled and shrank back, staring in sudden fear at the wild figure on the bridge. Was this in truth that bloodthirsty ogre of the southern seas who had so mysteriously vanished years ago, but who still lived in gory legends?

— The Hour of the Dragon

ZARIN THE RED

BACKER CHARACTER
Presented on the following page is a character created by a backer for the *Robert E. Howard's Conan: Adventures in an Age Undreamed Of* Kickstarter campaign, provided here for use by the gamemaster or as a player character.

Few have become so infamous as quickly as Zarin the Red, a threat to all who sail the whole of the Western Sea. Once he was a river smuggler, running slaves and other illicit goods along the Tybor River from Messantia to Shamar and back. Zarin was ruthless, throwing any rivals into his hold to be sold into slavery.

Hungering for more, he decided the next step was piracy, preying upon his competitors, slaying any who would not join him and selling their cargo as his own. He bought the loyalty of his crew with a generous cut of the loot, and coaxed potential enemies into allies, paying rival smugglers and pirates to turn on their own captains. Before long, he had a small fleet and a bloodthirsty crew of well-paid murderers and thieves, the scourge of the Argossean coast.

After a brutal assault on a Kushite merchant ship, Zarin found within the haul a small trinket — an obsidian medallion set with a glimmering red jewel. As he clasped it, his mind reeled with visions of vast wealth, loot pillaged from fleets afire on seas of blood. He took this as a sign, and has worn the amulet since, concealing its existence from even his closest crew.

From that day, his luck became legendary: chance encounters with merchant ships in open waters put him at the advantage; and freakish storms rose to seemingly thwart his pursuers. Emboldened, he expanded the range of his piracy, striking north- and southward. In that time, his excesses caused him to grow fat and grotesque, no depravity or sin he had not indulged in fully, often at the misery of others.

Several years of this gave Zarin wealth beyond that of many kings, and he relinquished direct captaincy of his fleet to his core of most trusted officers. He retired to the Barachas, managing his fleet from his villa, directing them as they raid the trade routes and coastal villages with impunity. Now, he rules like a debauched king, overseeing an endless feasts and orgies of increasing depravity. Despite his gross bulk and disgusting appearance, he is nonetheless still a capable fighter, able to move with surprising strength and speed when threatened.

A PIRATE OF THE AGE

ATTRIBUTES			
Awareness	Intelligence	Personality	Willpower
10	8	9	8
Agility	Brawn		Coordination
9	12		9

FIELDS OF EXPERTISE			
Combat	3	Movement	1
Fortitude	3	Senses	1
Knowledge	2	Social	1

STRESS AND SOAK

- **Stress:** Vigor 15, Resolve 11
- **Soak:** Armor —, Courage 3

ATTACKS

- **Cutlass (M):** Reach 2, 7⚔, Unbalanced, Vicious 1
- **Thrown Dagger (R):** Range C, 4⚔, 1H, Hidden 1, Volley
- **Thunderous Yell (T):** Range C, 4⚔ mental, Area, Stun

SPECIAL ABILITIES

- **Sixth Sense:** Zarin's experiences have given him a keen sense of how people behave, particularly pirates and criminals. Once per scene, he may attempt an Average (D1) Insight test as a Free Action to determine whether he is in danger, or to detect the true motives of those falsely representing themselves. He cannot determine someone's hidden identity, but will know if someone is lying about who they are.

DOOM SPENDS

- **Cursed Luck:** Zarin's strange amulet gives him uncanny luck, helping him escape capture and to stumble across unbelievable strokes of fortune. He may spend 2 Doom at any time to incur such a situation, using that Doom as if it were a Fortune point, but incurs a Complication which manifests in illness or a malady, a long-term condition he must accommodate. Thus, Zarin swells in size and becomes physically repugnant as he prospers, unknowingly exchanging prosperity and incredible luck for his former good looks.
- **Motley Horde:** Zarin is surrounded by a small army of hand-picked throat-slitters and murderers, chosen for their loyalty and lack of ambition. Once per round, he can spend 3 Doom to summon a Mob of 5 Minion pirates (**Conan** corebook, page 319) and can spend 1 additional Doom to trade a Minion for a Toughened pirate captain (also on page 319 of the **Conan** corebook).

ZARIN'S OBSIDIAN PENDANT

Unbeknownst to Zarin, the amulet he possesses is ancient beyond any measure of human understanding, a relic of the bygone ages before humanity first walked upon the earth. Crafted by a long-vanished race of winged humanoids from the lands beyond the shore of distant Khitai, this amulet has passed from owner to owner over the eons, originally brought to the Thurian continent by the ancient people who fled the ancient Lemurians.

If examined, a Daunting (D3) Lore test will realize its true origin, and a further Daunting (D3) Sorcery test will provide a clue as to its true use. If a sorcerer uses the amulet while casting a spell, it automatically rewards successful spell use with 1 Momentum, but also incurs an additional Consequence, as if it had been rolled on another d20. This additional Consequence does not count as an additional d20, however, and is not counted against the normal maximum dice allowed.

SHIP RECORD

NAME

SHIP DETAILS
- Ship Type
- Sailing Range
- Manuever
- Impact
- Qualities

CREW AND PASSENGERS
- Captain
- First Mate
- Crew (Req/Act)
- Passengers

STRESS AND HARMS
- Soak
- Structure
- Breaks

CARGO AND STOWAGE
- Stowage

NOTES

IMAGE

WEAPON	Reach/Range	Size	Size	Damage
Qualities				

WEAPON	Reach/Range	Size	Size	Damage
Qualities				

WEAPON	Reach/Range	Size	Size	Damage
Qualities				

SHIP RECORD

NAME

SHIP DETAILS
- Ship Type
- Sailing Range
- Manuever
- Impact
- Qualities

CREW AND PASSENGERS
- Captain
- First Mate
- Crew (Req/Act)
- Passengers

STRESS AND HARMS
- Soak
- Structure
- Breaks

CARGO AND STOWAGE
- Stowage

NOTES

IMAGE

WEAPON	Reach/Range	Size	Size	Damage
Qualities				

WEAPON	Reach/Range	Size	Size	Damage
Qualities				

WEAPON	Reach/Range	Size	Size	Damage
Qualities				

INDEX

Abobi ... 52
Akkad ... 47
Alimane River ... 31
Ancient Bloodlines ... 9
Anu ... 42, 45
Appearance ... 24–25
    Clothing ... 25
    Distinguishing Feature ... 25
Aquilonia ... 31
Archetypes ... 15–17
    Galley Slave ... 16
    Mariner ... 16
    Merchant Captain ... 17
    Smuggler ... 17
Argos ... 31–32, 36, 40–46
    Army ... 43
    Art ... 41
    Capital. *See* Messantia
    Culture ... 41
    History ... 41
    Navy ... 42
Argus ... 91
Asgalun ... 46
Barachan Isles ... 30, 36–38
Barachan Oracle ... 67–68
Bêlit ... 52, 91
Black Barnacle ... 62
Black Coast ... 29, 32, 52–53
    Politics ... 52
Black Kingdoms ... 35
Black River ... 31
Black Stranger ... 54
Bloody Tranicos ... 55
Bossonian Marches ... 31
Carousing ... 105
Castes ... 8–10
    Talents ... 10
Chagas ... 51
Complications ... 115
Conan the Pirate ... 93
Count Valenso ... 54
Crew Actions
    Commander ... 113
    General ... 113
    Helmsman ... 114
    Lookout ... 114
    Marine ... 114
    Piper ... 115
Davu ... 52
Educations ... 20–21
El Shebbeh ... 51
Encounters
    Black Octopus (Toughened) ... 76
    Black One (Toughened) ... 77
    Black Stranger (Nemesis) ... 78
    Black Zarono (Nemesis) ... 87
    Captain Strom (Nemesis) ... 84
    Captain Zaporavo (Nemesis) ... 86
    Count Valenso (Nemesis) ... 85
    Demetrio (Toughened) ... 82
    Dolphin (Minion) ... 72
    Ghostly Slave (Minion) ... 65
    Ghost Ship Sailor (Minion) ... 78
    Giant Crab (Toughened) ... 72
    Giant Hyena (Toughened) ... 79
    Giant Turtle (Toughened) ... 73
    Kraken (Nemesis) ... 79
    Marine (Minion) ... 69
    Marine Sergeant (Toughened) ... 69
    Monkey (Minion) ... 74
    N'Gora, Chief of the Black Corsairs (Toughened) ... 88
    N'Yaga, Shaman of the *Tigress* (Toughened) ... 89
    Pirate (Minion, Toughened) ... 71
    Publio (Toughened) ... 82
    Red Ortho (Nemesis) ... 83
    Sakumbe, King of Tombalku (Nemesis) ... 90
    Sancha of Kordava (Minion) ... 83
    Sargasso Strangler (Nemesis) ... 80
    Sea Serpent (Nemesis) ... 81
    Sergius of Khrosha (Nemesis) ... 84
    Shark (Toughened) ... 75
    Tito, Shipmaster of the *Argus* (Toughened) ... 85
    Vanir Raider (Toughened) ... 71
    Whale (Nemesis) ... 75
Equipment ... 26–28
Events
    Mortal ... 56–59
    Natural ... 59–60
    Preternatural ... 60
Freebooters ... 43
Gol-goroth ... 30
Great Pyramid of Set ... 50
Great Sargasso ... 38
Homelands ... 6
Hyperborea ... 32
Isle of Bal-Sagoth ... 30–31
Isle of Pirates' Doom ... 30
Isle of the Black Ones ... 30
Jullah ... 51
Karnath ... 49
Khemi ... 48–49
Khorotas River ... 31, 40
King Atreus ... 41, 42
King Tothmekri ... 55
King Valerio ... 31, 35
Kordava ... 35
Korvela ... 54
Koth ... 32, 40
Kulalo ... 52
Kush ... 50–53
Long Black Coast of Death ... 55
Luxur ... 48
Messantia ... 43–45
    Docks ... 45
Mitra ... 34, 42
Monster Quality (Immense) ... 74
Moving at Sea ... 112
Natures ... 18–19
Ophir ... 40
Pictish Coast ... 53–55
Pictland ... 31
Picts of the Kraken ... 40
Pillage ... 97
Pirate Code ... 23, 100
Plunder ... 98
Poitain ... 31
Princess Akivasha ... 50
Queen of the Black Coast. *See* Bêlit
Red Brotherhood ... 36, 95
Repairs ... 116
Sea Hags ... 62
Shem ... 32, 40, 46–47
Ship
    Qualities ... 111–112
    Weapons ... 117
    Argossean Fire ... 118
    Ballista ... 118
    Cheiroballistra ... 118
    Corvus ... 118
    Grapnel ... 118
    Iron Claw ... 118
Ship Combat
    Attacking ... 115
    Damaging ... 115
    Example ... 119
    Movement ... 110–111
Shipping Lanes ... 97
Ships
    Bireme ... 120
    Canoe, War ... 122
    Caravel ... 122
    Carrack ... 122
    Cog ... 123
    Dhow ... 123
    Galleon ... 123
    Galley ... 124
    Gondola ... 124
    Kayak ... 124
    Longboat ... 124
    Raft ... 125
    Ship ... 125
Ships of the Dead ... 65
Shirki River ... 31
Soothsayers of Zingg ... 61
Southern Isles ... 52
Spells
    Flames of the Deep ... 63
    Weave of Fate ... 64
Stories ... 11–15
Stowage ... 120
Stygia ... 32, 48–49
Talents ... 22–23
    Boarding Action (Parry) ... 23
    Deck Rat (Acrobatics) ... 22
    Fighting Dirty (Melee) ... 22
    Lodestone (Survival) ... 23
    Strength from the Sea (Resistance) ... 23
    Swashbuckler (Acrobatics) ... 22
Tananda ... 51
Thaala ... 42
Thoth-Amon ... 48
Thunder River ... 31
Thurian ... 29
Tigress ... 52, 88–90
Toragis ... 35–36
Tortage ... 36, 39–40
Trallibes ... 40
Treasure Cave of Tranicos ... 55
Valadelad ... 36
Valetta Island ... 35
Vanaheim ... 29, 35, 53
Vanir ... 31
Vilayet Sea ... 55
Western Continent ... 109
Western Ocean ... 29–31
Yanyoga ... 52
Zabhela ... 49, 51
Zarin the Red ... 126
Zarkheba River ... 53
Zingara ... 31–32, 36, 40
    Politics ... 33
    Style ... 33
Zingaran Freebooters ... 95
Zingg Valley ... 31

THE HYBORIAN AGE AWAITS YOU

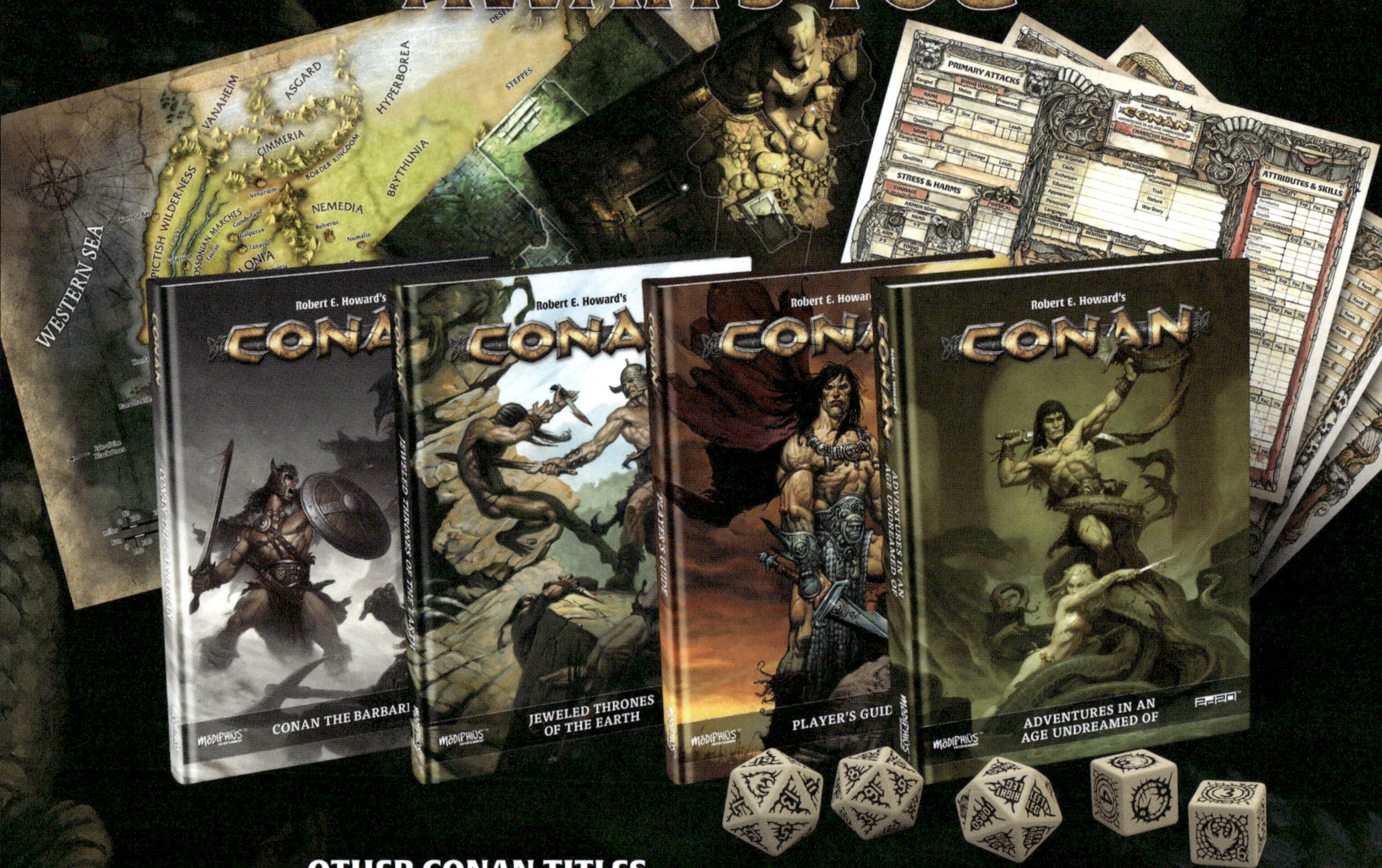

OTHER CONAN TITLES

- Conan the Adventurer
- Conan the Brigand
- Conan the King
- Conan the Mercenary
- Conan the Pirate
- Conan the Thief
- Conan the Scout
- Conan the Wanderer
- Ancient Ruins & Cursed Cities
- The Book of Skelos
- Horrors of the Hyborian Age
- Kull of Atlantis
- Nameless Cults
- Conan: The Exiles Sourcebook
- Conan: The Monolith Sourcebook
- The Art of Conan

CONAN ACCESSORIES

- Gamemaster Screen
- Geomorphic Tile Sets
- Q-Workshop Dice Set
- Doom & Fortune Card Deck
- Encounter Card Deck
- Location Card Deck
- Sorcery Card Deck
- Story Card Deck

modiphius.com/conan

© 2020 Conan Properties International LLC ("CPI"). CONAN, CONAN THE BARBARIAN, HYBORIA and related logos, characters, names, and distinctive likenesses thereof are trademarks or registered trademarks of CPI. All rights reserved. ROBERT E. HOWARD and related logos, characters, names, and distinctive likenesses thereof are trademarks or registered trademarks of Robert E. Howard Properties Inc. All rights reserved. The 2D20 SYSTEM and Modiphius Logos are copyright Modiphius Entertainment Ltd. 2015–2020. All 2D20 SYSTEM text is copyright Modiphius Entertainment Ltd.